Nature Tourism

In recent decades, the fast rise of emerging economies, like the BRICS nations, has propelled the growth of tourism worldwide. Meanwhile, a plethora of nature destinations has been developed to meet the diverse needs of the new wave of demand from emerging economies and to entice existing tourists from advanced and rich economies.

Nature Tourism augments the current literature on the benefits and pitfalls in recent developments of nature tourism, tracing the history in development, highlighting the ecological impacts and showcasing the current practices in nature tourism, along with discussions on specific tourist markets from holistic viewpoints embracing lessons learned from various destination nations and continents across the globe. A host of topics with global significance will be explored such as the effect of climate change on nature tourism, technological innovation in managing nature tourism, visitor management in nature tourism and market positioning in a highly competitive environment. These are reviewed in a wide range of countries from USA/Canada, South America, Scandinavian countries, the Swiss Alps, Middle-East countries, Africa, China and Australia/New Zealand.

This book will offer significant insight into nature-based tourism and its future development. It will be of interest to upper-level students, researchers and academics in tourism, environmental studies, development and sustainability.

Joseph S. Chen is Professor in Tourism, Hospitality and Event Management, the Department of Recreation, Park and Tourism Studies at Indiana University, Bloomington, USA. His research foci entail tourism marketing, tourist behaviors, social impacts of tourism, Arctic tourism and sustainability in hospitality and tourism.

Nina K. Prebensen is Professor at the University College of South East Norway and at UiT The Arctic University of Norway. She has published papers in various tourism journals. Her research highlights particularly the tourist decision and experience processes, where co-creation of value for hosts and guests is a focus.

Contemporary Geographies of Leisure, Tourism and Mobility

Series Editor: C. Michael Hall, Professor at the Department of Management, College of Business and Economics, University of Canterbury, Christchurch, New Zealand

The aim of this series is to explore and communicate the intersections and relationships between leisure, tourism and human mobility within the social sciences.

It will incorporate both traditional and new perspectives on leisure and tourism from contemporary geography, e.g. notions of identity, representation and culture, while also providing for perspectives from cognate areas such as anthropology, cultural studies, gastronomy and food studies, marketing, policy studies and political economy, regional and urban planning, and sociology, within the development of an integrated field of leisure and tourism studies.

Also, increasingly, tourism and leisure are regarded as steps in a continuum of human mobility. Inclusion of mobility in the series offers the prospect to examine the relationship between tourism and migration, the sojourner, educational travel, and second home and retirement travel phenomena.

For a full list of titles in this series, please visit www.routledge.com/series/SE0522

The series comprises two strands:

Contemporary Geographies of Leisure, Tourism and Mobility aims to address the needs of students and academics, and the titles will be published in hardback and paperback. Titles include:

10. Tourism and Climate Change
Impacts, adaptation and mitigation
C. Michael Hall, Stefan Gössling and Daniel Scott

11. Tourism and Citizenship
Raoul V. Bianchi and Marcus L. Stephenson

Routledge Studies in Contemporary Geographies of Leisure, Tourism and Mobility is a forum for innovative new research intended for research students and academics, and the titles will be available in hardback only. Titles include:

63. Women and Sex Tourism Landscapes
Erin Sanders-McDonagh

64. Nature Tourism
Edited by Joseph S. Chen and Nina K. Prebensen

65. Sport, Events, Tourism and Regeneration
Edited by Nicholas Wise and John Harris

Nature Tourism

**Edited by Joseph S. Chen and
Nina K. Prebensen**

Routledge
Taylor & Francis Group
LONDON AND NEW YORK

First published 2017 by Routledge

2 Park Square, Milton Park, Abingdon, Oxfordshire OX14 4RN
52 Vanderbilt Avenue, New York, NY 10017

*Routledge is an imprint of the Taylor & Francis Group,
an informa business*

First issued in paperback 2019

British Library Cataloguing in Publication Data
A catalogue record for this book is available from the British
Library

Library of Congress Cataloging in Publication Data
A catalog record for this book has been requested

ISBN: 978-1-138-96173-9 (hbk)
ISBN: 978-0-367-36894-4 (pbk)

Typeset in Times New Roman
by Deanta Global Publishing Services, Chennai, India

Contents

Lists of Figures   vii
List of Tables   viii
Notes on Contributors   ix

1 **Research Progress in Nature Tourism**   1
   JOSEPH S. CHEN AND NINA K. PREBENSEN

2 **Nature and Well-being: Explorer Travel Narratives of
   Transformation**   11
   JENNIFER LAING AND WARWICK FROST

3 **Well-being in Wildlife Experiences: Feeling Good for the Animals?**   23
   GIOVANNA BERTELLA

4 **The Impact of Korea's Nature-Based Recreation Settings on
   Tourists' Emotions, Satisfaction and Subjective Happiness**   34
   TIMOTHY J. LEE AND JINOK S. KIM

5 **Generation Y, Nature and Tourism**   46
   MELANIE SMITH

6 **Connectedness and Relatedness to Nature: A Case of
   Neo-Confucianism among Chinese, South Korean and
   Japanese Tourists**   57
   NINA K. PREBENSEN, YOUNG -SOOK LEE AND JOSEPH S. CHEN

7 **How Local Traditions and Way of Living Influence Tourism:
   Basecamp Explorer in Maasai Mara, Kenya and Svalbard, Norway**   68
   ØYSTEIN JENSEN, FRANK LINDBERG, DAMIANNAH M. KIETI, BJØRN WILLY ÅMO
   AND JAMES S. NAMPUSHI

8 **Impact of Climate Change on Tourism in World Heritage Sites:
   A Case Study from the Wet Tropics Region of Australia**   82
   BRUCE PRIDEAUX AND MICHELLE THOMPSON

9 **Quality Perspectives in Managing Visitor Experiences**   95
LYNN M. JAMIESON

10 **A National Park in Turmoil: The Case Study on Vanoise
   National Park in the Alps**   109
ISABELLE FROCHOT

11 **Listening to the Sounds of Silence: Forest-based Wellbeing
   Tourism in Finland**   120
RAIJA KOMPPULA, HENNA KONU AND NOORA VIKMAN

12 **Nature Tourism in Germany's Protected Areas**   131
MARIUS MAYER AND MANUEL WOLTERING

13 **Governing Nature Tourism in Eastern and Southern Africa**   146
RENÉ VAN DER DUIM, JAKOMIJN VAN WIJK AND MACHIEL LAMERS

14 **Emerging Trends in Wildlife and Tiger Tourism in India**   159
KRITHI K. KARANTH, SHIVANGI JAIN AND DINCY MARIYAM

15 **Chinese Approach to Sustainability: Challenges and Suggestions**   172
RUI SONG

16 **Tourism in Preserved Nature Areas in Taiwan**   184
YU-LIANG TSENG, NORIKO SATO, SHIH-SHUO YEH AND TZUNG-CHENG HUAN

17 **Forest as a Venue for Recreational Therapy in Japan**   196
NORIKO SATO, YU-LIANG TSENG, SHIH-SHUO YEH AND TZUNG-CHENG HUAN

18 **Final Remarks: Challenges and Research Directions**   208
NINA K. PREBENSEN AND JOSEPH S. CHEN

   Index   215

Figures

4.1   Results of the Research Model   41
5.1   The Benefits of Being in Nature   52
5.2   Activity Preferences in Nature Tourism   53
7.1   Maasai Preparing the Bonfire, by Øystein Jensen   72
7.2   Maasai Guide from Sekenany Camp and Tourist on
       Walking Safari, by Øystein Jensen   73
7.3   Lions Resting in the Shadow, by Øystein Jensen   74
7.4   Walking with Maasai Guides, by Øystein Jensen   75
7.5   With the Dog-Sledges by Trapper's Hut, by Frank Lindberg   76
7.6   On the Way with the Dogs, by Frank Lindberg   77
7.7   Ship Frozen in the Ice, by Per Østergaard   78
8.1   Flow Diagram Illustrating the Impact of Climate Change on a
       Protected Area and How it Can Be Responded to
       by the Tourism Industry   84
12.1   Guided Tour through the Wadden Sea in Lower Saxony
       Wadden Sea National Park, by Marius Mayer   134
12.2   Hiking Trail through Dead Wood Areas in Bavarian Forest
       National Park, by Marius Mayer   134
12.3   Large-scale Protected Areas in Germany   136
12.4   Decision Tree to Determine Visitors with High
       National Park Affinity   142
14.1   Annual Tourist Growth Rate from 2005 to 2015 across 69
       Wildlife Reserves in India Including 17 Tiger Reserves   164
14.2   Gate Fees in 2014-2015 across 96 Wildlife Reserves in India
       Including 20 Tiger Reserves   166

Tables

3.1 The Respondents of the In-depth Interviews Listed According to Their Experience of Well-being and Some Relevant Characteristics 28

4.1 Demographic Characteristics of the Respondents 38

4.2 Results of Confirmatory Factor Analysis 40

4.3 Measure Correlations, Squared Correlations and AVE 41

6.1 Mean Scores for Nature Relatedness and Connectedness in Tourism 64

9.1 Activities Prohibited in Yellowstone 106

9.2 Prohibitive Activities in Yosemite 106

12.1 Protected area categories in Germany 135

12.2 Tourism Indicators for Selected German National Parks, Biosphere Reserves and Nature Parks 140

13.1 Logics in the Conservation Discourse 148

13.2 Overview of the Key Events in the Emergence of the Institutional Arrangements under Study 149

14.1 Visitors and Gate Fees in Indian Wildlife Reserves 163

15.1 National Natural Protection Systems in China 174

Contributors

Bjørn Willy Åmo is Associate Professor at Nord University Business School, Norway. His field of expertise is within entrepreneurship and innovation. His current work investigates entrepreneurship education, social entrepreneurship and entrepreneurship in the tourism industry.

Giovanna Bertella is Associate Professor at the School of Business and Economics, UiT The Arctic University of Norway in Tromsø, Norway. Topics covered in her research include rural tourism, tourism networking and innovation, tourism entrepreneurship, nature-based tourism, animals in tourism and sustainability.

Joseph S. Chen is Professor in Tourism, Hospitality and Event Management, the Department of Recreation, Park and Tourism Studies at Indiana University, Bloomington, USA. His research foci entail tourism marketing, tourist behaviors, social impacts of tourism, Arctic tourism and sustainability in hospitality and tourism.

Isabelle Frochot received her PhD from Manchester Metropolitan University, UK and has been Senior Lecturer in Tourism Marketing since 2000 at the University of Savoie Mont Blanc, France. Her research interests include tourists' psychographic segmentation studies (benefit segmentation), service quality scales and experiential marketing.

Warwick Frost is Associate Professor in Tourism and Events in the Department of Management and Marketing at La Trobe University, Australia. His research interests include heritage, regional development, events, tourism and the media and national parks.

Tzung-Cheng Huan is Professor in the Department of Marketing and Tourism Management, National Chiayi University, Taiwan. His research interests are forest recreation and tourist behavior.

Shivangi Jain is a research assistant with the Centre for Wildlife Studies, with research interests in how resource management policies can be improved to serve both conservation interests and economic development.

Lynn M. Jamieson is Interim Chair and Professor at the Department of Recreation, Park and Tourism Studies, Indiana University, Bloomington, USA. Her research centres on government policy regarding sport and leisure, management impacts in the leisure industry, competencies in recreation sports, sport and violence and tourism image salience.

Øystein Jensen is Professor at University of Stavanger and Nord University Business School in Norway. His main fields of research during the last 30 years have included destination marketing, tourist experiences, co-operation in distribution channels and sustainable tourism development.

Krithi K. Karanth is Associate Conservation Scientist with the Wildlife Conservation Society and adjunct faculty at Duke University, USA. She has over 17 years of research experience examining species distributions, wildlife tourism, human–wildlife conflicts, voluntary resettlement and land use change.

Damiannah M. Kieti is Associate Professor at Moi University in Kenya and a tourism expert with over 15 years of experience. Her research interests include: services management, tourism planning and development, sustainable tourism, community-based tourism, tourism and poverty reduction.

Jinok S. Kim is a lecturer in the Department of Tourism at Kyung Hee University, South Korea. Her research particularly focuses on psychological health and restorative components of environments, aspects of health tourism behavior and health tourism development impacts.

Raija Komppula is Professor of Marketing and Tourism Business from the University of Eastern Finland. Her research interests include tourist experience, customer involvement in new service development, destination leadership, branding, small business, entrepreneurship, co-operation and networks.

Henna Konu is a Project Manager and a researcher in the Center for Tourism Studies, University of Eastern Finland. Her research interests include service development, customer involvement, consumer/tourist experiences, experiential services and wellbeing and nature tourism.

Jennifer Laing is Associate Professor in Management in the Department of Management and Marketing at La Trobe University, Australia. Her research interests include travel narratives, heritage tourism, wellness tourism and exploring extraordinary tourism experiences.

Machiel Lamers is Assistant Professor at the Environmental Policy Group at Wageningen University, the Netherlands. His research focuses especially on tourism, conservation and environmental motilities in sub-Saharan Africa and the Polar Regions.

Timothy J. Lee is Professor at Ritsumeikan Asia Pacific University (APU) and Founding Director of the APRI-HOT (Asia Pacific Research Institute for Health-Oriented Tourism). His research interests include medical/wellness/health tourism, ethnic identity, cultural heritage tourism and tourism development which incorporates East Asian values.

Young-Sook Lee is Associate Professor and Department Head of Tourism and Northern Studies, UiT The Arctic University of Norway. Areas of her research interest include East Asian cultural philosophies, sustainable Arctic tourism and literature and language in tourism.

Frank Lindberg is Associate Professor of Marketing at Nord University Business School, Norway. His current research focuses on experience marketing, tourism marketing and consumer research, especially as it relates to Consumer Culture Theory.

Dincy Mariyam is a scientific consultant with the Centre for Wildlife Studies, with research interests in community ecology, climate science and invasion biology.

Marius Mayer has been Junior Professor for Economic Geography and Tourism at Ernst-Moritz-Arndt Universität Greifswald, Germany since 2013. His research interests are economic geography, with a focus on tourism, leisure and parks research, especially economic impact and park-people-relationships.

James S. Nampushi is a lecturer at Maasai Mara University, Kenya. He received his PhD in Parks, Recreation and Tourism Management (PRTM) at Clemson University, USA. His research interest is ecotourism focusing on creative and innovative leadership skills towards sustainable solutions.

Nina K. Prebensen is Professor at the University College of South East Norway and at UiT The Arctic University of Norway. She has published papers in various tourism journals. Her research highlights the tourist decision and experience processes in particular, where co-creation of value for hosts and guests is in focus.

Bruce Prideaux is the Director of the Centre for Tourism and Regional Opportunities at the Cairns campus of Central Queensland University, Australia and is the Program Director of the Masters of Sustainable Tourism Management. He has a wide range of research interests including climate change.

Noriko Sato is Professor in the Faculty of Agriculture and Graduate School of Bioresource and Bioenvironmental Sciences, Kyushu University, Fukuoka, Japan. Her current research interests are forest therapy, forest recreation, sustainable forest management and urban forestry.

Melanie Smith is Associate Professor at Budapest Metropolitan University, Hungary and co-author of the book *Health, Tourism and Hospitality: Spas, Wellness and Medical Travel* (2013). She has worked for over 15 years on cultural, city and health tourism.

Rui Song is Director of the Tourism Research Center in the Chinese Academy of Social Sciences, Editor in Chief of the Tourism Green Book of China, and Editor in Chief of the Leisure Green Book of China, with a focus on sustainability, tourism and leisure management.

Michelle Thompson is Associate Lecturer in Tourism at the School of Business and Law, Central Queensland University, Cairns, Australia. Michelle's research expertise extends across regional areas, including nature-based tourism research in the north Queensland region of Australia, and developing tourism in agricultural regions.

Yu-Liang Tseng received his PhD from Kyushu University, Japan, and Associate Professor in the Department of Geography, National Changhua University of Education, Changhua, Taiwan. His research interests are green tourism, forest creation and forest therapy.

René van der Duim is Personal Professor at the Cultural Geography Chair Group at Wageningen University, the Netherlands. His research focuses on tourism, conservation and development, especially in sub-Saharan Africa.

Jakomijn van Wijk is Assistant Professor at Maastricht School of Management, the Netherlands. Her research interest focuses on processes of institutional change towards sustainability, frequently in the tourism industry.

Noora Vikman is Senior Lecturer and a soundscape researcher in the School of Humanities, University of Eastern Finland. Her research interests are soundscape studies, travel experiences, sustainable, nature and culture tourism and ethnomusicology.

Manuel Woltering has been Research Associate at Julius-Maximilians-Universität Würzburg, Germany, since 2008. His research interest is economic geography focusing on the theory and practice of regional development, especially in protected area regions.

Shih-Shuo Yeh received his PhD from the University of Waikato, New Zealand, and is Assistant Professor in the Department of Tourism Management, National Quemoy University, Kinmen, Taiwan. His research interests are tourism marketing, hospitality management and service brand management.

1   Research Progress in Nature Tourism

Joseph S. Chen and Nina K. Prebensen

Progress and Woes of Nature Tourism Development

In developing and developed economies, nature environment has been constantly exploited for economic ends and social development that inevitably deprives certain groups of people, such as city dwellers, from nature on a daily base. This situation motivates people to come in contact with nature as a rewarding leisure pursuit thought various types of activities such as hiking and wildlife viewing. Meanwhile, the tourism business regards nature as a viable resource to stage optimal tourist experiences for the sake of business growth.

The development of modern technologies enables the travelling public to amply indulge in nature environment on a gigantic piece of land that has not been easily accessible to the masses up to now. In China, for instance, due to the completion of the high-mountain rail passage through the Tibetan Plateau, masses of tourists have now been able to visit a vast majority of the 4,000-meter-high mountainous area in Tibet. In the Arctic, ocean cruises have brought tourists to experience singular natural phenomena (e.g. midnight sun, iceberg, and arura) and view wildlife on the brink of extinct (e.g. polar bear and Arctic fox). Indeed, tourism has for long been regarded as a powerful apparatus for economic growth and social development in developed and under-developed nations. Place (1991) has highlighted the relationship between nature tourism and rural development and that ecotourism is a valuable tourist venue for community development and an economic contributor to the economy of Costa Rica.

However, in some cases, the inflow of masses of tourists has been viewed as an activity that hampers the maintenance of tranquility of the environment in the area. It is unarguably evident that development of large-scale tourism is in conflict with the goal of preservation of nature. In the last decades, as fast-rising emerging economies, represented by the BRICS nations, have propelled the growth of tourism worldwide, a plethora of nature destinations in these locations have been renovated or constructed to provide for the growing needs of the tourists and entice tourists from far-flung locations and other developing economies. In sum, as the robust growth of emerging economies persists, it shall continue to significantly increase the number of visitors.

Could the foreseeable expansion of the market of nature tourism benefit human beings economically, socially and environmentally? It is high time that tourism stakeholders contemplated to what extent nature environment should be exposed to tourists and what sorts of sustainable developmental strategies that enhance the tourist experiences in specific and human welfare as a whole should be considered. In a bid to facilitate tourism researchers, professionals, and policy makers to reflect on those pressing issues, this book is in an attempt to furnish a scholarly forum gathering updated cases from different parts of the world in connection with nature tourism.

Specifically, the book encompasses three parts of synopses concerning the phenomenon of nature tourism. In the first part (i.e. Chapters 2 and 3), the book centers on wellbeing—an optimal benefit of nature tourism—illustrated by two different kinds of analyses drawing from both non-empirical and empirical data. In the second part (i.e. Chapters 4–9), contemporary issues from both supply and demand sides of tourism are further examined. The last section (i.e. Chapters 10–17) of the book reports case studies from five developed economies (i.e. Japan, Norway, Finland, Germany and France), two most populous emerging economies (i.e. China and India), two newly industrialized countries (i.e. South Korea and Taiwan) and African nations. Furthermore, the concluding part (i.e. Chapter 18) of this book summarizes the updated knowledge presented throughout the book while giving recommendations for future research. The following section traces the empirical works on nature tourism that have transpired in the last three decades and delivers analytical remarks on four investigative realms of significance: (1) environmental rows and conservation, (2) tourist experiences, (3) impacts on community and nature, and (4) management and development.

Environmental Rows and Conservation

In recent decades, the literature with regards to nature tourism has touched on diverse streams of context. Nevertheless, scholarly debates on environmental issues in relation to the development of nature tourism have frequently appeared. It has been recognized that environmental goods and resources are latent primary factors of production in tourism (Marcouiller, 1998). Akama (1996) further enunciated that Western environmental values influence the creations of nature destinations in the case of wildlife conservation in Kenya. As illustrated by Wilson and Tisdell (2003) through their investigation of wildlife-based attractions, conservation of species leads to economic benefits and political support for the wildlife affected.

In order to gain a competitive edge for nature destinations, Huybers and Bennett (2003) called attention to an environmental management scheme, involving voluntary environmental protection actions by the private sector and the reinforcement of regulations by public entities, as an influential concept of operation. In respect of nature tourism, Blanco (2011) further exhibited the determinants of voluntary environmental initiatives by using a social–ecological system approach that consists of presence of leadership, norms of behaviors among the people involved in voluntary environmental initiatives, shared mental mode, salience of resource for users, and substantial productivity of source system.

Not surprisingly, as presented in the work of Bury (2008), tourism stakeholders have been concerned about the expansion of nature tourism that inadvertently engenders the negative impacts of economy, culture, and environment on the host community given that the contributions to community wellbeing and the magnitude of impact on the environment are not often measured and monitored along different developmental stages. In this regard, researchers (e.g. Bury, 2008; Edwards & Thompson, 2010; Rudendyke & Son, 2005) have advocated concerted actions toward developing efficacious strategies on conservation as a defining agenda to help nature tourism thrive.

A recent study (Sliva & Motzer, 2014) showed that people suffering from economic and social hardship are apt to embrace neoliberal conservation projects in the hope of combining economic opportunities generated by nature tourism with traditional livelihood practices.

In their evaluation of the outcome of a conservation action, Rudendyke & Son (2005) divulged that the resettled people affected by the development of a national park in Vietnam do not benefit much from nature tourism which is in principle regarded as an alternative means of survival for those settlers. Nevertheless, from a story of a different type of tourism stakeholder, Edwards and Thompson (2010) found that private conservation centers for research and education in environmentally affected locations contribute economic welfare to the local communities. They stressed that active conservation centers, which are most likely located in remote locations, could yield significant impacts on rural communities in Africa.

Drawing from a Delphi survey of factors affecting the development of sustainable nature tourism in southern Africa, Spenceley (2008) identified 159 essential and incompatible factors relevant to four emphases: (1) policy and planning, (2) tourism and business management, (3) environment and conversation management, and (4) social and culture issues. Recently, a renewed methodological effort on identifying critical success factors has been developed as Perez, Guerrero, Gonzalez, Perez, and Caballero (2014) constructed a composite indicator in assessment of sustainability of nature destinations. These studies supplied refreshing methodological and practical notes from which the practitioners can learn to advance their efforts on conversation and development.

Tourist Experiences

A growing amount of literature has weighed upon tourist experiences resulting from tourists' contact with nature as well as their participation in physical activity in nature, given the fact that the leisure engagement in nature creates positive effects on human health (Brymer, Cuddihy, & Sharma-Brymer, 2010). Empirical data drawing from a recent study (Chang, 2014) of the health benefits of traveling to nature destinations shows that the frequency of participation in domestic nature tourism has a direct contribution to the function of the nervous system and stress release. Moreover, nature attractions could lead to the fulfillment of a higher hierarchical need in spirituality as indicated in a study by Heintzman (2009).

Through a qualitative study, he further described the scopes of spiritual attainment as spiritual experience, spiritual wellbeing and spiritual coping.

Dorwart, Moore, and Leung (2009), in their grounded theory research explicating recreational experiences in nature, evaluated the influences of visitor experiences from five aspects including nature details, scenic values, management influences, presence of other people, and depreciative behavior. Their study evokes a conceptual framework encompassing the attributes affecting tourist experiences in nature. Hearne and Salinas (2002) added that improved infrastructure is one of the critical attractors for eco-tourists. Meanwhile, from a different perspective evaluating the moderators of tourist experiences, Lee, Huang, and Yeh (2010) illustrated 23 attributes influencing individuals' desires to indulge in the forest environment. Among them, unique forest landscape and special climate phenomena are two salient determinants. Apropos of aesthetic experiences in nature, Breiby (2014) pointed out that harmony, variation/contrast, scenery/viewing, genuineness, and art/architecture are influential factors impacting the effect of viewing experience.

Place attachment is also regarded as a moderator of tourist experiences in nature (Kil, Holland, Stein, & Ko, 2012). Berry and Wolf-Watz (2014), criticizing a current theory of environmental psychology involving concepts of nature and environmental connectedness, called for attentive actions toward the interpretation of nature as a place to avoid simplistic and reductionist views on the concept of nature. They implied that nature should not be portrayed as a geographically undefined agent, as current literature suggests, when examining an individual's environmental connectedness. It is important to consider the influence of the place-related bond between human and the environment. Thus, in nature tourism settings, environmental connectedness is akin to place attachment in concept.

Packer, Ballantyne, and Hughes (2014), in their investigation of the differences in tourist experiences between Chinese and Australian tourists in respect of a nature-centered island resort, argued that nationality could be seen as a moderator of tourist experiences. Their finding shows that Chinese people tend to have more anthropologic views of nature and a fear or less experience of contact with wildlife. Certainly, it cannot be argued that the level of competence and the traits of tour operators/providers could also moderate the tourist experience. In nature settings, tour operators could be seen as resource managers who are able to provide educative information to the tourists and therefore could influence the tourists' attitude toward the environment. Weiler and Davis (1993) listed knowledge, skills, and attitudes as the qualifiers of tour leaders that affect the success in delivering educative messages to the tourists. Powell, Kellert, and Ham (2009) shared their notion that characteristics of service providers (e.g. rafting guide) could affect tourist experiences so as to enhance the tourists' awareness toward pressing issues occurring in protected areas. In addition, the presence of the other tourists could affect the tourist experience. For example, the perceived crowdedness concerning the number of tourists in a given space has been identified as a key moderator of the tourist experience in nature (Wei & Lu, 2014).

Impacts on Community and Nature

Scholars have shown notable interest in exploring the impacts of tourism on nature and community. Bushell, Staiff, and Conner (2002) suggested that the role of tourism in protected areas is significant in connection with the conservation effort and enhancement of quality of life in rural communities and in underdeveloped nations; this has been seen as a pro-poor intervention (Hill, Nel, & Trotter, 2006) concerning the appropriate form of development—in the case of Costa Rica, Sandbrook (2010)—examining spending patterns among different types of tourist activities in Bwindi National Park in Uganda, affirming that the relationship between local benefits and conversation outcomes remains contentious. High-cost forms of tourism are less effective than other forms of tourism in terms of contributing to local benefit.

Studies have been concerned with disturbances caused by human activities to wildlife as the visitor market grows. Huhia and Sulkava (2014) investigated the impact of the presence of tourists on bird nesting behavior, concluding that no significant behavioral change is apparent. However, Steven, Pickering, and Gastley (2001), after reviewing 69 research articles published from 1978 to 2010 on impacts of recreation on birds, ascertained that 88 percent of the articles show negative impacts. As for the contact experience with different types of species, Aguilar-Melo, Andresen, Cristóbal-Azkarate, Arroyo-Rodríguez, Chavira, Schondube, Serio-Silva, and Cuarón (2013) claimed that monkeys' behaviors would be altered due to the presence of humans in nature preserved areas. They observed that as the number of people increase, monkeys tend to spend more time at lower-quality habitations and decrease their social interaction. Bessa and Gonçalves-de-Freitas (2014) monitored the negative impact of nature tourism on fish's social and spawning behaviors and suggest actions to avoid the impact by avoiding stepping on the river bed and reducing the number of visitors.

Moreover, environmental impacts have been reported in other types of recreational activities including fishing, sandboarding, four-wheel driving, and sightseeing, which cause environmental degradation as perceived by the tourists (Priskin, 2003a). Pickering, Bear, and Hill (2007) conveyed that tourism in protected areas results in negative impacts on the environment and further noted that there is an association between tourism infrastructure and diversity of exotic plants according to their investigation of exotic plants in Koscluszko National Park in Australia. In other words, different types of exotic plants introduced via different stages in tourism development may threaten domestic vegetation.

Management and Development

Comprehending consumer behaviors is a critical task complementing service delivery and product development in the realm of marketing management. In the context of nature tourism, studies have evaluated socio-economic (e.g. Slabbert & Plessis, 2012) and psychographic (e.g. Silverberg, Backman, & Backman, 1996) variances. Some focus on a particular demographic, behavioral or trip characteristic that includes but is not limited to gender (e.g. Meng & Uysal, 2015), loyalty (e.g. Moore, Rodger, & Taplin, 2013), motivation (e.g. Tangeland, 2011), satisfaction (e.g. Meng, Tepanon, & Uysal, 2008; Naidoo, Ramseook-Munhurrun, & Seegoolam, 2011), seasons and activity (e.g. Tkaczynski, Rundle-Thiele, & Prebensen, 2015), tourist activity (e.g. Chen, Wang, & Prebensen, 2016) and trust perception (e.g. Zillifor & Morais, 2004). Marketing researchers also utilized socio-demographic (e.g. Tangeland & Aas, 2011) psychological (e.g. Chen, Prebensen, Chen, & Kim, 2013; Mehmetoglu, 2007) traits along with trip characteristics (e.g. Priskin, 2003b) to draw tourist typology (e.g. Arnegger, Woltering, & Job, 2010), as well as to uncover different mutually exclusive market segments in nature tourism and compare the differences in demographics, psychology, and trip characteristics between/among the segments. This type of analysis provides pragmatic insights for developing service and product strategies.

Managerial studies have also considered other issues arising from the demand-related context. Orams (1995), in response to concerns over impact deriving from tourists' increasing use of the natural environment, challenged developing interpretation programs that say that it is sufficient enough to diminish the level of environmental impact caused by tourist activities and called for evaluative schemes to monitor the impacts of interpretation programs. Gaede, Stricker, and Jurin (2011) stressed that tourism providers should encourage their clients to forge a meaningful bond with nature by the use of environmental interpretation programs which could be seen as a way of enhancing tourist experiences. Biggs, Ban, and Hall (2012) articulated personal lifestyle and values as likely to affect business owners and staffs' desire to work in nature environment. Lunderberg, Fredman, and Wall-Reinius (2014) explained that the mindset of tourism entrepreneurs toward profit-making is rather complex. They further argued that profit-making and business growth may not necessarily be a critical agenda for business operators.

Literature has often reported the challenges facing tourism development and planning. In regard to resource assessment, scholars utilized Geographic Information System (GIS) as a tool to assess the possible opportunities for the development of nature tourism. For example, Marzuki, Hussin, Mohamed, Othman, and Puad (2011), using an application of GIS, classified different types of tourism zones guided by three criteria, including physical feature, infrastructure, and accessibility. Using a different approach, Priskin (2001) deployed both qualitative and quantitative methods to identify different tourism sites. Speaking of successful factors and constraints in tourism development, Hiwaski (2006), in a study of national parks, shared four successful factors relying on institutional arrangements, self-regulation towards conservation, high environmental awareness, and the existence of environmental partnerships. Matysek and Kriwoken (2003) highlighted the advantage of implementing an accreditation process as a way to boost the tourist experience and grow the business. Meanwhile research has also shown barriers in development as presented in a Swedish study by Lundmark and Muller (2010) who found accessibility and a lack of suitable products as limitations for tourism development in rural communities. Auger (2004) also pointed to accessibility as a shortcoming when assessing the market potential enticing nature tourists to Canadian-protected nature areas.

Conflict in development between local tourism actors and central government has been occasionally discussed in recent literature. Amundsen (2012), for example, observed tourism development in the Arctic and found that the locals had different goals in development compared to that of nationally defined agendas and are reluctant to embrace national development agendas. Scholars have long advocated building community-based tourism as a sustainable solution for development. In a similar vein, Viljoen and Naicker (2000) demonstrated a successful story involving the tourism business in a communal trust land. Further, literature has suggested analytical mechanisms to assess the effectiveness of community-based tourism. For example, Reimer and Walter (2013), in their investigation of community-based ecotourism in Cambodia, analyzed the benefits and pitfalls of community-based tourism from seven perspectives (e.g. involving travel to destination and minimizing impacts) following the conceptual framework proposed by Honey (2008). They further suggested adding gender as a consideration when evaluating the social dimension of ecotourism since their study revealed a gendered division of labor in ecotourism.

In aggregate, the above review of literature summarizes essential issues familiar to the practitioners of tourism research. The following chapters of this book supplements updated knowledge linking the four thematic notes aforementioned. Chapters 2, 3, 4, 9, and 11 relate to tourist experiences. Chapters 5, 6, 8, 10, 12, 13, 14, 16, and 17 deal with management and development. Chapter 7 covers impacts on community and nature and Chapter 15 touches on environmental rows and conservation.

References

Akama, J. S. (1996). Western environmental values and nature-based tourism in Kenya. *Tourism Management*, 17(8), 567–574.

Arnegger, J., Woltering, M., & Job, H. (2010). Toward a product-based typology for nature-based tourism: A conceptual framework. *Journal of Sustainable Tourism*, 18(7), 915–928.

Auger, D. (2004). Profile of Canada's network of protected areas and its link to potential nature-based tourism and outdoor recreation development. *Tourism (Zagreb)*, 52(4), 329–340.

Beery, T. H., & Wolf-Watz, D. (2014). Nature to place: Rethinking the environmental connectedness perspective. *Journal of Environmental Psychology*, 40, 198–205.

Bessa, E., & Gonçalves-de-Freitas, E. (2014). How does tourist monitoring alter fish behavior in underwater trails? *Tourism Management*, 45, 253–259.

Biggs, D., Ban, N. C., & Hall, C. M. (2012). Lifestyle values, resilience, and nature-based tourism's contribution to conservation on Australia's Great Barrier Reef. *Environmental Conservation*, 39(4), 370–379.

Blanco, E. (2011). A social-ecological approach to voluntary environmental initiatives: The case of nature-based tourism. *Policy Sciences*, 44(1), 35–52.

Breiby, M. A. (2014). Exploring aesthetic dimensions in a nature-based tourism context. *Journal of Vacation Marketing*, 20(2), 163–173.

Brymer, E., Cuddihy, T. F., & Sharma-Brymer, V. (2010). The role of nature-based experiences in the development and maintenance of wellness. *Asia-Pacific Journal of Health, Sport and Physical Education*, 1(2), 21–27.

Bury, J. (2008). New geographies of tourism in Peru: Nature-based tourism and conservation in the Cordillera Huayhuash. *Tourism Geographies*, 10(3), 312–333.

Bushell, R., Staiff, R., & Conner, N. (2002). The role of nature-based tourism in the contribution of protected areas to quality of life in rural and regional communities in Australia. *Journal of Hospitality and Tourism Management*, 9, 24–36.

Chang, L. C. (2014). The relationship between nature-based tourism and autonomic nervous system function among older adults. *Journal of Travel Medicine*, 21(3), 159–162.

Chen, J. S., Prebensen, N., Chen, Y., & Kim, H. (2013). Revelation of nature-minded tourists: A study of Swedish. *Tourism Analysis*, 18, 651–661.

Chen, J. S., Wang, W., & Prebensen, N. (2016). Travel companions and activity preferences of nature-based tourists. *Tourism Review*, 71(1), 45–57.

Dorwart, C. E., Moore, R. L., & Leung, Y. F. (2009). Visitors' perceptions of a trail environment and effects on experiences: A model for nature-based recreation experiences. *Leisure Sciences*, 32(1), 33–54.

Edwards, R. C., & Thompson, E. (2010). The role of conservation research and education centers in growing nature-based tourism. *Great Plains Research*, 20(spring 2010), 51–70.

Gaede, D., Strickert, D., & Jurin, R. R. (2011). Nature-based tourism businesses in Colorado: Interpreting environmental ethics and responsible behavior. *Journal of Tourism Insights*, 1(1), 52–58.

Hearne, R. R., & Salinas, Z. M. (2002). The use of choice experiments in the analysis of tourist preferences for ecotourism development in Costa Rica. *Journal of Environmental Management*, 65(2), 153–163.

Heintzman, P. (2009). Nature-based recreation and spirituality: A complex relationship. *Leisure Sciences*, 32(1),72–89.

Hill, T., Nel, E., & Trotter, D. (2006). Small-scale, nature-based tourism as a pro-poor development intervention: Two examples in Kwazulu-Natal, South Africa. *Singapore Journal of Tropical Geography*, 27(2), 163–175.

Hiwasaki, L. (2006). Community-based tourism: A pathway to sustainability for Japan's protected areas. *Society and Natural Resources*, 19(8), 675–692.

Honey, M. (2008). *Ecotourism and sustainable development: Who owns paradise?* (2nd ed.). Washington, DC: Island Press.

Huybers, T., & Bennett, J. (2003). Environmental management and the competitiveness of nature-based tourism destinations. *Environmental and Resource Economics*, 24(3), 213–233.

Kil, N., Holland, S. M., Stein, T. V., & Ko, Y. J. (2012). Place attachment as a mediator of the relationship between nature-based recreation benefits and future visit intentions. *Journal of Sustainable Tourism*, 20(4), 603–626.

Lee, C. F., Huang, H. I., & Yeh, H. R. (2010). Developing an evaluation model for destination attractiveness: Sustainable forest recreation tourism in Taiwan. *Journal of Sustainable Tourism*, 18(6), 811–828.

Lundberg, C., & Fredman, P. (2012). Success factors and constraints among nature-based tourism entrepreneurs. *Current Issues in Tourism*, 15(7), 649–671.

Lundmark, L., & Müller, D. K. (2010). The supply of nature-based tourism activities in Sweden. *Turizam: znanstveno-stručni časopis*, 58(4), 379–393.

Marcouiller, D. W. (1998). Environmental resources as latent primary factors of production in tourism: The case of forest-based commercial recreation. *Tourism Economics*, 4(2), 131–145.

Marzuki, A., Hussin, A. A., Mohamed, B., Othman, A. G., & Puad, A. (2011). Assessment of nature-based tourism in South Kelantan, Malaysia. *Tourismos: An International Multidisciplinary Journal of Tourism*, 6(1), 281–295.

Matysek, K. A., & Kriwoken, L. K. (2003). The natural state: Nature-based tourism and ecotourism accreditation in Tasmania, Australia. *Journal of Quality Assurance in Hospitality & Tourism*, 4(1–2), 129–146.

Mehmetoglu, M. (2007). Typologising nature-based tourists by activity: Theoretical and practical implications. *Tourism Management*, 28(3), 651–660.

Meng, F., & Uysal, M. (2008). Effects of gender differences on perceptions of destination attributes, motivations, and travel values: An examination of a nature-based resort destination. *Journal of Sustainable Tourism*, 16(4), 445–466.

Meng, F., Tepanon, Y., & Uysal, M. (2008). Measuring tourist satisfaction by attribute and motivation: The case of a nature-based resort. *Journal of Vacation Marketing*, 14(1), 41–56.

Moore, S. A., Rodger, K., & Taplin, R. (2013). Moving beyond visitor satisfaction to loyalty in nature-based tourism: A review and research agenda. *Current Issues in Tourism*, 1–17.

Naidoo, P., Ramseook-Munhurrun, P., & Seegoolam, P. (2011). An assessment of visitor satisfaction with nature-based tourism attractions. *International Journal of Management and Marketing Research*, 4(1), 87–89.

Orams, M. B. (1995). Towards a more desirable form of ecotourism. *Tourism Management*, 16(1), 3–8.

Packer, J., Ballantyne, R., & Hughes, K. (2014). Chinese and Australian tourists' attitudes to nature, animals and environmental issues: Implications for the design of nature-based tourism experiences. *Tourism Management*, 44, 101–107.

Pérez, V., Guerrero, F., González, M., Pérez, F., & Caballero, R. (2014). The sustainability of Cuban nature based tourism destinations: a quantitative approach. *Tourism & Management Studies*, 10(2), 32–40.

Pickering, C. M., Bear, R., & Hill, W. (2007). Indirect impacts of nature based tourism and recreation: The association between infrastructure and the diversity of exotic plants in Kosciuszko National Park, Australia. *Journal of Ecotourism*, 6(2), 146–157.

Powell, R. B., Kellert, S. R., & Ham, S. H. (2009). Interactional theory and the sustainable nature-based tourism experience. *Society and Natural Resources*, 22(8), 761–776.

Priskin, J. (2001). Assessment of natural resources for nature-based tourism: The case of the Central Coast Region of Western Australia. *Tourism Management*, 22(6), 637–648.

Priskin, J. (2003a). Tourist perceptions of degradation caused by coastal nature-based recreation. *Environmental Management*, 32(2), 189–204.

Priskin, J. (2003b). Characteristics and perceptions of coastal and wildflower nature-based tourists in the central coast region of Western Australia. *Journal of Sustainable Tourism*, 11(6), 499–528.

Reimer, J. K., & Walter, P. (2013). How do you know it when you see it? Community-based ecotourism in the Cardamom Mountains of southwestern Cambodia. *Tourism Management*, 34, 122–132.

Rugendyke, B., & Son, N. T. (2005). Conservation costs: Nature-based tourism as development at Cuc Phuong National Park. *Vietnam. Asia Pacific Viewpoint*, 46(2), 185–200.

Sandbrook, C. (2010). Local economic impact of different forms of nature-based tourism. *Conservation Letters*, 3(1), 21–28.

Silva, J. A., & Motzer, N. (2014). Hybrid uptakes of neoliberal conservation in Namibian tourism-based development. *Development and Change*, 46(1), 48–71.

Silverberg, K. E., Backman, S. J., & Backman, K. F. (1996). A preliminary investigation into the psychographics of nature-based travelers to the Southeastern United States. *Journal of Travel Research*, 35(2), 19–28.

Slabbert, E., & Plessis, L. D. (2012). The influence of demographic factors on travel behaviour of visitors to nature-based products in South Africa. *Tourism & Management Studies*, 1118–1121.

Spenceley, A. (2008). Requirements for sustainable nature-based tourism in transfrontier conservation areas: A southern African Delphi consultation. *Tourism Geographies*, 10(3), 285–311.

Steven, R., Pickering, C., & Guy Castley, J. (2011). A review of the impacts of nature based recreation on birds. *Journal of Environmental Management*, 92(10), 2287–2294.

Tangeland, T. (2011). Why do people purchase nature-based tourism activity products? A Norwegian case study of outdoor recreation. *Scandinavian Journal of Hospitality and Tourism*, 11(4), 435–456.

Tangeland, T., & Aas, Ø. (2011). Household composition and the importance of experience attributes of nature based tourism activity products: A Norwegian case study of outdoor recreationists. *Tourism Management*, 32(4), 822–832.

Tkaczynski, A., Rundle-Thiele, S. R., & Prebensen, N. K. (2015). Segmenting potential nature-based tourists based on temporal factors: The case of Norway. *Journal of Travel Research*, 54(2), 251–265.

Viljoen, J. H., & Naicker, K. (2000). Nature-based tourism on communal land: The Mavhulani experience. *Development Southern Africa*, 17(1), 135–148.

Wang, E., Wei, J., & Lu, H. (2014). Valuing natural and non-natural attributes for a national forest park using a choice experiment method. *Tourism Economics*, 20(6), 1199–1213.

Weiler, B., & Davis, D. (1993). An exploratory investigation into the roles of the nature-based tour leader. *Tourism Management*, 14(2), 91–98.

Wilson, C., & Tisdell, C. (2003). Conservation and economic benefits of wildlife-based marine tourism: Sea turtles and whales as case studies. *Human Dimensions of Wildlife*, 8(1), 49–58.

Zillifro, T., & Morais, D. B. (2004). Building customer trust and relationship commitment to a nature-based tourism provider: The role of information investments. *Journal of Hospitality & Leisure Marketing*, 11(2–3), 159–172.

2 Nature and Well-being

Explorer Travel Narratives of Transformation

Jennifer Laing and Warwick Frost

Introduction

Perhaps as a reaction to the artificiality of modern life, there is increasing interest in the role that time spent in nature can play in improving health, quality of life, individual well-being and even happiness (e.g. MacKerron & Mourato, 2013; Smith *et al.*, 2013; Thompson Coon *et al.*, 2011). The traveller may experience 'a total merging of self and environment' (Ittelson, Franck & O'Hanlon, 1976), allowing them to discover who they are and their place in the world, in a form of self-actualisation (Hall, 2002; Laing & Crouch, 2011) or existential authenticity (Wang, 1999). The visceral quality of these nature-based experiences, involving potential or real risks, appear to lead some travellers to challenge themselves, transcend self-imposed boundaries, achieve goals or to be receptive to new identities (Laing & Frost, 2014; Robledo & Batle, 2015).

The profound impacts of time spent in the natural surrounds have been described by various travel writers, in an attempt to give the reader some understanding of what such an experience might be like. The writer often refers to the experience as *transformative*. For example, blind mountaineer Eric Weihenmayer illustrates the connections between nature and self during a day climbing:

> A feeling of such intensity swept over me that I could feel my body shaking. I had only stood on the summit for a few minutes, but the experience had forged itself into me, more powerful than any memory, fusing so tight that it was impossible to distinguish me from it. I could still feel the blasting wind, the storms, and the staggeringly long days. I could feel it all, from the bumpy plane ride in, to the immense openness of the summit, and it was all within me, changing my life forever, no longer a dream but flesh and bone and blood. I had never known, never truly known, that this awesome place could exist inside me.
>
> (Weihenmayer, 2001, pp. 196–197)

Previous studies on the role of travel writing have considered whether it may encourage 'more globally conscious and socially responsible' travel (McWha, Frost, Laing & Best, 2016, p. 85), facilitate reflections on the self (Blanton, 2002) or influence travel imaginings (Laing & Frost, 2012). We feel there is scope to go further; analysing travel texts in order to broaden our understanding of some of the deeper psychological benefits of travel. Travel in the modern era is often criti- cised for the heavy footprint it leaves on both the physical and social landscape, with less emphasis placed on the potentially positive outcomes for individuals (Brosnan, Filep & Rock, 2015). Travel narratives could be used to explore how the process of travel shapes and changes us in a positive sense, perhaps using theories drawn from positive psychology; a body of work which examines con- cepts such as happiness, optimism, well-being and quality of life (Filep, 2012a; Filep & Pearce, 2014).

In this chapter, we examine the potential contributions that nature-based travel can make to well-being through a qualitative thematic analysis of three non-fiction explorer travel narratives. The term *explorer traveller* is used here to describe those individuals who walk in the footsteps of those who have gone before them:

> Imagining ourselves to be explorers like them gives purpose and status to our travels. Rather than just being a tourist on holidays, we are seeking, search- ing, discovering. There is a primal urge to keep moving, looking over the next hill for new lands, peoples and adventures.
>
> (Laing & Frost, 2014, p. 4)

Both authors conducted the analysis together, categorising the well-being out- comes that emerged from the texts and comparing them to the extant literature. These texts were selected to encompass a mix of genders and a variety of natural landscapes (mountains, water and wetlands and desert) and wildlife. They are all still in print; in Muir's case over a century after first being published. Before moving to the three case studies, we introduce the theoretical framework used in the analysis.

Eudaimonia, Hedonia and Subjective Well-being

In choosing well-being as the focus of this chapter, we were aware that there are a number of models or theoretical frameworks which could have been used to underpin this study. For example, the elements of Seligman's (2011) theoretical model of well-being known as PERMA (positive emotions, engagement, rela- tionships, meaning and achievement) were found to be present in an exploratory study of contemporary long-distance walkers (Saunders, Laing & Weiler, 2014). We felt there was value however in considering other theories of well-being and extending the inquiry beyond long-distance walking to nature-based experiences more generally.

Despite the large body of work on well-being that has developed, there is still a divergence of opinions on the role of eudaimonia and hedonia in well- being outcomes, as well as a lack of consensus on an agreed definition of each concept. Huta and Waterman (2014) have provided an overview of conceptual definitions, to assist researchers moving forward, and we found this to be a use- ful starting point for this study. The concept of *eudaimonia* can be traced back to Aristotle (384–322 BC), and its philosophical underpinnings are encapsulated in the idea of 'activity reflecting virtue, excellence, the best within us, and the full development of our potentials' (Huta & Waterman, 2014, p. 1427). It can be contrasted with *hedonia* or hedonism, where 'the principal, and sometimes exclusive, focus is placed on happiness as pleasure, enjoyment, and absence of discomfort understood as subjective affective states' (p. 1427). According to Voigt (2017), both concepts are important in order to 'comprehensively understand psychological well-being', although there has been a greater emphasis on the hedonic aspects of tourism to date (Filep, 2012b; 2016). For this reason, we will focus on both hedonic and eudaimonic elements of nature travel experiences in this chapter.

The four common elements of eudaimonia, according to Huta and Waterman (2014) appear to be growth, authenticity, meaning and excellence. The element of *growth* includes personal growth, reaching one's potential and self-actualisation, while *authenticity* covers such things as identity, autonomy and personal expressiveness. The element of *meaning* includes seeing a purpose in what one is doing and taking a long-term perspective, while *excellence* can be understood as involving the attainment of a high standard and developing signature strengths. However, other eudaimonic elements have also been identified in the literature, notably *positive relationships* and *competence/environmental mastery*. In terms of hedonia, common elements appear to be *pleasure, enjoyment* and *life satisfaction*. There is conjecture over whether *absence of distress* also plays a part. In this chapter, we will consider whether some or all of the elements appear to be present for the writers of the three texts we have chosen for analysis.

My First Summer in the Sierra (John Muir, 1911)

In the spring of 1868, thirty-year-old Muir wants to venture into the Sierra Nevada Mountains of California; he has already made a short trip to Yosemite and he dreams of going further. Born in Scotland, his family migrated to the USA. After an industrial accident almost leaves him blind, the restless Muir resolves to travel and experience the natural world (Hall, 2010; Mark & Hall, 2009). However, funding is a restraint. A Mr Delaney, for whom he had worked previously, asks him to accompany a flock of sheep, which will be herded into the mountains for the summer. Muir protests that 'I was in no way the right man for the place ... I feared that half or more of the flock would be lost' (Muir, 1911, pp. 153–4). Delaney is not concerned; he just needs a reliable man and is happy for Muir to engage in nature studies as he travels. It is an interesting time for nature travels into the American West. An instructive contrast may be drawn between Muir's trip and the 1870 Washburn Expedition that results in the establishment of Yellowstone National Park (Frost & Laing, 2015). Both venture into territory that has been touched upon by trappers and prospectors, but lay claim to be 'discoverers' by virtue of being the first to produce a written record of their travels.

Muir is in raptures as he advances higher and higher into the mountains. Following the literary conventions of travellers in the nineteenth century, he romanticises the wild scenery that he views through the concept of the sublime. Thus, upon entering the Yosemite Valley, he refers to:

> its sublimes domes and cañons, dark upsweeping forests, and glorious arrays of white peaks deep in the sky ... Never before had I seen so glorious a landscape, so boundless an affluence of sublime mountain beauty. The most extravagant description I might give of this view to any one who had not seen similar landscapes with his own eyes would not so much as hint at the grandeur and the spiritual glow that covered it. I shouted and gesticulated in a wild burst of ecstasy.
>
> (Muir, 1911, p. 219)

In such a passage, Muir starts by describing a physical view and then proceeds to explain his inability to fully convey what he sees. The latter was an especially common trope in nineteenth century travel writing about mountains. However, he then goes one step further, describing how he is so transformed into a state of ecstasy that this has a physical manifestation.

Eleven days later, he provides another passage invoking transformation and religious imagery. On that day he has travelled higher into the Sierra, aiming for the summit of Mt Hoffman at 11,000 feet. For Muir, this is 'the highest point in life's journey my feet have yet touched'. This alpine environment is all new to him and he relates how he is 'eagerly, tremulously hopeful of some day knowing more, learning the meaning of the divine symbols crowded together on this wondrous page' (Muir, 2011, p. 240). He finds the alpine meadows to be full of unusual plants and crystals and writes again of a physical effect 'in the midst of such beauty, pierced with its [the sun's] rays, one's body is all one tingling palate'. And again he veers towards ecstatic exclamation: 'Who wouldn't be a mountaineer! Up here all the world's prizes seem nothing' (p. 243). Returning downhill towards his camp, he notes that he is 'enjoying wild excitement and excess of strength' (p. 244).

The next day, he strikes out for the glacial Lake Tenaya. It is:

> another big day, enough for a lifetime ... joyful, wonderful, enchanting, banishing weariness and sense of time ... on I sauntered in freedom complete, body without weight as far as I was aware ... everything is perfectly clean and pure and full of divine lessons ... Nature as a poet ... becomes more and more visible the farther and higher we go.
>
> (Muir, 2011, p. 244)

At this stage, Muir is still with the shepherd. However, after an argument with Mr Delaney, the shepherd quits. With autumn coming, Delaney has to leave Muir to fetch supplies. When his boss returns, Muir reflects that he 'felt not a trace of loneliness while he was gone. On the contrary, I never enjoyed grander company. The whole wilderness seems to be alive and familiar' (p. 293). As they guide the sheep back down the mountains, Muir ponders the future and wonders if he will be ever able to return.

Muir's writing suggests that these outdoor environments are emotional territories (Shafer & Mietz, 1972), linked to nineteenth century romantic views of nature. The focus is on the majestic landscape, and to a lesser extent the flora within the alpine setting. Muir's experience in nature is largely hedonic, involving moments of pure happiness and joy, illustrated by his references to 'wild excitement' and 'wild burst of ecstasy', yet it goes beyond that. There are hints at eudaimonic well-being involving the deeper meaning behind these travel experiences, manifested in his comments about 'the world's prizes' seeming to be empty or worthless, as well as aspects like mastery and excellence, both in terms of what he is learning about nature but also about the pinnacle of his own physical achievements. There are hints at the transformative power of what he has seen and done. It does not appear however that this journey has affected his relationships with others. Muir likes being on his own. If anything, the most positive relationship he has on his travels is with nature, which he describes in human terms ('never enjoyed grander company'). While the epiphany of the book is not made explicit, Muir will now go back into nature on a regular basis.

Ring of Bright Water (Gavin Maxwell, 1960)

Gavin Maxwell is staying with a friend. One morning, the friend remarks that he has bought a Scottish Estate, with a vacant cottage, which Gavin can have if he wants. So begins his adventure. There is very little exposition as to why Gavin takes up the offer. The author explains that while he is not a native of the Highlands, it has always fascinated him. He describes himself as 'an earnest member of the Celtic fringe', though as an 'arrant snob', the 'robust enthusiasm of tartaned hikers from the industrial cities inspired in me a nausea' (Maxwell, 1960, p. 4). He might also be escaping financial difficulties. A five-year stint at establishing a fishing business has brought him to the verge of bankruptcy and that is where his friend steps in.

However, there is much more background to Maxwell that is not covered in the book. According to his biographers, his life was characterised by restlessness, a series of crackpot ventures and a range of unsuccessful personal relationships. It has been suggested that he was bi-polar and/or suffered other psychological issues. During World War Two, he served in London during the Blitz and later was a specialist training officer of under-cover operatives for the elite Special Operations Executive (Botting, 1993; Lister-Kaye, 2014). Nature might have been a form of escape. We also have hints that Maxwell saw the West Highlands in romantic terms. According to Botting (1993), he invoked Arthurian references, calling it his Avalon, though such terminology is not used in Maxwell's book. Such omissions create challenges for readers as they try to understand Maxwell's motivations for embracing the natural world.

The first third of the book covers Maxwell settling into his new home at Sandaig Bay, opposite the Isle of Skye. In one of his few references to the War, Maxwell is enthusiastic about the appeal of remoteness:

It brings a sense of isolation that is the very opposite of the loneliness a stranger finds in the city ... but to be quite alone where there are no other human beings is sharply exhilarating; it is as though some pressure has suddenly been lifted, allowing an intense awareness of one's surroundings, [and] a sharpening of the senses ... I experienced it first as a very young man, travelling alone on the tundra ... of the Arctic Circle ... paradoxically, for the external circumstances were the very opposite, I had the same or an allied sensation during the heavy air-raids in 1940, as though life was stripped of inessentials.

(Maxwell, 1960, pp. 22–23)

Maxwell's book is an interesting variation on many nature narratives. He does not characterise the landscape as wilderness; for he notes that it is inhabited by people – albeit sparsely – and these are working farms, forests and fisheries. It is wild animals, rather than wilderness, that he concentrates on. Accordingly, there are long passages of interactions with the likes of deer, wildcats, porpoises, fish and birds. Maxwell notes a profound difference in how his visiting friends react to nature, for they are 'usually struck inarticulate by the desolate grandeur of the landscape and the splendour of pale blue and gold spring mornings, [yet] they are entirely articulate in their amazement at the variety of wild life by which I am surrounded' (pp. 24–5).

About a third of the way into the book, the tone and prose change dramatically as Maxwell undertakes a bold experiment. He convinces Wilfred Thesiger to take him on an expedition to Iraq. Again this seems to be the result of a combination of restlessness and the need to prove himself as a worthy explorer (Botting, 1993), though Maxwell provides very little elaboration on his motivations. Once in Iraq, he becomes focussed on acquiring an otter. This leads to a series of comical interludes. Whilst a master of fieldcraft and wilderness survival, Maxwell is disorganised in more normal social settings. Returning to Britain, he takes his otter on the plane as hand luggage. Naturally, it escapes, and the flight attendant must step in to retrieve it.

The otter, who is given the name Mijbil, is completely out of place in urban environments. However, once Maxwell takes him to his Scottish cottage, Mijbil is in his element. There are lengthy passages describing his play and adventures in waterfalls, streams and the sea. These are the best-written and most enchanting passages within the book and it is this interaction between human and otter which made this story famous. Mijbil functions as a sort of alter-ego for Maxwell. When they are both together in Scotland, life is idyllic. Encounters with modernity cause stress and chaos for both of them.

When Mijbil is killed by a truck, Maxwell is heart-broken and goes into a decline. He does not visit Scotland for a year, writing that Mijbil, 'had filled the landscape so completely ... that it seemed, after he had gone from it, hollow and insufficient' (Maxwell, 1960, p. 150). During this period of mourning, Maxwell becomes obsessed with possessing exotic animals. He buys a lemur, which tries to kill him, then a bush-baby and a dozen tropical birds. He arranges for the importation of three otters from Iraq, but they all die within days. Another attempt results in the death of two more otters, finally forcing Maxwell to realise that people like him, 'by their patronage keep alive the nauseating market in wild animals, and after this I was determined that I would try no more importing of otters' (p. 157).

Having made this resolution, Maxwell has a chance encounter with a couple who have an African otter they are trying to find a home for. This second otter, called Edal, quickly bonds with Maxwell and they return to Scotland. The book concludes with an optimistic Maxwell looking to the future. Unfortunately, this was not to be. Amongst other things, his book was an instant best-seller and this attracted large numbers of tourists to his remote Scottish cottage, while Edal proves to be difficult and dangerous (Botting, 1993).

Like Muir, Maxwell also refers to a mixture of hedonic and eudaimonic well-being outcomes in his book, the result of being within nature. Mostly this is connected to the wildlife he encounters, which is not the case with Muir. Perhaps, for a person who has not experienced many positive human relationships over his life, the time Maxwell spent with animals was balm for his soul. While he refers to the hedonic enjoyment of being alone as 'exhilarating', his time with Thesiger suggests that he sought the company of a famous explorer and a challenging environment to achieve outcomes of mastery or excellence. Unfortunately, this doesn't seem to have worked. Yet there is a sense that Maxwell has achieved some personal growth and self-actualisation by the end of the book, learning that he functions best in remote settings. His relationship with animals also undergoes examination, with Maxwell realising that his mania for possessing wild animals is paradoxically taking them out of the very environment that he prizes. There is also a suggestion that Maxwell is slowly beginning to understand that their wildness, while attractive to him, will never make them the companions he desires.

Tracks (Robyn Davidson, 1980)

Robyn Davidson is clear about her reasons for wanting to trek across the Australian Outback solo with camels. Her desire for change is palpable: 'The most difficult thing had been the decision to act ... One really could act to change and control one's life; and the procedure, the process, was its own reward' (Davidson, 1980, p. 37). The journey is partly a way of escaping the ennui of her life in the city, but is also something positive that will give her a purpose and direction:

> I had ... been vaguely bored with my life and its repetitions – the half-finished, half-hearted attempts at different jobs and various studies; had been sick of carrying around the self-indulgent negativity which was so much the malaise of my generation, my sex and my class.
>
> (Davidson, 1980, p. 37)

The first thing she notices in the Outback is 'a feeling of release; a sustained buoyant confidence as I strolled along' (p. 109). The desert is visually a place of enchantment, with references to 'an infinitely extended bowl of pastel blue haze with writhing hills and crescents floating and shimmering in it and fire-coloured dunes lapping at their feet and off in the distance some magical, violet mountains' (p. 218). It is also a transcendent experience. Davidson writes that the desert makes her feel:

> as if I were made of some fine, bright, airy, musical substance and that in my chest was a source of power that would any minute explode, releasing thousands of singing birds ... I felt like dancing and calling to the great spirit. Mountains pulled and pushed, wind roared down chasms. I followed eagles suspended from cloud horizons. I wanted to fly in the unlimited blue of the morning.
>
> (Davidson, 1980, p. 101)

The result was that 'I was seeing it all as if for the first time, all fresh and bathed in an effulgence of light and joy' (p. 101). The process of being in nature cleanses Davidson of the dirt and detritus of urban life (p. 154): 'My mind was rinsed clean and sparkling and light'. Davidson's prose is evocative, as she compares herself to a snake with the shedding of conventions built up through exposure to Western society. Time spent in the Outback leads to a new self emerging: 'This desocial-izing process – the sloughing off, like a snakeskin, of the useless preoccupations and standards of the society I had left, and the growing of new ones that were more tuned to my present environment – was beginning to show' (p. 181). This process of purification extends to her relationships:

> It was a giant cleansing of all the garbage and muck that had accumulated in my brain, a gentle catharsis. And because of that, I suppose, I could see much more clearly into my present relationships with people and with myself.
>
> (Davidson, 1980, p. 181)

Perhaps the transformative moment for Davidson is when she realises after two weeks in the desert – 'hey, where was the great clap of the thunder of awareness that as everyone knows, knocks people sideways in deserts. I was exactly the same person that I was when I began' (p. 127). Despite all the joy of being in nature and captivated by its beauty and majesty, and her satisfaction in dealing with challenges, Davidson comes to understand that transformation in this environment takes time. Gradually she starts to relax and the changes gradually unfold. She stops worrying about how she looks ('I liked myself this way, it was such a relief to be free of disguises and prettiness and attractiveness' – p. 196). There is a realisation however that these changes could be short-lived if she is not careful ('I didn't want ever to leave this desert. I knew that I would forget' – p. 197).

She starts to embrace the moment and her euphoria is recorded in a letter she writes to a friend. While knowing it won't be posted for months, Davidson needs to get the sentiment down on paper, or she will burst: 'I FEEL GREAT. Life's so joyous, so sad, so ephemeral, so crazy, so meaningless, so goddam funny. What's wrong with me that I feel this good? ... This is paradise, and I wish I could give you some' (p. 204). This is juxtaposed with the wretchedness she later feels when her beloved dog is poisoned, reminding her that life could be arbitrary and she was not invincible: 'That night I received the most profound and cruel lesson of all. That death is sudden and final and comes from nowhere. It had waited for my moment of supreme complacency and then it had struck' (p. 221).

The end of her trek leaves her musing on what it has all meant and what she has learnt. While there is the danger that the seductions of urban living will lead her to fall back into bad habits, she is aware of how the trip has changed her:

> I had discovered capabilities and strengths that I would not have imagined possible in those distant dream-like days before the trip. I had rediscovered people in my past and come to terms with my feelings towards them. I had learnt what love was. That love wanted the best possible for those you cared for even if that excluded yourself ... I had learnt to use my fears as stepping stones rather than stumbling blocks, and best of all I had learnt to laugh.
>
> (Davidson, 1980, p. 220)

Davidson's travels, like those of Muir and Maxwell, appear to exhibit both eudaimonic and hedonic elements. The difference here is that *all* the key eudaimonic elements noted in the literature appear to be present for her, such as growth, authenticity, meaning, excellence, positive relationships and competence. They relate to all aspects of the natural environment – landscape, the weather, and the animals she takes with her and also encounters in the wild. She also learns from the indigenous people she meets on the way. Her trip is also clearly highly pleasurable at different stages, and the enjoyment bubbles through her writing; when she sees something beautiful or feels a sense of peace about what she is doing or simply when she surrenders to the moment. The upsetting or painful circumstances at different periods during her travels – her dog dying, the camels escaping, lack of food and water – perhaps heighten the delight she experiences at other times. This suggests that the hedonic concept of well-being as a function of *absence of distress* is not as relevant in this type of travel experience, where the challenges faced make the journey deeper, richer and more meaningful. Unlike Muir and Maxwell, there is an express acknowledgement that Davidson has been transformed during her travels in nature, while being on guard against slipping back into old habits. Like Muir, this was the start of a number of journeys into nature for Davidson.

Conclusion

This study demonstrates the value of applying positive psychology theories in a tourism setting in order to gain a deeper understanding of the benefits of nature-based travel. The analysis of the three narratives examined in this chapter supports the view that nature-based travel can be a powerful and transformative experience that may contribute to both hedonic and eudaimonic well-being. These findings support the calls by Voigt (2017) and Filep (2012b; 2016) for tourism studies to encompass exploration of both hedonic and eudaimonic forms of well-being, as opposed to concentrating on hedonic elements such as pleasure. We recognise however that further work is needed to understand these outcomes in more depth, perhaps based on a broader study of travel narratives, including films and documentaries, or the conduct of long interviews with travellers to tease out subtle nuances connected to well-being. In addition, Voigt's research considered well-being at three different levels: experiential (focused on the tourist experience), motivational (considering the benefits sought by the tourist, which form their motives for travel) and global (examining well-being outcomes outside the tourist experience). It was beyond the scope of this chapter to look at well-being in this level of detail. This suggests another area for future research.

A second finding of this study is that well-being outcomes were mentioned in travel narratives spanning nearly one hundred years. This is thus not merely a modern phenomenon. Whether a study spanning a greater time period would be useful however is up for debate. While the three narratives considered in this chapter provided a great amount of detail about the impact of their time in nature on the *self*, the lack of such content in travel narratives of a previous generation, where there is often a greater emphasis on factual information rather than personal stories (Blanton, 2002), may prove a stumbling block to comparing well-being outcomes over time.

The small number of books covered in this chapter made it difficult to assess whether gender made a difference in terms of the findings. This would be a fruitful area for a follow-up study. The books were also largely drawn from a Western, Anglo-Saxon canon, and thus different findings might have been present in a study of books written by authors from outside these cultural settings. A more diverse set of texts might therefore be useful, particularly as a basis of comparison with the findings outlined in this chapter. Nevertheless, the study shows some of the potential of using travel narratives such as books as texts to be analysed. It is to be hoped that more tourism researchers will avail themselves of what is still a largely underused resource at their disposal.

References

Blanton, C. (2002). *Travel writing: The self and the world*. New York: Routledge.

Botting, D. (1993). *Gavin Maxwell: A life*. London: Harper Collins.

Brosnan, T., Filep, S. & Rock, J. (2015). Exploring synergies: Hopeful tourism and citizen science. *Annals of Tourism Research*, 53, 96–98.

Davidson, R. (1980). *Tracks*. London: Pan Macmillan.

Filep, S. (2012a). Positive psychology and tourism. In M. Uysal, R. Perdue & J. Sirgy (Eds.), *Handbook of tourism and quality-of-life research* (pp. 31–50). London: Springer.

Filep, S. (2012b). Moving beyond subjective well-being: A tourism critique. *Journal of Hospitality and Tourism Research*, 38, 266–274.

Filep, S. (2016). Tourism and positive psychology critique: Too emotional? *Annals of Tourism Research*, 59, 113–115.

Filep, S. & Pearce, P. (Eds.) (2014). Introducing tourist experience and fulfilment research. In S. Filep & P. L. Pearce (Eds.), *Tourist experience and fulfilment: Insights from positive psychology* (pp. 1–14). New York, NY: Routledge.

Frost, W. & Laing, J. (2015). *Imagining the West through film and tourism*. London: Routledge.

Hall, C. M. (2002). The changing cultural geography of the frontier: National parks and wilderness as frontier remnant. In S. Krakover & Y. Gradus (Eds.), *Tourism in frontier areas* (pp. 283–298). Lanham, MA: Lexington Books.

Hall, C. M. (2010). John Muir: Pioneer of nature preservation. In R. W. Butler & R. A. Russell (Eds.), *Giants of tourism* (pp. 229–242). Wallingford UK: CABI.

Huta, V. & Waterman, A. S. (2014). Eudaimonia and its distinction from hedonia: Developing a classification and terminology for understanding conceptual and operational definitions. *Journal of Happiness Studies*, 15, 1425–1456.

Ittelson, W. H., Franck, K. A. & O'Hanlon, T. J. (1976). The nature of environmental experience. In S. Wapner, S. B. Cohen & B. Kaplan (Eds.), *Experiencing the environment* (pp. 187–206). New York: Plenum Press.

Laing, J. & Frost, W. (2012). *Books and travel: Inspiration, quests and transformation*. Bristol: Channel View.

Laing, J. & Frost, W. (2014). *Explorer travellers and adventure tourism*. Bristol: Channel View.

Laing, J. H. & Crouch, G. I. (2011). Frontier tourism: Retracing mythic journeys. *Annals of Tourism Research*, 38(4), 1516–1534.

Lister-Kaye, J. (2014). *The genius of Gavin Maxwell, The Telegraph,* 4 July 2014. Retrieved from http://www.telegraph.co.uk/news/earth/wildlife/10943319/The-genius-of-Gavin-Maxwell.html

MacKerron, G. & Mourato, S. (2013). Happiness is greater in natural environments. *Global Environmental Change*, 23(5), 992–1000.

McWha, M., Frost, W., Laing, J. & Best, G. (2016). Writing for the anti-tourist? Imagining the contemporary travel magazine reader as an authentic experience seeker. *Current Issues in Tourism*, 19(1), 85–99.

Mark, S. R. & Hall, C. M. (2009). John Muir and William Gladstone Steel: Activists and the establishment of Yosemite and Crater Lake National Parks. In W. Frost & C. M. Hall (Eds.), *Tourism and national parks: International perspectives on development, histories and change* (pp. 88–101). London: Routledge.

Maxwell, G. (1960). *Ring of bright water*. New York: E. P. Dutton.

Muir, J. (1911). *My first summer in the Sierra*. In *John Muir nature writings, 1997*. New York: Library of America.

Robledo, M. A. & Batle, J. (2015). Transformational tourism as a hero's journey. *Current Issues in Tourism*, 1–13, doi:10.1080/13683500.2015.1054270

Saunders, R., Laing, J. & Weiler, B. (2014). Personal transformation through long-distance walking. In S. Filep & P. L. Pearce (Eds.), *Tourist experience and fulfilment: Insights from positive psychology* (pp. 127–146). New York, NY: Routledge.

Seligman, M. E. P. (2011). *Flourish*. Sydney: Random House.

Shafer, E. L. Jr. & Mietz, J. (1972). Aesthetic and emotional experiences rate high with northeast wilderness hikers. In J. F. Wohlwill & D. H. Carson (Eds.), *Environment and the social sciences: Perspectives and applications* (pp. 207–216). Washington DC: American Psychological Association.

Smith, L. M., Case, J. L., Smith, H. M., Harwell, L. C. & Summers, J. K. (2013). Relating ecosystem services to domains of human well-being: Foundation for a US index. *Ecological Indicators*, 28, 79–90.

Thompson Coon, J., Boddy, K., Stein, K., Whear, R., Barton, J. & Depledge, M. H. (2011). Does participating in physical activity in outdoor natural environments have a greater effect on physical and mental well-being than physical activity indoors? A systematic review. *Environmental Science & Technology*, 45(5), 1761–1772.

Voigt, C. (2017). Employing hedonia and eudaimonia to explore differences between three groups of wellness tourists on the experiential, the motivational and the global level. In S. Filep, J. Laing & M. Csikszentmihalyi (Eds.), *Positive tourism*. London: Routledge.

Wang, N. (1999). Rethinking authenticity in tourism experience. *Annals of Tourism Research*, 26, 349–370.

Weihenmayer, E. (2001). *Touch the top of the world: A blind man's journey to climb higher than the eye can see*. Sydney: Hodder.

3   Well-being in Wildlife Experiences

Feeling Good for the Animals?

Giovanna Bertella

This study concerns wildlife experiences and investigates the link between human and animal well-being. The research question is: How and to what extent can human well-being related to wildlife encounters be described and explained in terms of empathy toward the animals?

Here, well-being is understood as identifying a hedonic aspect—experiencing pleasure and happiness—and a eudaimonic aspect—experiencing a sense of meaning and self-realization (Ryan & Deci, 2001). Several scholarly contributions from various fields argue that experiences that occur in nature, including those relative to wildlife encounters, can be sources of well-being in both these senses (Curtin, 2009; Filep, 2012; Kaplan, 1995; Keniger, Gastone, Irvine, & Fuller, 2013; McDonald, Wearing, & Pointing, 2009; Russel et al., 2013).

Based on these considerations, and in order to investigate the link between animal and human well-being, this study adopts the concepts of empathy and empathic well-being. The study's focus and empirical research concern encounters with whales. This choice depends on the assumption of the high probability that such encounters provoke a form of well-being in humans that goes beyond the hedonic aspect (Allen, 2014; DeMares & Krycka, 1999; Webb & Drummond, 2001).

Conceptualizing Empathy and Empathic Well-being

Discussing empathy in the context of wildlife experiences, Bulbeck (2005) notes the following definition: empathy is about "putting ourselves in the other's place, seeing the world to some degree from the perspective of another with needs and experiences both similar to and different from our own" (Plumwood, 2002, p.132, as cited in Bulbeck, 2005, p. 196). Based on this definition, empathy is understood here as the capacity to recognize the similarities and differences between humans and non-human animals and to put ourselves in their place. Empathy is a broader concept than compassion and it includes not only concern for the suffering others, but also perspective taking and emotional sharing (Pfattheicher, Sassenrath, & Schindler, 2015).

Empathy can be further conceptualized by referring to the notion of care and, more specifically, to the four dimensions of knowledge, attentiveness, respon-sibility, and connectedness (Donovan & Adams, 2007). The philosopher Mary

Midgley commented on our knowledge of the animal world as follows: "The more we know about their [the animals'] detailed behavior, the clearer and more interesting [the] continuity [between human and non-human animals] becomes" (Midgley, 1998, p. 14). According to Midgley such continuity does not imply the possibility of fully understanding the animal world but for those who are willing to give time and attention to animals, it allows them the potential for understanding. Thus, empathy relies on the individual's knowledge as well as on their attentiveness.

Some studies argue that humans can feel a sense of responsibility and a sense of affinity and connectedness towards nature and animals, and these aspects are also viewed in relation to the concept of empathy (Donovan & Adams, 2007; Wilson, 1984). It could be proposed that wildlife encounters are capable of reawakening emotional connections between humans and the natural world, including wild animals (Clement, 2007; Curtin & Kragh, 2014).

The four dimensions of empathy presented above can be related to the concept of wildlife value orientation. Different orientations toward wildlife are identified on the basis of various beliefs about the human use of wildlife, and care for wild animals is among these as a dimension of mutualism (Dayer, Stinchfield, & Manfredo, 2007). Care is about feeling emotionally attached to animals, and feeling well when coming into contact with them and when helping them.

On the basis of these considerations, this study describes the concept of empathic well-being in the context of wildlife encounters in the following way: a sense of happiness and meaningfulness when witnessing the animal's well-being and, at the same time, a sense of being partly responsible for such a state.

Whale Watchers' and Whales' Well-being

Whale watching is a consumptive non-lethal activity centered on the potential for tourists to observe whales in their natural environment. Whale watching activities performed in an irresponsible way can interfere in the animals' lives and have negative effects on their well-being (Higham, Bejeder, & Williams, 2014). The latter is here understood in relation to the "five freedoms": freedom from hunger and thirst; freedom from discomfort; freedom from pain, injury or disease; freedom to express normal behavior; and freedom from fear and distress (Fennel, 2012). The freedom related to the expression of normal behavior is viewed here in relation to the potentials that the animals have, including physical as well as cognitive and affective ones (Kalof & Fitzgerald, 2007).

The issue concerning the distance that is kept between the whale watching boats and the animals is relevant to the whales' well-being as well as to the tourist experience. With regard to this, the literature shows some contrasting results. On the one hand, Finkler and Higham (2004) observe that whale watchers can sometimes experience contrasting feelings of wanting to be close to the whales whilst, at the same time, being concerned about disturbing the animals. Similarly, a recent report by the Whale and Dolphin Conservation indicates that whale watchers tend to consider following the guidelines concerning the proximity to the whales and maintaining a safe distance very important (Harms, Asmutis-Silvia, & Rosner 2013). On the other hand, Kessler, Harcourt, and Bradford (2014) suggest that, given the possibility, whale watchers would prefer to approach closer to the whales than is currently permitted. Some studies suggest that there is a variety of attitudes among whale watchers, with some being concerned about the animals' well-being, and others focused on their desire to get as close as possible to them (Moscardo, 2000; Muloin, 1998; Orams, 2000). This is in line with the recognition of various wildlife orientations and the description of wildlife watchers as a heterogeneous group (Lemelin & Wiersma, 2007; Wilson & Tisdell, 2003).

Method

The empirical investigation for this study focuses on northern Norway, where whale watching activities, both touristic and recreational, have increased considerably since 2011. The data collection was divided into two phases. An explorative phase was based on the collection and analysis of secondary data. In the second phase, in-depth interviews were conducted with the aim of gaining a good understanding of the emotions and reflections linked to the whale encounters. The interviews were performed in the researcher's and the respondents' mother tongue.

The secondary data are 124 TripAdvisor reviews concerning the three whale watching companies indicated on the webpage of the northern Norwegian destination management organization. A content analysis was conducted in which the units of analysis were the expressions used to describe the animals and the feelings and reflections provoked by the whale encounters. The analysis focused on those elements that can be related to three of the dimensions of empathic well-being. The knowledge dimension is difficult to observe in the reviews and, therefore, the analysis considers attentiveness, responsibility, and connectedness. Attentiveness is related to comments about the behavior and the condition of the whales, in particular, their aesthetics, mood, aliveness, intention, and reciprocity, and the way in which these features are interpreted in terms of well-being (DeMares, 2000). Comments about responsibility are categorized in two groups: responsibility at the individual level and responsibility at the collective level (Harms, Asmutis-Silvia, & Rosner, 2013). The dimension of connectedness is related to comments about a sense of affinity and fellowship with the whales.

Interviews were performed using the recollection technique and they focused on the emotional and reflective responses to whale encounters (Ballantyne, Packer, & Sutherland, 2011). Similar approaches have been adopted in other studies concerning cetacean encounters (Curtin, 2006; DeMares, 2000). The findings of these studies are used here as references to identify relevant themes investigated with probing questions.

The 10 interview respondents were selected from people who had experienced one or more whale encounters as a recreational activity performed privately, by using a tourism provider, or as part of their job. The selection began with some acquaintances and, using a snowball method, attempted to identify people who differed in terms of factors that the literature indicated as relevant to wildlife value orientations: in particular, gender and age (Christensen, Needham, & Rowe, 2009; Deruiter, 2002). Other possible relevant factors, such as socialization, personal experience, spirituality, and places of residence, were explored during the interviews.

The interviews were organized in three sections following a line of reasoning that developed from the description of one or more specific whale encounters, to more general considerations about whales, and then back to considerations about the specific encounter(s). The first part centered on the respondents' memories. Here, the respondents were invited to tell their stories and to describe in detail what they had felt and thought before, during, and after the encounter(s). Particular attention was paid to the themes identified as relevant in the literature, for example the animals' intentionality and their aliveness (Curtin, 2006; DeMares, 2000; Muloin, 1998).

The interview then focused on the respondents' personal characteristics that might be relevant to their wildlife orientation, their interest and knowledge about the whale, their habitat and their vulnerability. The researcher provided some information about the commercial whaling moratorium introduced by the International Whaling Commission in 1986, and Norway's 1993 objection, and the recent oil and gas explorations along the northern Norwegian coast. The respondents were asked if they were familiar with these events and to comment on them. In addition, a local episode of human–whale interaction was presented to the respondents: a suspected collision between the boat of a recreationist and a whale.

In the final part of the interview, respondents were asked to think back to the whale encounter(s) reported at the beginning of the interview and to comment on it in relation to the aspects that had emerged during the interview, in particular, on the possible effects on the animals.

Findings from the Explorative Phase

The findings of the first phase suggest that whale encounters are usually remembered as extraordinary experiences characterized by fun and wonder. The aspect of well-being that seems to dominate is the hedonic one, with only a few comments that can be related to the eudaimonic one.

The findings show that there are various ways of experiencing whale encounters and that some of the empathy dimensions can be useful for describing some of the encounters. In relation to attentiveness, the tourists tend to observe the animals very carefully. An influential factor here is that only a very limited view of the whales is possible and, usually, only for a short time. Comments often concerned the way that the whales moved, based exclusively on sightings of their tales and dorsal fins.

Some comments about the whales' behaviors included assumptions about their condition and well-being. Some tourists tended to experience the whales' behaviors in quite an unproblematic way. For example, some reviews reported whales swimming away from the boat as "shy" and not as possibly scared or disturbed. Similarly, active whales were sometimes described as "playing" and as being "curious", without any consideration about the possibility of that such behavior may be a sign of stress. A few tourists describe the whales' active behavior as a "show", something that can indicate an underlying perception of the animals more as objects of entertainment than individuals with their own will. Some observations of whales feeding were described positively, and no concern was reported about the possibility of disturbing the animals at such a critically important moment.

Several tourists commented positively on the condition of freedom of the whales, and on the importance of keeping a distance from them. At the same time, several tourists perceived the distance from the animals as being surprisingly short, and this was usually reported in positive terms. A few comments were critical and suggested that the whales could feel "pressed" and "chased" by the boats.

With regard to the sense of responsibility, the boat captains and the guides were reported as the ones who were responsible for not disturbing the animals. Responsibility at the individual level was not mentioned. One tourist commented critically about Norwegian whaling, and this could be related to the issue of collective responsibility in terms of protecting the whales.

Two reviews could be related to the theme of connectedness: one reporting the whales as our "marine cousins", and the other describing the whales as fellow earthlings who need our protection.

The findings of this explorative phase indicated the following aspects as relevant to the concept of empathic well-being:

- the extent and the way in which the whale encounter is viewed with a sense of discomfort due to concern about the animals' well-being;
- the sense of responsibility at the individual level.

These aspects were further investigated through in-depth interviews.

Main Findings

The respondents' group included six men and four women. Their ages ranged from 27 to 58 (average 43.8, median 45). All respondents defined themselves as being mainly urban, but attracted to non-urban environments, as demonstrated by their favorite leisure activities (for example, hiking, hunting, and sailing). Their whale watching activity was, in most of the cases, related to their general interest in nature. Three respondents had experienced numerous whale encounters either as a leisure activity, performed privately or by joining organized tours, or in relation to their jobs (biologists, tour guide). All respondents had a Catholic background and, apart from three, they had all moved away from this religion, with one being interested in spirituality independent of any religion, and another Buddhism.

The findings show that two respondents did not experience a sense of well-being during their encounter with the whales, two experienced well-being—with

Table 3.1 The Respondents of the In-depth Interviews Listed According to Their Experience of Well-being and Some Relevant Characteristics.

		Experienced Whale Watcher	Context	Level of Knowledge (Whales)	Level of Interest (Whales and Habitat)
No Wellbeing	respondent 1	no	as a tourist	not particularly high	not particulalry high
Wellbeing (Hedonic)	respondent 2	no	as a tourist	not particularly high	not particulalry high
	respondent 3	no	as a tourist	not particularly high	not particulalry high
	respondent 4	no	job (tourism)	not particularly high	not particulalry high
Wellbeing (Hedonic Eudaimonic)	respondent 5	yes	recreational-tourism – job (research-biology, tourism)	high	high
	respondent 6	yes	recreational – job (research-biology, tourism)	high	high
	respondent 7	yes	recreational – job (research-biology)	high	high
	respondent 8	no	recreational – job (research-geology)	not particularly high	high
	respondent 9	no	recreational	not particularly high	high
	respondent 10	no	recreational	not particularly high	high

a marked emphasis on the hedonic aspect—and the remainder experienced a sense of well-being that shows some elements that can be related to the eudaimonic aspect. Table 3.1 shows a list of the respondents organized in groups according to their experience of well-being and noting the potentially relevant characteristics.

No Well-being Experienced

One respondent had difficulty in remembering his encounters. The only clear memory he had was of his attempts to get a good view of the animals. For this respondent, the lack of any hedonic value seems to have compromised the eudaimonic aspect of the experience. The disappointment in not getting close to the animals seems to have dominated his memories. Reflecting on what could have happened to turn the encounter into a positive experience, he mentioned the possibility of interacting with the animals. Although recognizing this expectation as unrealistic, he said: "If I can't interact with the animal, I can, at most, enjoy its view as 'something beautiful' but I can't feel emotionally attached to it".

Another respondent described his whale encounter in a detailed way. When asked how he had felt, he answered: "I didn't feel anything, no emotion, zero!" This respondent is an experienced hunter and during the interview he mentioned that he usually feels excited and also fascinated by wild animals. Reflecting on this point, he mentioned the possibility that in the case of the whale there was no intention or possibility of interacting in any way, whereas on his hunting trips he aimed to develop an interaction with the animals in the form of a hunter–prey relationship.

The Hedonic Aspect of Well-being

Two interviewees indicated that their whale encounters were extraordinary experiences characterized by fun and wonder. These respondents tended to underestimate the possible disturbance that their presence may have caused the animals. Referring to the fact that several boats were following the animals, one respondent described the whale encounter "almost as a dance", thus highlighting her belief that the animals were not "bother[ed] that much by the human presence".

Both respondents commented from what they considered to be the whales' perspective. One said: "If I were a whale, I wouldn't care that much about these small boats". Similarly, the other respondent commented on the possible disturbance referring to the considerable size of the animals as a sign of strength. In her words: "It must feel like when we have a fly or a mosquito flying close to us". Moreover, they indicated that the encounter took place in the animals' habitat, thus, in their view, the animals knew how to behave in order to survive and avoid disturbance. These respondents also indicated that they relied on the boat captains' knowledge, competence, and sense of respect toward the animals.

The Eudaimonic Aspect of Well-being

Six of the respondents attached a deeper meaning to the whale encounters. This can be related to the eudaimonic aspect of well-being and, to a certain extent, to empathy in terms of attentiveness, knowledge, sense of connectedness, and responsibility.

Three respondents can be qualified as competent as they have an educational background relevant to the understanding of whales. In addition, they also have personal experience of numerous whale encounters that had occurred in connection with their jobs (biologists, tour guides) and leisure activities.

Two of the respondents had experienced very close encounters with the whales while diving. One vividly described how his attention was captured by the eyes of the whales. He reflected on this close encounter saying that he was sure that the whale was aware of his presence, and he felt that they were interacting.

The other respondent who had dived in the presence of whales, was particularly concerned about the vulnerable condition of wild animals. During the interview he particularly highlighted the importance of having the necessary knowledge about the whales in order to have an authentic experience. He said:

> To be valuable, the experience has to be somehow authentic. I mean that we have to know how to interpret the whales' behavior, the way they move and so on. If they jump ... it might be a sign of stress, not a greeting to us, as someone might like to believe.

The third of these competent respondents is an experienced whale watching guide. He highlighted the importance of viewing each encounter as unique. He commented:

> We might observe a whale ... that is not just a generic whale ... it is a unique whale. For some of the whales in our area we also have names. They are individuals, like me and you... well ... not exactly like me and you, but still unique.

The concern about the commodification of whale watching was highlighted by these competent respondents and also by two others. One of the latter has had a lifelong interest in the whales. Both these respondents expressed a sense of fascination with the whales and explained it in relation to the particular habitat where the whales live (the sea, the Arctic). They said that they were not particularly eager for any close contact and were satisfied watching the whales from the land.

Finally, one respondent reported that in some cases she had not only seen but had also smelled the whales, and heard the sound of the air coming from their blowholes. During the interview she also reported her feeling of discomfort when she once came close to a sleeping whale. She said that she had felt responsible for disturbing the animal, in her words: "We approached and we didn't realize what it was at the beginning. When I saw that it was a sleeping whale... I felt like an intruder". Although having a limited knowledge about the biology of the whales, this respondent appeared to be very interested and informed about the whale-related issues concerning their protection and also their value in different cultures.

Conclusions

This study concludes that, in some cases, well-being related to wildlife encounters can be described and explained in terms of empathy. The results suggest that the value attached to wildlife encounters by some people is both hedonic and eudaimonic, and the four dimensions of empathy—attentiveness, knowledge, connectedness, and responsibility—are relevant to these cases. It can be proposed that these people tend to be characterized by a high level of knowledge and/or interest in the specific animal and its habitat.

The sense of responsibility at the individual level has emerged as a particularly critical element. Its absence is particularly observed in the cases of whale watchers who join organized tours and are not especially knowledgeable or interested in whales. Although showing some elements relative to perspective taking, these tourists might have the tendency to attribute the responsibility exclusively to the tour providers.

A further element that has emerged is in relation to attentiveness that, ultimately, it depends heavily on the objective possibility of observing the animals. This is a challenge that is particularly relevant to the case of marine animals. Such limitation can influence the empathy dimension of connectedness. Similarly, the lack of interaction with the animals can prevent some people from recognizing the animals as living beings and not as a mere "entertainment" show. In relation to this, it can be noted that the underlying perception of animals as resources, as in the case of hunting and also tourism commodification, clearly limits the application of the concept of empathy.

This study has some practical implications for the tourism industry. One such factor is related to the necessity for the industry to rely on responsible tourism providers. Moreover, it is important to develop interpretation programs that can encourage a sense of responsibility among the tourists. In this way, the tourists can be given information and inspiration and feel empowered in relation to animal and environmental debates and actions.

Whilst in the context of tourism, knowledge and responsibility can be encouraged in the way indicated above, in the case of personal interest—that also has emerged as relevant—this can be taken into account when profiling the tourism offer and segmenting the market. This suggests the advisability of moving away from mass tourism and to focus on niche tourism.

Finally, one element that has emerged in this study concerns the challenges related to the conceptualization of animal well-being. Animal well-being is mainly iterated in relation to welfare. There is clearly some difficulty in identifying a deeper sense of well-being that, as suggested by recent studies about cetaceans, some animals might feel.

References

Allen, S. J. (2014). From exploitation to adoration. In J. Higham, L. Bejder, & R. Williams (Eds.), *Whale-watching: Sustainable tourism and ecological management* (pp. 31–47). Cornwall: Cambridge University Press.

Ballantyne, R., Packer, J., & Sutherland, L. A. (2011). Visitors' memories of wildlife tourism: Implications for the design of powerful interpretive experiences. *Tourism Management*, 32, 770–779.

Bulbeck, H. (2005). *Facing the wild: Ecotourism, conservation and animal encounters.* London: Earthscan.

Christensen, A., Needham, M. D., & Rowe, S. (2009). Whale watchers' past experience, value orientation, and awareness of consequences of actions on the marine environment. *Tourism in Marine Environment*, 5(4), 271–285.

Clement, G. (2007). The ethic of care and the problem of wild animals. In J. Donovan & C. J. Adams (Eds.). *The feminist care tradition in animal ethics* (pp. 301–315). New York: Columbia University Press.

Curtin, S. (2006). Swimming with dolphins: A phenomenological exploration of tourist recollections. *International Journal of Tourism Research*, 8, 301–315.

Curtin, S. (2009). Wildlife tourism: The intangible, psychological benefits of human-wildlife encounters. *Current Issues in Tourism*, 12(5–6), 451–474.

Curtin, S., & Kragh, G. (2014). Wildlife tourism: Reconnecting people with nature. *Human Dimensions of Wildlife: An International Journal*, 19(6), 545–554.

Dayer, A. A., Stinchfield, H. M., & Manfredo, M. J. (2007). Stories about wildlife: Developing an instrument for identifying wildlife value orientations cross-culturally. *Human Dimensions of Wildlife: An International Journal*, 12(5), 307–315.

DeMares, R. (2000). Human peak experience triggered by encounters with cetaceans. *Anthrozoös: A Multidisciplinary Journal of the Interactions of People and Animals*, 13(2), 89–103.

DeMares, R., & Krycka, K. (1999). Wild-animal-triggered peak experiences: Transpersonal aspects. *The Journal of Transpersonal Psychology*, 30(2), 161–177.

Deruiter, D. S. (2002). A qualitative approach to measuring determinants of wildlife value orientations. *Human Dimensions of Wildlife: An International Journal*, 7(4), 251–271.

Donovan, J., & Adams, C. J. (2007). *The feminist care tradition in animal ethics*. New York: Columbia University Press.

Fennel, D. (2012). *Tourism and animal ethics*. New York: Routledge.

Filep, S. (2012). Positive psychology and tourism. In M. Uysal, R. R. Perdue, & M. J. Sirgy (Eds.). *Handbook of tourism and quality-of-life research: Enhancing the lives of tourists and residents of host communities* (pp. 31–50). London: Springer Science+Business Media B.V.

Finkler, W., & Higham, J. (2004). The human dimensions of whale watching: An analysis based on viewing platforms. *Human Dimensions of Wildlife: An International Journal*, 9(2), 103–117.

Harms, M., Asmutis-Silvia, R., & Rosner, A. (2013). *Whale watching: More than meets the eyes*. Report by Whale and Dolphin Conservation to NOAA's Fisheries Northeast Region Program Office (NERO), Award Number NA11NMF4720240.

Higham, J., Bejeder, L., & Williams, R. (Eds.) (2014). *Whale-watching, sustainable tourism and ecological management*. Cambridge: Cambridge University Press.

Kalof, L., & Fitzgerald, A. (2007). *The animal's reader: The essential classic and contemporary writings*. Oxford: Berg.

Kaplan, S. (1995). The restorative benefits of nature: Toward an integrative framework. *Journal of Environmental Psychology*, 15, 169–182.

Keniger, L., Gaston, K. J., Irvine, K. N., & Fuller, R. A. (2013). What are the benefits of interacting with nature? *International Journal of Environmental Resources and Public Health*, 10(3), 913–935.

Kessler, M., Harcourt, R., & Bradford, W. (2014). Will whale watchers sacrifice personal experience to minimize harm to whales? *Tourism in Marine Environments*, 10(1–2), 21–30.

Lemelin, R. H., & Wiersma, E. C. (2007). Perceptions of polar bear tourists: A qualitative analysis. *Human Dimensions of Wildlife: An International Journal*, 12(1), 45–52.

McDonald, M. G., Wearing, S., & Pointing, J. (2009). The nature of peak experience in wilderness. *The Humanistic Psychologist*, 37(4), 370–385.

Midgley, M. (1998). *Animals and why they matter*. Athens: University of Georgia Press.

Moscardo, G. (2000). Understanding wildlife tourism market segments: An Australian marine study. *Human Dimensions of Wildlife: An International Journal*, 5(2), 36–53.

Muloin, S. (1998). Wildlife tourism: The psychological benefits of whale watching. *Pacific Tourism Review*, 1(3–4), 199–213.

Orams, M. B. (2000). Tourist getting close to whales, is it what whale-watching is all about? *Tourism Management*, 21, 561–569.

Pfattheicher, S., Sassenrath, C., & Schindler, S. (2015). Feelings for the suffering of others and the environment: Compassion fosters pro-environmental tendencies. *Environment and Behavior*, 47, 1–17.

Russel, R., Guerry, A. D., Balvanera, P., Grould, R. K., Basurto, X., Chan, K. M. A., Klain, S., Levine, J., & Tam, J. (2013). Humans and nature: How knowing and experiencing nature affect well-being. *Annual Review of Environmental Resources*, 38, 473–502.

Ryan, R., M., & Deci, E. (2001). On happiness and human potentials: A review of research on hedonic and eudaimonic well-being. *Annual Review of Psychology*, 52, 141–166.

Webb, N., & Drummond, P. D. (2001). The effect of swimming with dolphins on human well-being and anxiety. *Anthrozoös*, 14(2), 81–85.

Wilson, E. O. (1984). *Biophilia*. Cambridge, MA: Harvard University Press.

Wilson, C., & Tisdell, C. (2003). Conservation and economic benefits of wildlife-based marine tourism: Sea turtles and whales as case studies. *Human Dimensions of Wildlife: An International Journal*, 8(1), 49–58.

4 The Impact of Korea's Nature-Based Recreation Settings on Tourists' Emotions, Satisfaction and Subjective Happiness

Timothy J. Lee and Jinok S. Kim

Introduction

Interest in health has increased worldwide and nature-based tourism for the pursuit of health has also grown (Hales & Low Choy, 2012). Nature-based activities are reported as providing people with a range of health-related benefits including stress-relief, attention-improvement, social relationships, physical health and emotional well-being (Doherty, Lemieux & Canally, 2014; Korpela et al., 2014; Richardson, Pearce, Mitchell & Kingham, 2013; Vella, Milligan & Bennett, 2013). As a result, the popularity of nature-based tourism and nature-based activities for the pursuit of health has also increased (Beeco & Brown, 2013; Cordell, 2012; Oftedal & Schneider, 2013).

According to the Attention Restoration Theory, perceived environmental restorativeness can restore exhausted directed attention without the expenditure of any attention (Berto, 2005; Kaplan, 1995). The perceived environmental restorativeness in nature has been shown to have a greater attention restoration effect than other restorative environments. The purpose of this study is to examine the effect of nature-based activities, a part of health tourism, on the subjective happiness of tourists by applying the Attention Restoration Theory. Modern people feel psychological fatigue caused by the expenditure of directive attention in city life, and they try to restore their directive attention through natural environments. Following this desire, modern people come to seek nature-based tourism. Thus, by targeting participants in nature-based activities, this study examines their impact on subjective happiness.

Perceived Environmental Restorativeness

The Attention Restoration Theory (ART) helps to understand nature's cognitive and affective impact on directed attention (Kaplan, 1995). In general, restoration refers to the process that renews or restores exhausted physical, psychological and social ability because of additional demands (Hartig & Staats, 2005). The ART views nature as a major means of helping the attention restoration ability and aims to facilitate positive atmospheres to promote welfare (Nikunen & Korpela, 2012). The feature of a restoration environment in attention restoration can be measured in four perspectives, including 'being-away', 'fascination', 'coherence' and 'compatibility' (Berto, 2005). Berto (2005) maintains that scope refers to a wide place without the limit of movement. A perceived environmental restorativeness scale based on this characteristic was created to evaluate the potential ability of restoration in other environments (Sonntag-Öström et al., 2014).

Pazhouhanfar and Kamal (2014) examined the influential relationship between restorative environment elements (being away, fascination, compatibility) through relevant photos and four elements of visual prediction in a favorite scene (coherence, complexity, legibility, mystery). Nikunen et al. (2014) studied the relationship between the restorative environment (being away, fascination, range and compatibility) and lighting attributes (brightness, distribution, glare, colour quality, feeling of safety and pleasantness) to observe whether each outdoor lighting quality affects the perceived restorativeness at night. Tyrväinen et al. (2014) examined the relation of a perceived restorative environment in cities, parks and forests in Helsinki, Finland. As per the results of the study, cities were considered as a lowest restorative environment, parks ranked in the middle and forests had the highest scale. Korpela et al. (2014) conducted the empirical analysis of the relationship between the average time of nature-based outdoor recreation and the emotional comfort through a restorative experience and a recent nature-based recreation visit. Stevens (2015) investigated the differences between urban and natural environments. The results revealed an influential effect for two components (being away and fascination). Fascination components showed a significant interaction of affective-prime and the environment, a high effect being seen for natural environments.

Previous studies related to restorative environment elements and restorative environments in general have addressed how urban and natural environments support perceived restorativeness. Therefore, natural environment elements are important factors for emotional recovery.

Emotion

Emotions are characterized as experiences of intense feelings about a specific event (Cohen & Areni, 1991), when emotion comes to be considered important in a consumer's purchasing of products (Eggert & Ulaga, 2002; Jones et al., 2006; Voss et al., 2003). In particular, tourism products pursue not only functional aspects as experience goods but emotional as well (Ryu et al., 2010). Emotion also affects the decision-making in tourism and leisure activities (Prayag et al., 2013). Emotion, including fun, fantasy, pleasure, excitement and rest felt through leisure experience, completes satisfaction (Hirschman & Holbrook, 1982). At the post-decision process stage, emotions influence satisfaction and behaviour intention.

Folmer et al. (2013) examined the relationship between wildlife and emotional attachment to a nature-based tourism destination. The study suggests that motivation to visit wildlife, the perceived intensity of the wildlife experience and interest in guided wildlife encounters explain the emotional attachment to a nature-based tourism wildlife park. Song, Ahn and Lee (2015) studied the relationships among strategic experiential modules, emotion and satisfaction with a mega event. The mega event studied was the Yeosu Expo held in South Korea and the theme was 'The Living Ocean and Coast'. The results reveal that the event experience is an important factor and affects satisfaction through positive emotional experience (sense, feel, think, act, relate). Lee et al. (2014) examined the impact of environmental cues on emotion, satisfaction, loyalty and support for the revitalization. Environmental cues from the revitalization's positive emotions lead to satisfaction and loyalty.

All these previous studies suggest tourists generally gain experiences through positive emotions and satisfaction. Emotions largely influence peoples' decision to purchase tourism and leisure activities. Also, emotions affect antecedents of satisfaction and behavioural intentions (Prayag et al., 2013).

Satisfaction

Satisfaction explains the possibility of the purchasing intention better than any other factors (Kim et al., 2014). This customer satisfaction has been regarded as the prerequisite of loyalty (Kim et al., 2013). Tourism satisfaction was considered as the result of perceiving external information gained from tourism experience, but presently satisfaction is being recognized as an emotional response to experience (del Bosque & Martin, 2008). General satisfaction can be measured by referring to expectation, and the level of agreement on revisits should be higher than that of expectation (Žabkar et al., 2010). In the tourism industry, satisfaction could determine the survival or failure of companies; thus, considering customer satisfaction is always important (Williams & Uysal, 2003). This customer satisfaction has been considered as preceding the behaviour intention (Kim et al., 2013).

Meng et al. (2008) examined the relationship between destination attribute importance and performance, motivation and satisfaction at a nature-based resort. The results of the study show that friendly service/quality and lodging performance are important factors in decided overall satisfaction. Travel motivation explains the overall tourist satisfaction of a nature-based resort. Kim and Park (2016) studied the relationship between perceived value, satisfaction and loyalty at a nature-based ecotourism destination and found that three values (functional, social, emotion) influenced the overall value. Overall value and satisfaction in turn influenced loyalty. Perera and Vlosky (2013) examined the relationship between previous visits, trip quality, perceived value, satisfaction and behavioural intentions in nature-based ecotourism and report that trip quality and perceived value were significant influencers of satisfaction.

On the basis of previous studies, nature-based tourists' satisfaction experience is an important predictor of intention to revisit and recommend the destination. Nature-based tourists' participation in the healing program is significantly related to their quality of life increases (Kim et al., 2015). Also, quality of life increases were positively affected by the natural environment and healing programs.

Subjective Happiness

Subjective happiness can be defined as the psychological state of well-being, joy and self-contentment. As such, subjective happiness is a significant part of human life and an important goal for every human being (Lyubomirsky et al., 2005). Previous researches implied that subjective happiness is connected with subjective well-being (McCabe & Jonhnson, 2013; Pavot & Diener, 2013), satisfying relationships (Pillow, Malone & Hale, 2015), life satisfaction (Diener, 2000), positive emotions (Gruber et al., 2013) and emotional intelligence (Ruiz-Aranda et al., 2014).

Kim, Lee, and Ko (2016) studied the differences of perception between health tour seekers and non-seekers of subjective well-being. Health tourism seekers perceived the level of influence of the health tour on subjective well-being to be more positive than did non-seekers. Cini et al., (2013) examined the relationship between motivation for a nature-based national park visit, that is, more autonomous reasons for visiting and less autonomous reasons for visiting and subjective well-being. They found that more autonomous reasons for visiting resulted in larger subjective well-being increases, while less intrinsically motivated had lower subjective well-being associated. Kim et al., (2015) studied the relationship between motivation, values, subjective well-being and revisit intention and showed that revisit intention is influenced by motivation and subjective well-being. Motivation and values are influences of subjective well-being.

Methods

Measurement

This study intends to reveal how the perceived restorative environment affects positive emotion and satisfaction subjective happiness. Therefore, the perceived restorative environment is divided into five different elements in Berto's (2005) simple scale. Subjective happiness was assessed by using three items adapted from studies by Lyubomirsky and Lepper (1999). Emotion was measured through a scale used in previous researches (Lee et al., 2008). Satisfaction was also measured through a scale used in previous researches (Choi, Kim, Lee & Hickerson, 2015; Kim et al., 2014). All measurement elements were measured by five scales on a Likert Scale (1. Strongly disagree, 2. Disagree, 3. Neutral, 4. Agree, 5. Strongly agree).

Sampling and Data Collection

The data were collected at four times only on weekends from 12 to 20 July 2012 at the entrance of Mt Dobong in the Mt Bukhan National Park in Seoul. The places of data collection included the subway station of Mt Dobong and bus stops, where there were the greatest numbers of pedestrians (Mt Bukhan National Park Service, 2014). Researchers selected every fifth visitor for systematic sampling. In terms of the number of questionnaires that each researcher had, the total was 1,125 over four times, out of which 420 questionnaires were distributed. Based on this process, the rate of response for this research was 58.16 per cent. From the 420 collected questionnaires, except for 20 questionnaires that included unanswered items, 400 questionnaires were used for the empirical analysis.

Data Analysis

SPSS 21.0 was used for the data analysis of the 400 questionnaires for frequency analysis, exploratory factor analysis and reliability analysis. Also, in this study, the two-stage testing procedure was adopted by using AMOS 21.0. In the first stage, confirmatory factor analysis was executed to identify the reliability and validity of the underlying structure of factors and to systematically purify measured indicators of constructs.

Results

Respondents' Demographic Characteristics

The general characteristics of respondents are shown in Table 4.1. The rate of the genders of the respondents is similar between males and females, 49.5 and 50.5 per cent, respectively. In terms of marital status, singles accounted for 37.3 per cent, married 61.5 per cent and 1.3 per cent unknown. Concerning the ages, 14.0 per cent consisted of the below 19-year-old group; 14.0 per cent fell into 19–29 year olds; 16.8 per cent belonged to 30–39 year olds; 21.0 per cent represented 40–49 year olds, 24.3 per cent entailed 50–59 year olds and 10.0 per cent were over 60 years

Table 4.1 Demographic Characteristics of the Respondents

Characteristics		Sample	%	Characteristics		Sample	%
Gender	Male	198	49.5	Marital	Single	149	37.3
	Female	202	50.5	Status	Married	246	61.5
					Other	5	1.3
Education	High school or	149	37.3	Age	Below 19	56	14.0
	less	53	13.3		19–29	56	14.0
	Junior college	183	45.8		30–39	67	16.8
	University	15	3.8		40–49	84	21.0
	Graduate				50–59	97	24.3
	school				60 or over	40	10.0
Occupation	Professional	49	12.3	Monthly	US$		
	Business	50	12.5	household	Below 1,000	74	18.5
	Service	49	12.3	income	1,000–2,999	126	31.5
	Clerical	54	13.5	(US$)	3,000–4,999	129	32.3
	Official	19	4.8		5,000–6,999	43	10.8
	House wife	50	12.5		7,000–8,999	18	4.5
	Student	89	22.3		9,000 or more	10	2.5
	Unemployed	19	4.8				
	Others	21	5.3				
Total		400	100	Total		400	100

old. As for the education level, 37.3 per cent had completed high school or less; 13.3 per cent had obtained a junior college degree; 45.8 per cent had received a university diploma and 3.8 per cent had a graduate degree. As for respondent's work status, professional comprised 12.3 per cent, business owner 12.5 per cent, service staff 12.3 per cent, clerical person 13.5 per cent, government official 4.8 per cent, house wife 12.5 per cent, students 22.3 per cent, the unemployed 4.8 per cent and 5.3 per cent fell into none of the above categories. As far as the monthly household income was concerned, 18.5 per cent of the respondents earned less than 1 million Korean won (US$1,000), 31.5 per cent 1–2.99 million won, 32.3 per cent 3–4.99 million won, 10.8 per cent 5–6.99 million won, 4.5 per cent 7–8.99 million won and 2.5 per cent over 9 million won.

Measurement Model

This study used Confirmatory Factor Analysis to analyze structural relationships and a structure model for the two-stage testing procedure (Anderson & Gerbing, 1988). The Measurement Model and Structural Model in this study were found to be suitable (See Table 4.2), because the compatibility was higher than average. As shown in Table 4.2, the measurement model indicated a good fit to the data: Normed x^2 =1.912, NFI =.947, TLI =.967, CFI =.974 and RMSEA =.048; these were higher than the cut-off values (Hair et al., 2010). The convergent validity was confirmed, because the factor loadings ranged from .655 to .863, average variance extracted ranged from .546 to .702 and the construct reliability ranged from .841 to .904, which is relatively higher than the average (Hair et al., 2010). Therefore, the convergent validity in this study is found to be suitable.

The Discriminatory Validity was verified by comparing squared correlations with AVE (Hair et al., 2014). There are three kinds of methods for testing discriminant validity that demonstrate the differences between the latent variables (Anderson & Gerbing, 1992). Table 4.3 indicates that, generally, AVE values were higher than squared correlations, which confirms the discriminatory validity.

Structural Model

Figure 4.1 shows the results of the proposed research model in this study. Maximlikelihood estimates for the various parameters of the overall fit of the model are given. The Structural Model fits the data well: x^{22} = 183.174, df = 96, x^2/df = 1.908, GFI = .947, NFI = .947; TLI = .967, CFI = .974 and RMSEA = .048. The explained variance in the endogenous constructs was 40.3 per cent for emotion, 44.4 per cent for satisfaction and 19.7 per cent for subjective happiness.

The results showed that the perceived environmental restorativeness (PER) had a significant positive effect on emotion (EM) (γPER → EM = .634, t = 8.858, p<.001), satisfaction (SA) (γPER → SA = .356, t = 4.610, p<.001). EM had a significant positive effect on subjective happiness (SH) (βEM → SH = .381, t = 5.429, p<.001), however, it did not have an effect on SH. SA has a significant positive effect on SH (βsA → SH = .360, t = 4.951, p<.001).

Table 4.2 Results of Confirmatory Factor Analysis

Constructs and Items	Convergent Validity			
	λ	C.R.	AVE	CR
Perceived Environmental Restorativeness				
'This is a place away from everyday demands where I would be able to relax and think about what interests me (being away)'.	.793			
'This place is fascinating; it is large enough for me to discover and be curious about things' (Fascination).	.836	12.508		
'That is a place where the activities and the items are ordered and organized' (Coherence).	.721	9.104	.546	.856
'That is a place that is very large, with no restrictions to movements; it is a world of its own' (Scope).	.674	8.337		
'In this place, it is easy to find my way, move around, and do what I like' (Compatibility).	.655	8.378		
Emotion				
It was interesting to go trekking.	.817			
I was pleasant when trekking.	.871		.702	.904
I was happy when trekking.	.846			
I felt good when climbing.	.816			
Satisfaction				
Trekking satisfies my expectations.	.758			
I am satisfied with my decision to go trekking.	.841	17.217	.636	.875
I feel very good with the trekking.	.795	15.327		
Overall, I am satisfied with the trekking.	.794	15.268		
Subjective Happiness				
In general, I consider myself happy.	.861		.641	.841
Compared to most of my peers, I consider myself happy.	.863	17.293		
Some people are generally very happy. They enjoy life regardless of what is going on, getting the most out of everything. To what extent does this characterization describe you?	.662	13.652		

Goodness-of fit	x^2	df	Normed x^2	NFI	TLI	CFI	RMSEA
	181.611	95	1.912	.947	.967	.974	.048

Notes. λ: Factor loading, C.R.: Critical Ratio, AVE: Average Variance Extracted, CR: Construct Reliability, α: Cronbach's Alpha. Parameter fixed at 1.0 for the maximum-likelihood estimation and thus, *t*-values were not available (Back et al., 2011).

Table 4.3 Measure Correlations, Squared Correlations and AVE

	PER	*EM*	*SA*	*SW*
PER	.546			
EM	.632*** (.399)	.702		
SA	.595*** (.354)	.607*** (.368)	.636	
SH	.348*** (.121)	.336*** (.112)	.430*** (.184)	.641

Notes. PER: Perceived Environmental Restorativeness, EM: Emotion, SA: Satisfaction, SW: Subjective Happiness. The number is measure correlations. The number in the parentheses indicate R Squared (R^2), Diagonal Bold text is Average Variance Extracted (AVE), All correlations were significant at ***$p<.001$.

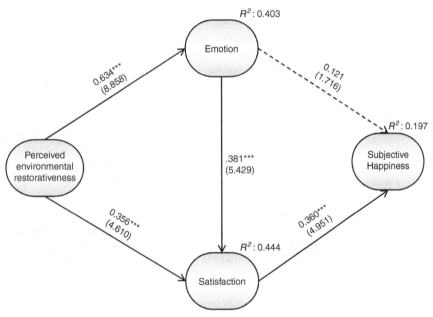

Notes : * $p<0.05$, ***$p<0.001$
The numbers in the parentheses indicate t-values
x^2 = 183.174, df = 96, x^2/df = 1.908, GFI = 0.947,
NFI = 0.947, TLI = 0.967, CFI = 0.974, RMSEA = 0.048

Figure 4.1 Results of the Research Model

Conclusions and Implications

In the contemporary world, due to scientific development, human lifespan has expanded and people have pursued health for improvements in quality of life (Smith, 2013). As the interest in health has increased, the relevant industry for health and wellness has rapidly grown and nature-based tourism relating to health and wellness in tourism has developed significantly (Laesser, 2011). Recently, in leisure activities, nature-based tourism has increased not only for leisure itself, but also for health-pursuits (Cordell, 2012). In this respect, this study explored how naturally perceived environmental restorativeness affects satisfaction and subjective happiness.

This study result indicates that the subjective happiness of tourists can be improved through nature-based activities. In addition, it turned out that the perceived environmental restorativeness of nature-based activities significantly influences satisfaction. This result echoes previous research that emphasizes the effect of nature-based restorative environments (White et al., 2013). Perceived environmental restorativeness could be a defining agent to enhance tourist satisfaction in participating in nature-based activities as researches have investigated the effect of perceived environmental restorativeness for nature-based activities on satisfaction and loyalty via the wellness felt during the activities (Kim et al., 2014). In this context, this study suggests theoretical implications by analyzing the structural relationships between the perceived environmental restorativeness, emotion, satisfaction and subjective happiness of visitors in a nature-based national park.

One of the findings that perceived environmental restorativeness influences both emotion and satisfaction perceived by the visitors, indicates the importance of the natural environment in the national parks. Consequently, it should be noted that visitors have an interdependent relationship with the natural environment: thus, the business of creating Dulegil (Korean for designated trekking course) and eco-trails could seek to provide long-term experiences for visitors and conserve the natural environment. The study results could support policy makers and park managers in understanding the decision-making processes of nature-based visitors in order to frame and implement policies regarding construction of eco-trails. However, it would be difficult to generalize the study's results, because this empirical survey was conducted only in the Mt Bukhan National Park and therefore there is a need for future studies to reflect the characteristics of various types of nature-based national parks such as mountain marine and seashore national parks.

References

Anderson, J. C., & Gerbing, D. W. (1988). Structural equation modeling in practice: A review and recommended two-step approach. *Psychological Bulletin, 103*(3), 411–423.

Anderson, J. C., & Gerbing, D. W. (1992). Assumptions and comparative strengths of the two-step approach: Comment on Fornell and Yi. *Sociological Methods & Research, 20*(1), 321–333.

Beeco, J. A., & Brown, G. (2013). Integrating space, spatial tools and spatial analysis into the human dimensions of parks and outdoor recreation. *Applied Geography, 38*, 76–85.

Berto, R. (2005). Exposure to restorative environments helps restore attentional capacity. *Journal of Environmental Psychology, 25*(3), 249–259.

del Bosque, I. R., & Martín, H. S. (2008). Tourist satisfaction a cognitive-affective model. *Annals of Tourism Research, 35*(2), 551–573.

Choi, Y., Kim, J., Lee, C. K., & Hickerson, B. (2015). The role of functional and wellness values in visitors' evaluation of spa experiences. *Asia Pacific Journal of Tourism Research, 20*(3), 263–279.

Cini, F., Kruger, S., & Ellis, S. (2013). A model of intrinsic and extrinsic motivations on subjective well-being: The experience of overnight visitors to a national park. *Applied Research in Quality of Life, 8*(1), 45–61.

Cohen, J. B., & Areni, C. S. (1991). Affect and Consumer Behavior. In T. S. Robertson & H. H. Kassarjian (Eds.), Handbook of Consumer Behavior (pp. 188–240). Englewood Cliffs, NJ: Prentice Hall.

Cordell, H. K. (2012). *Outdoor recreation trends and futures: A technical document supporting the Forest Service 2010 RPA Assessment. General Technical Report-Southern Research Station, USDA Forest Service*, (SRS-150).

Diener, E. (2000). Subjective well-being: The science of happiness and a proposal for a national index. *American Psychologist, 55*(1), 34–43.

Doherty, S. T., Lemieux, C. J., & Canally, C. (2014). Tracking human activity and well-being in natural environments using wearable sensors and experience sampling. *Social Science & Medicine, 106*, 83–92.

Eggert, A., & Ulaga, W. (2002). Customer-perceived value: A substitute for satisfaction in business markets? *Journal of Business & Industrial Marketing, 17*(2/3), 107–118.

Folmer, A., Haartsen, T., & Huigen, P. P. (2013). The role of wildlife in emotional attachment to a nature-based tourism destination. *Journal of Ecotourism, 12*(3), 131–145.

Gruber, J., Kogan, A., Quoidbach, J., & Mauss, I. B. (2013). Happiness is best kept stable: Positive emotion *variability is associated with poorer psychological health. Emotion, 13*(1), 1–6.

Hair, J. F., Black, W. C., Babin, B. J., & Anderson, R. E. (2010). *Multivariate data analysis: A global perspective* (7th ed.). New Jersey: Pearson Education.

Hair Jr, J., Sarstedt, M., Hopkins, L., & G. Kuppelwieser, V. (2014). Partial least squares structural equation modeling (PLS-SEM): An emerging tool in business research. *European Business Review, 26*(2), 106–121.

Hales, R., & Low Choy, D. (2012). 'Swings and roundabouts': A case study of trends in outdoor recreation participation in South East Queensland. *Annals of Leisure Research, 15*(2), 115–131.

Hartig, T., & Staats, H. (2005). Linking preference for environments with their restorative quality. In B. Tress, G. Tress, G. Fry, & P. Opdam (Eds.), *From landscape research to landscape planning: Aspects of integration, education and application* (pp. 279–292). Dordrecht: Springer.

Hirschman, E. C., & Holbrook, M. B. (1982). Hedonic consumption: Emerging concepts, methods and propositions. *Journal of Marketing, 46*, 92–101.

Jones, M. A., Reynolds, K. E., & Arnold, M. J. (2006). Hedonic and utilitarian shopping value: Investigating differential effects on retail outcomes. *Journal of Business Research, 59*(9), 974–981.

Kaplan, S. (1995). The restorative benefits of nature: Toward an integrative framework. *Journal of Environmental Psychology*, 15(3), 169–182.

Kim, H., Woo, E., & Uysal, M. (2015). Tourism experience and quality of life among elderly tourists. *Tourism Management, 46*, 465–476.

Kim, H., Lee, S., Uysal, M., Kim, J., & Ahn, K. (2015). Nature-Based Tourism: Motivation and Subjective Well-Being. *Journal of Travel & Tourism Marketing, 32*(sup1), S76–S96.

Kim, H. J., Lee, T. J., & Ko, T. G. (2016). A comparative study of health tourism seekers and non-seekers' satisfaction and subjective well-being evaluation: The case of Japanese and Korean tourists. *Journal of Travel & Tourism Marketing, 33*(5), 742–756. DOI:10.1080/10548408.2016.1167392.

Kim, J. O., Lee, J. E., & Kim, N. J. (2014). An influence of outdoor recreation participants' perceived restorative environment on wellness effect, satisfaction and loyalty. In *SHS Web of Conferences* (Vol. 12, p. 01082). EDP Sciences.

Kim, K. H., & Park, D. B. (2016). Relationships among perceived value, satisfaction and loyalty: Community-based ecotourism in Korea. *Journal of Travel & Tourism Marketing*, 1–21. DOI:10.1080/10548408.2016.1156609.

Kim, M., Vogt, C. A., & Knutson, B. J. (2013). Relationships among customer satisfaction, delight and loyalty in the hospitality industry. *Journal of Hospitality & Tourism Research*, *39*(2), 170–197.

Kim, M. J., Lee, C. K., Chung, N., & Kim, W. G. (2014). Factors affecting online tourism group buying and the moderating role of loyalty. *Journal of Travel Research*, *53*(3), 380–394.

Korpela, K., Borodulin, K., Neuvonen, M., Paronen, O., & Tyrväinen, L. (2014). Analyzing the mediators between nature-based outdoor recreation and emotional well-being. *Journal of Environmental Psychology*, *37*, 1–7.

Laesser, C. (2011). Health travel motivation and activities: insights from a mature market–Switzerland. *Tourism Review*, *66*(1/2), 83–89.

Lee, Y. K., Lee, C. K., Lee, S. K., & Babin, B. J. (2008). Festivalscapes and patrons' emotions, satisfaction and loyalty. *Journal of Business Research*, *61*(1), 56–64.

Lee, Y. K., Lee, C. K., Choi, J., Yoon, S. M., & Hart, R. J. (2014). Tourism's role in urban regeneration: Examining the impact of environmental cues on emotion, satisfaction, loyalty and support for Seoul's revitalized Cheonggyecheon stream district. *Journal of Sustainable Tourism*, *22*(5), 726–749.

Lyubomirsky, S., & Lepper, H. S. (1999). A measure of subjective happiness: Preliminary reliability and construct validation. *Social Indicators Research*, *46*(2), 137–155.

Lyubomirsky, S., Sheldon, K. M., & Schkade, D. (2005). Pursuing happiness: The architecture of sustainable change. *Review of General Psychology*, *9*(2), 111–131.

McCabe, S., & Johnson, S. (2013). The happiness factor in tourism: Subjective well-being and social tourism. *Annals of Tourism Research*, *41*, 42–65.

Meng, F., Tepanon, Y., & Uysal, M. (2008). Measuring tourist satisfaction by attribute and motivation: The case of a nature-based resort. *Journal of Vacation Marketing*, *14*(1), 41–56.

Nikunen, H., & Korpela, K. M. (2012). The effects of scene contents and focus of light on perceived restorativeness, fear and preference in nightscapes. *Journal of Environmental Planning and Management*, *55*(4), 453–468.

Nikunen, H., Puolakka, M., Rantakallio, A., Korpela, K., & Halonen, L. (2014). Perceived restorativeness and walkway lighting in near-home environments. *Lighting Research and Technology*, *46*(3), 308–328.

Oftedal, A., & Schneider, I. (2013). Outdoor recreation availability, physical activity and health outcomes: County-level analysis in Minnesota. *Journal of Park & Recreation Administration*, *31*(1), 34–56.

Pazhouhanfar, M., & Kamal, M. (2014). Effect of predictors of visual preference as characteristics of urban natural landscapes in increasing perceived restorative potential. *Urban Forestry & Urban Greening*, *13*(1), 145–151.

Perera, P., & Vlosky, R. P. (2013). How previous visits shape trip quality, perceived value, satisfaction and future behavioral intentions: The case of forest-based ecotourism in Sri Lanka. *International Journal of Sport Management, Recreation and Tourism*, *11*(1), 1–24.

Pillow, D. R., Malone, G. P., & Hale, W. J. (2015). The need to belong and its association with fully satisfying relationships: A tale of two measures. *Personality and Individual Differences*, *74*, 259–264.

Prayag, G., Hosany, S., & Odeh, K. (2013). The role of tourists' emotional experiences and satisfaction in understanding behavioral intentions. *Journal of Destination Marketing & Management, 2*(2), 118–127.

Richardson, E. A., Pearce, J., Mitchell, R., & Kingham, S. (2013). Role of physical activity in the relationship between urban green space and health. *Public Health, 127*(4), 318–324.

Ruiz-Aranda, D., Extremera, N., & Pineda-Galán, C. (2014). Emotional intelligence, life satisfaction and subjective happiness in female student health professionals: The mediating effect of perceived stress. *Journal of Psychiatric and Mental Health Nursing, 21*(2), 106–113.

Ryu, K., Han, H., & Jang, S. (2010). Relationships among hedonic and utilitarian values, satisfaction and behavioral intentions in the fast-casual restaurant industry. *International Journal of Contemporary Hospitality Management, 22*(3), 416–432.

Smith, M. (2013). Transforming quality of life through wellness tourism. In Y. Reisinger (Ed.), Transformational tourism: Tourist perspectives (pp. 55–67). Wallingford, CT: CABI.

Song, H. J., Ahn, Y. J., & Lee, C. K. (2015). Structural relationships among strategic experiential modules, emotion and satisfaction at the Expo 2012 Yeosu Korea. *International Journal of Tourism Research, 17*(3), 239–248.

Sonntag-Öström, E., Nordin, M., Lundell, Y., Dolling, A., Wiklund, U., Karlsson, M., & Slunga Järvholm, L. (2014). Restorative effects of visits to urban and forest environments in patients with exhaustion disorder. *Urban Forestry & Urban Greening, 13*(2), 344–354.

Stevens, P. (2014). Affective priming of perceived environmental restorativeness. *International Journal of Psychology, 49*(1), 51–55.

Tyrväinen, L., Ojala, A., Korpela, K., Lanki, T., Tsunetsugu, Y., & Kagawa, T. (2014). The influence of urban green environments on stress relief measures: A field experiment. *Journal of Environmental Psychology, 38*, 1–9.

Vella, E. J., Milligan, B., & Bennett, J. L. (2013). Participation in outdoor recreation program predicts improved psychosocial well-being among veterans with post-traumatic stress disorder: A pilot study. *Military Medicine, 178*(3), 254–260.

Voss, K. E., Spangenberg, E. R., & Grohmann, B. (2003). Measuring the hedonic and utilitarian dimensions of consumer attitude. *Journal of Marketing Research, 40*(3), 310–320.

White, M. P., Pahl, S., Ashbullby, K., Herbert, S., & Depledge, M. H. (2013). Feelings of restoration from recent nature visits. *Journal of Environmental Psychology, 35*, 40–51.

Williams, J. A., & Uysal, M. (2003). *Current issues and development in hospitality and tourism satisfaction.* New York: Routledge.

Žabkar, V., Brenčič, M. M., & Dmitrović, T. (2010). Modelling perceived quality, visitor satisfaction and behavioural intentions at the destination level. *Tourism Management, 31*(4), 537–546.

5   Generation Y, Nature and Tourism

Melanie Smith

Introduction

Research has suggested that young people may be at risk of losing contact with nature and developing what Louv (2005, 2012) describes as 'Nature-Deficit Disorder'. This involves an outdoor to indoor migration and intensive use of electronic media (Barton, 2012). However, studies have shown that the young can benefit the most from exposure to nature in terms of health (Barton & Pretty, 2010). Forest settings have been shown to benefit children and adolescents, especially those with behavioural problems and mental disorders (Roe & Aspinall, 2011; Bell & Ward Thompson, 2014). Kuo (2001) showed that even very small green spaces in cities can lead to an improvement in children's' ability to pay attention and manage impulses.

This chapter will discuss in more depth the relationship between nature, wellbeing and tourism with a particular emphasis on young people. The questionnaire research discussed here focused on Generation Y (aged 18+) and compared the frequency of young peoples' visits to the countryside in four countries (Hungary, Poland, Romania and Israel), their reasons for visiting or not visiting the countryside, the types of landscape and activities they prefer and the benefits derived from time spent there. Although the emphasis was partly on leisure, the respondents were also asked about trips to the countryside and nature-based tourism.

The Relationship between Nature, Wellbeing and Tourism

Numerous studies have emerged which focus on the relationship between nature and wellbeing or quality of life. For example, in quality of life studies Sirgy & Cornwell (2001) as well as Rahman et al. (2005) emphasise the domain of environmental quality and aesthetics in quality of life. An increasing number of studies emphasise the importance of environmental quality and Ecosystem Services for human wellbeing (e.g. Millennium Ecosystem Assessment, 2005; Happy Planet Index (New Economics Foundation, 2012); Knight & Rosa, 2013). The New Economics Foundation (2008) suggest that the more you relate to nature, the more positive your emotions and the greater your life satisfaction. Louv (2005) takes this argument a stage further and argues that lack of contact with nature can be highly detrimental to health. In his book *The Nature Principle* he states that 'reconnection to the natural world is fundamental to human wellbeing' (ibid., 2012: 82).

The philosopher Alain de Botton (2003) suggested that nature is an important component of the tourism experience and described how travellers are attracted to 'sublime' landscapes that benefit their soul by making them feel small, yet part of an infinite and universal cycle. Kaur Kler (2009) discusses theories of environmental psychology which explain tourists' preferences for nature and restorative environments. The spiritual nature of landscapes is also significant, and spiritual wellbeing can be partly enhanced through contact with nature, especially awe-inspiring locations. Todd (2009) suggests that this notion goes beyond conventional notions of 'the picturesque' and sentimental or romanticised simplifications of nature. His theories are more in line with those authors who have highlighted the connection between nature, spirituality and sustainability, arguing that care for and love of nature is something like a 'green religion' (e.g. Carroll, 2004; Taylor, 2009). Taylor (2009) describes how nature-based 'religion' has been re-kindled because of the global sustainability movement.

There is a growing interest in some of the more intangible elements of nature-related wellbeing enhancement. The Millennium Ecosystem Assessment (2005) describes Cultural Ecosystem Services (CES) as 'The non-material benefits people obtain from ecosystems through spiritual enrichment, cognitive development, reflection and aesthetic experiences'. Their categorization includes spiritual, aesthetic, inspirational, place-related, educational and heritage-based experiences, as well as recreation and tourism. Andersson et al. (2014) suggest that unlike other Ecosystem Services, CES are more visible to people and are more easily experienced without specialist ecological and other scientific knowledge. They also state that there is a strong connection between CES, civic engagement and Ecosystem Service stewardship. That is to say, if people understand and appreciate the landscape better, they are more likely to want to look after it. Most of the research on CES so far has been undertaken on recreation and tourism (Plieninger et al., 2013; Hernández-Morcillo et al., 2013), but other results suggest that aesthetic values were the most frequently mentioned Ecosystem Service (Plieninger et al., 2013).

Several studies have suggested that nature-based experiences can improve health and wellbeing (e.g. Ulrich, 1984; Kaplan, 1989; Kaplan & Kaplan, 1995; Louv, 2005; Barton and Pretty, 2010; Bell & Ward Thompson, 2014; Tyrväinen et al., 2014).

Research shows that viewing natural scenes can improve mental wellbeing, increase alertness, and reduce stress (e.g. Kaplan and Kaplan, 1989). Typical metrics for assessment include: directed attention, concentration, memory, mood, stress and includes SRT (stress reduction theory) and ART (attention restoration theory).

Hujbens (2013) writes of 'therapeutic landscapes' which can help to achieve physical, mental, and spiritual healing. According to Howard Clinebell, who wrote a 1996 book on the topic, 'ecotherapy' refers to healing and growth nurtured by healthy interaction with the earth. He also called it 'green therapy' and 'earth-centered therapy'. Ecotherapeutic work as Clinebell conceived it takes guidance from an Ecological Circle of three mutually interacting operations or dynamics:

- Inreach: receiving and being nurtured by the healing presence of nature, place, Earth.
- Upreach: the actual experience of this more-than-human vitality as we relocate our place within the natural world.
- Outreach: activities with other people that care for the planet.

Nature-based tourism can have some of the most important benefits to human health. Smith and Puczkó (2009: 252) discuss the role of nature in health and wellness tourism:

> [n]ature plays a significant role in health and wellness in many countries, especially those which have a sea coast. ... Mountains are another feature which have always attracted health visitors, especially the Alps in Europe. Jungles and national parks (e.g. in Central and South America, Africa) make ideal locations for adventure and ecospas. ... To a lesser (but increasing extent) deserts (e.g. in the Middle East or North Africa) are being used as locations for yoga and meditation holidays.

Several studies in spa and wellness tourism have highlighted the importance of nature. For example, the Tourism Observatory for Health Wellness and Spa (2012) stated that Northern Europe, in particular, Nordic countries, will be the most important hub for outdoor recreation combined with nature-based wellbeing tourism. The Global Spa Summit (2011) quoted one Finnish interviewee as stating that location and environment are playing a huge role in wellness and that such experiences can be deeply spiritual. Consumers are becoming more attuned to the importance and value of green, eco, sustainable and organic practices and products. They are also more open to re-connecting with nature. The Global Spa and Wellness Summit (2013) mentioned getting back to nature and 'earthing' as major new trends in spas and wellness. This means promoting direct contact with the earth's electron-rich surface, such as walking or hiking barefoot. More classes (e.g. yoga, tai chi) are being held outside in natural surroundings. Spa design is also becoming more focused on views of nature and some are even being built in remote wildernesses (e.g. 'pop-up' spas which can be removed again later without impacting on the environment permanently).

Smith and Kelly's (2006) research showed that the location of holistic retreats is important in terms of the type of landscape rather than specific countries or regions. For example, most retreats tend to be in quiet, beautiful locations such as a small village, by the sea or a lake, near a forest or wood. Retreat Finder (2013) includes a category for so-called Eco Retreats which are described as 'Environmentally sustainable retreats and retreat centres employing a wide variety of tactics to help the planet including: solar power, rain barrels, organic farming, recycling, and much more!' The Retreat Company (2013) lists over eighty Eco Retreats around the world, which shows the growing importance of sustainability and nature-based experiences in the holistic sector as well as in spas.

Slow tourism has also been growing in popularity. Slow tourism respects local cultures and history, protects the environment and is socially responsible. Slow tourists want to enjoy a more authentic experience of living in a place, rather than just holidaying there. Although some forms of slow tourism take place in so-called 'slow cities', many of the typical slow tourism experiences tend to take place in peaceful natural environments.

As a summary, some of the latest trends in nature-based health tourism include:

- ecotherapy;
- green spirituality;
- use of organic and bio products;
- local and seasonal foods;
- exercise in the fresh air (including outdoor recreation and adventure sports, 'Green Gyms' and Nordic Walking);
- slow city and slow food movements;
- natural locations for spas and retreats;
- greening of spas and eco-friendliness;
- interest in local and indigenous treatments.

Going to the countryside and re-connecting with nature may help to overcome what Richard Louv (2005) described as 'Nature-Deficit Disorder' (NDD). He said that NDD is not a medical condition; but a description of the human costs of alienation from lack of contact/connection with nature. The symptoms include attention problems, obesity, anxiety and depression. It can be partly caused by too much time spent indoors with TV, computers and mobile phones. Increasing numbers of tourists live in big cities and have relatively little contact with green spaces in their everyday lives. Holiday time may be one of the few occasions when they can enjoy nature. People living in visiting green areas or areas by water ('blue-green areas') tend to be more physically active (e.g. walking, cycling, swimming). The combination of increased exercise, fresh air, sunshine, open spaces, wildlife and views can be just some of the advantages. This includes interaction with nature and oneself.

Research is increasingly emphasising that 'blue spaces' (i.e. those by water) are some of the most healing spaces (Völker & Kistemann, 2013; Bell et al., 2015). Another growing trend is forest therapy. Recently, studies on the healing effects of nature have been carried out in Northern Europe, Japan and Korea, focusing on forest healing in the fields of psychology and forest science (Bell & Ward Thompson, 2014; Song et al., 2014; Tyrväinen et al., 2014).

Overall, as stated by Maller et al. (2006: 54):

> natural areas can be seen as one of our most vital health resources. In the context of the growing worldwide mental illness burden of disease, contact

with nature may offer an affordable, accessible and equitable choice in tackling the imminent epidemic, within both preventative and restorative public health strategies.

Young People and their Connection to Nature

Despite all of the benefits mentioned above, there is a growing concern that young people do not engage as much with nature or the countryside because of lack of time, cost, transportation issues and competition from electronic entertainment (Barton, 2012). Kaplan and Kaplan (2002) also stated that young people have a lower preference for natural settings than for certain kinds of developed areas. The proliferation of shopping malls and other forms of indoor entertainment in cities, for example, are not conducive to encouraging young people to spend more time outdoors or in countryside areas. However, Barton (2012) suggests that young people may appreciate nature differently, for example as the backdrop for specific social and sporting activities. This could include mountain biking, hiking, camping or adventure sports.

In order to investigate young peoples' relationship to nature and the tendency to visit the countryside for leisure and tourism, a questionnaire was undertaken to demonstrate the importance of nature and rural activities for Generation Y (aged 18–33). The questionnaire was completed by 483 respondents: 153 respondents in Hungary, 143 in Romania, 119 in Poland and 68 from Israel. The questionnaires were designed by the author and distributed within the context of an EU COST Project on Tourism, Wellbeing and Ecosystem Services. The sample was a convenience sample generated by volunteers from one of the project Working Groups in which researchers from the given countries offered to translate and distribute the questionnaires. Israel was offered as a contrast to the other countries which have a much more similar geography, climate and nature-based traditions. Israel's climate is hotter, dryer, less green and more desert-like. The coastal resorts are also used for more months of the year. It was decided that the questionnaire sample should include only those young people who are over the age of 18 to facilitate permission and the resolution of ethical issues.

67.9 per cent were female and all of them were tourism students from higher education institutions. Such programmes tend to attract larger numbers of girls than boys. The decision to focus on higher education students provided convenient and guaranteed access to a large sample of respondents due to snowball sampling (i.e. lecturers and students distributed and forwarded the questionnaire to more students). A self-completion questionnaire was designed both in hard copy and for Survey Monkey. The hard copy version data was then input into Survey Monkey and the results were transferred to Excel. The questionnaire consisted of 11 questions. These were mainly closed questions; however, in many cases respondents were able to choose more than one answer, to state their own opinion in an 'other' category, and sometimes they were asked to rank or prioritise their answers. Before the final self-completion questionnaire was distributed, a hard copy pilot questionnaire was undertaken with 20 students in

Hungary and the results were analysed and discussed, after which the questions were refined.

The questionnaire aimed to investigate young peoples' reasons for going regularly to the countryside or not; preferred activities and types of landscape; perceptions of the health benefits of being in nature; and propensity to take holidays in nature.

It should be noted that the landscapes of the countries in question were somewhat different in that Hungary has no sea coast or mountains but lakes and rivers are very important. Israel has fewer green spaces than the other countries, however it has more deserts and the sea coast is also highly valued as a natural landscape (even if more sun-sea-sand tourism takes place there). Poland is rich in forests, mountains and lakes, but also has a sea coast. Nature-based activities such as mushroom picking are very popular there. Romania has very diverse natural resources, such as mountains, plains, lakes, rivers, sea and the unique Danube Delta. Rural areas in Hungary, Poland and Romania tend to be quite traditional and sometimes quite poor compared to cities. Thermal baths or spas are also frequently located in natural landscapes in Hungary, Romania and Poland, therefore these were included in the questionnaire (even Israel has one or two). Hungary has 22 wine regions and vinotherapy is a growing trend in spa and wellness tourism, therefore this dimension was also included in the research.

The most relevant results are presented here. Not all 11 questions are included as some of the questions focused on the profile of respondents. It should be noted that the students were living in the city where they were studying, but their parents sometimes lived in the countryside or they had a second home there (second home ownership is relatively high in Hungary, Poland and Romania). This influenced the frequency of visits and affected the reasons for going (i.e. necessity or obligation rather than personal desire for a nature-based experience).

The majority of students stated that they go to the countryside several times per year. The main reason for going was because their parents or family live in the countryside and they went to visit. However, the second most-quoted reason was that the countryside is relaxing, followed by the countryside is beautiful. The countryside may represent a positive contrast to big city life (the majority of the respondents are currently living in the city where they study). As stated earlier, aesthetics (or beauty) is one of the most important reasons for spending time in natural landscapes and relaxation is one of the major benefits.

When students were asked about why they do not go to the countryside, they cited lack of time as the main reason (70 per cent), followed by the difficulties of reaching or accessing rural areas (15 per cent), lack of interest (12 per cent) and lack of comfort (12 per cent). When asked about which facilities and services would most improve their experience of being in the countryside, access or transport improvements were the most important answer followed by better accommodation. There is also a perceived lack of visitor facilities, services and entertainment. To young people living in a big city with a vibrant nightlife, the countryside can perhaps seem too quiet or dull. However, better visitor centres and trails could be attractive to young people, and nature and wildlife trails or

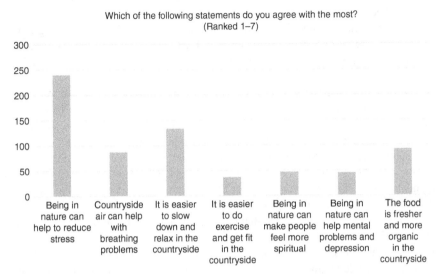

Figure 5.1 The Benefits of Being in Nature

walks are very important, too. These often form part of educational visits or so-called 'forest schools'.

The respondents were asked to rank several statements which related to the benefits or the attractions of being in the countryside. Stress reduction seems to be the most important benefit, followed by relaxation and slowing down. Food is perceived to be fresher and more organic in the countryside too. Perhaps surprisingly, the lowest-scoring benefit is exercise and fitness, even though it was suggested by Barton (2012) that nature can serve as a backdrop for sports for young people. Another problem can be the extreme climate in some of the countries, for example, the desert heat in Israel and the 35–40 degrees Celsius summers in Hungary are not very conducive to exercising unless it is swimming in the sea or a lake.

When asked about which rural or nature-based activities they like to do, the respondents ranked hiking, walking and cycling the highest followed by water-based activities including swimming in lakes, rivers and sea. Wildlife watching scored somewhat lower than might be expected, but it is possible that wildlife is more interesting for younger children and/or that the wildlife present in these countries is not particularly 'exotic' or unusual (e.g. compared to an African safari, for example). Eating local food scores relatively highly, but it was suggested in the open questions that having parties, grilling and drinking alcohol in the countryside is relatively popular with young people.

Relatively large numbers of respondents (almost 80 per cent) find spending time in nature important on holidays. However, this does not necessarily mean that they actually take rural or nature-based holidays regularly. They were asked which environments or activities they would consider for a holiday. The results can be seen in Figure 5.2.

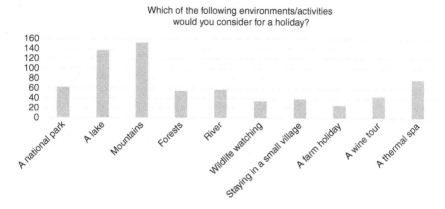

Figure 5.2 Activity Preferences in Nature Tourism

It should be noted here that 'beach' was not included as a category, as it was assumed that the activities that take place there are more connected to 'sun-sea-sand' activities than nature-based ones. However, the Israeli respondents in particular suggested that 'beach' should have been included as a nature-based landscape. It should also be emphasised that lakes are often used in a similar way to beach spaces (e.g. Lake Balaton in Hungary during the summer months). Mountains and lakes are the first choice, but thermal spas feature quite prominently (more than they would in some other countries which do not locate their spas in the countryside).

A significant number of the respondents (around 40 per cent) stated that they planned to take more holidays in the countryside in the future and 30 per cent intended to take more day trips. Many would also like to live in the countryside and/or bring their children up there (more than 40 per cent). However, very few of them (10 per cent) wanted to work in rural tourism despite all of them being tourism students.

When asked about who they thought were the main markets for rural tourism, the respondents listed families with children, older retired people (aged 60+) and active couples without children before young people aged 18–30. This suggests that rural and nature-based tourism is not as popular with young people as they perhaps are with older ones.

Some of the open questions generated a few comments, for example, bathing and tanning by the sea are seen as part of nature (especially in Israel). Sailing, picnics, grilling, camping, working in a garden and extreme sports are also important (as well as drinking strong alcohol outdoors) in Eastern Europe. Some respondents mention that being in nature can make the family closer, being away from computers and electronic devices and just spending fun time in the outdoors together.

Conclusions and Recommendations

The main findings from this research suggested that although a relatively large number of respondents went to the countryside several times a year for leisure or tourism purposes (75 per cent), many of them had parents who lived there permanently or had a summer or weekend home there. However, the second most important reason to go to the countryside after visiting parents or a second home was relaxation (40 per cent). This is a positive finding which suggests that young people associate the countryside or nature-based activities with some dimensions of wellbeing. The main barrier for not going to the countryside was lack of time (most respondents were full-time students). However, many respondents thought that transport access and accommodation could be improved, as well as more visitor information and interpretation (e.g. trails). The countryside can seem dull and lacking in excitement for many young people who are used to urban and technology-based entertainment. More should be done to create active and inter-active visitor experiences.

The most interesting activities in order of importance are: hiking or walking, cycling, visiting lakes and rivers (swimming) (at least 50 per cent for each), followed by eating local farm fresh foods (40 per cent). The latter is a surprising response, perhaps, but may be due to the food consumed during parties, picnics or grills. The main health benefits in order of importance were considered to be: stress reduction, relaxing and slowing down, breathing fresher air and eating local and organic foods. Spiritual dimensions and easing depression were not rated so highly, and exercising or getting fit were considered the least important. This means that although hiking, cycling or swimming are attractive in theory, they are not considered to be major motivations or benefits. It is not surprising that spirituality is ranked quite low. Moal-Ulvoas and Taylor (2014) suggest that older adults tend to be more motivated by spirituality during leisure and tourism time, and connecting more closely with nature is also more important as people age.

At least 85 per cent of respondents thought that having some time in nature during a holiday was important or very important; however, this does not mean that this will necessarily translate into bookings of nature-based holidays. Almost none wanted to work in rural tourism, which is perhaps a worrying finding for the sector. However, a high number of respondents stated that they would like to spend more time in the countryside in the future: 40 per cent said they would like to take more holidays in the countryside, 30 per cent would like to take more day trips and almost half would like to live in the country and bring their children up there later. It seems that the benefits of nature are recognized, but responses to the question about target markets suggested that nature-based activities and holidays are considered to be later life experiences – once people have children or are retired, rather than while they are young.

Acknowledgements

My thanks go to members of the EU-funded COST Project on Tourism, Wellbeing and Ecosystem Services (TObeWELL ISCH COST Action IS1204) – Gabriela Slusariuc, Andrzej Tucki and Anna Dłuewska – as well as Dr Hezi Israeli for collecting some of the data which was used in this paper.

References

Andersson, E., Tengö, M., McPhearson, T. & Kremer, P. (2014). Cultural ecosystem services as a gateway for improving urban sustainability. *Ecosystem Services*, 12, 165–168.

Barton, K. S. (2012). Colorado's millennial generation: Youth perceptions and experiences of nature. *Journal of Geography*, 111, 6.

Barton, J. & Pretty, J. (2010). what is the best dose of nature and green exercise for improving mental health? A multi-study analysis. *Environmental Science and Technology*, 44(10), 3947–3955.

Bell, S. & Ward Thompson, C. (2014). Human Engagement with Forest Environments: Implications for Physical and Mental Health Wellbeing. In T. Fenning (ed.) *Challenges and Opportunities for the World's Forests in the 21st Century*. Forestry Sciences. Dordrecht: Springer.

Bell, S. L., Phoenix, C., Lovell, R. & Wheeler, B. W. (2015). Seeking everyday wellbeing: The coast as a therapeutic landscape. *Social Science & Medicine*, 142, 56–67.

Carroll, J. E. (2004). *Sustainability and Spirituality*. New York, NY: Sunny Press.

Clinebell, H. (1996). *Ecotherapy: Healing Ourselves, Healing the Earth*. London: Routledge.

De Botton, A. (2003). *The Art of Travel*. London: Penguin.

Global Spa Summit/GSS (2011). *Wellness Tourism and Medical Tourism: Where do Spas Fit?* New York, NY: Global Spa Summit.

Hernández-Morcillo, M., Plieninger, T. & Bieling, C. (2013). An empirical review of cultural ecosystem service indicators. *Ecological Indicators*, 29, 434–444.

Hujbens, E. H. (2013). Natural Wellness: The Case of Icelandic Wilderness Landscapes for Health and Wellness Tourism. In M. K. Smith & L. Puczkó, L. (eds) *Health, Tourism and Hospitality: Spas, Wellness and Medical Travel* (pp. 413–416). London: Routledge.

Kaplan, R. & Kaplan, S. (1989). *The Experience of Nature: A Psychological Perspective*. Cambridge: Cambridge University Press.

Kaplan, R. & Kaplan, S. R. (2002). Adolescents and the Natural Environment: A Time Out? In P. H. Kahn & S. R. Kellert (eds) *Children and Nature: Theoretical, Conceptual and Empirical Investigations* (pp. 227–258). Cambridge, MA: MIT Press.

Kaplan, S. (1995). The restorative benefits of nature: Towards an integrative framework. *Journal of Environmental Psychology*, 15, 169–182.

Kaur Kler, B. (2009). Tourism and Restoration. In J. Tribe (ed.) *Philosophical Issues in Tourism* (pp. 117–134). Bristol: Channel View.

Knight, K. W. & Rosa, E. A. (2011). The environmental efficiency of well-being: A cross-national analysis. *Social Science Research*, 40, 931–949.

Kuo, F. E. (2001). Coping with poverty: Impacts of environment and attention in the inner city. *Environment and Behavior*, 33, 5–34.

Louv, R. (2005). *Last Child in the Woods: Saving our Children from Nature Deficit Disorder*. London: Atlantic Books.

Louv, R. (2012). *The Nature Principle: Human Restoration and the End of Nature Deficit Disorder*. Chapel Hill, NC: Algonquin Books.

Maller, C., Townsend, M., Pryor, A., Brown, P. & St Leger, L. (2006). Healthy nature healthy people: 'contact with nature' as an upstream health promotion intervention for populations. *Health Promotion International*, 21(1), 45–54.

Millennium Ecosystem Assessment (2005). *Ecosystems and Human Well-being: Synthesis*. Washington, DC: Island Press.

Moal-Ulvoas, G. & Taylor, V. A. (2014). The spiritual benefits of travel for senior tourists. *Journal of Consumer Behaviour*, 13, 453–462.

New Economics Foundation (NEF) (2008). *Five Ways to Wellbeing*. Retrieved February 25, 2016, from www.fivewaystowellbeing.org

New Economics Foundation (NEF) (2012). *Happy Planet Index*. Retrieved February 24, 2013, from: http://www.neweconomics.org/publications/entry/happy-planet-index-2012-report

Plieninger, T., Dijks, S., Oteros-Rozas, E. & Bieling, C. (2013). Assessing, mapping, and quantifying cultural ecosystem services at community level. *Land Use Policy*, 33, 118–129.

Rahman, T., Mittelhammer, R. C. & Wandschneider, P. (2005). *Measuring the Quality of Life Across Countries: A Sensitivity Analysis of Well-being Indices*. Research paper No. 2005/06 in World Institute for Development Economics Research (WIDER) established by United Nations University (UNU).

The Retreat Company (2013). Retrieved March 24, 2013, from www.theretreat company.com

Retreat Finder (2013). Retrieved March 3, 2013, from www.retreatfinder.com

Roe, J. & Aspinall, P. (2011). The restorative outcomes of forest versus indoor settings in young people with varying behaviour states. *Urban for Urban Green*, 10, 205–212.

Sirgy, M. J. & Cornwell, T. (2001). Further validation of the Sirgy et al.'s measure of community quality of life. *Social Indicators Research*, 56(2), 125.

Smith, M. K. & Kelly, C. (2006). Holistic tourism: Journeys of the self? *Journal of Tourism Recreation Research*, 31(1), 15–24.

Smith, M. K. & Puczkó, L. (2009). *Health and Wellness Tourism*. Oxford: Butterworth Heinemann.

Song, C., Ikei, H. & Miyazaki, Y. (2014). Elucidation of the physiological adjustment effect of forest therapy. *Japanese Journal of Hygiene*, 69(2), 111–116.

Taylor, B. (2009). *Dark Green Religion: Nature, Spirituality and the Planetary Future*. Oakland, CA: University of California Press.

Todd, C. S. (2009). Nature, Beauty and Tourism. In Tribe, J. (ed.) *Philosophical Issues in Tourism* (pp. 154–170). Bristol: Channel View.

Tourism Observatory for Health, Wellness and Spa (TOHWS) (2012). *International Wellness & Spa Tourism Monitor*. Retrieved February 6, 2016, from https://drive.google.com/file/d/0Bzev74rN3_ysdUVHWlRHRzJnWDhPZjRrOERRR2ltaE1rNE1Z/view?pli=1

Tyrväinen, L., Ojala, A., Korpela, K., Lanki, T., Tsunetsugu, Y. & Kagawa, T. (2014). The influence of urban green environments on stress relief measures: A field experiment. *Journal of Environmental Psychology*, 38, 1–9.

Ulrich, R. S. (1984). View through a window may influence recovery from surgery. *Science*, 224, 420–442.

Völker, S. & Kistemann, T. (2013). Reprint of: 'I'm always entirely happy when I'm here!' Urban blue enhancing human health and well-being in Cologne and Düsseldorf, Germany. *Social Science & Medicine*, 91, 141–152.

6 Connectedness and Relatedness to Nature

A Case of Neo-Confucianism among Chinese, South Korean and Japanese Tourists

Nina K. Prebensen, Young-Sook Lee, and Joseph S. Chen

Introduction

In developing economies, it seems to be an upcoming trend to embrace a popular ideology relevant to environmental stewardship such as a growing feeling of interconnectedness with nature (Schultz, 2000). Consequently, the scientific community is increasingly focusing on the human–nature relationship and its impact on environmentally sustainable behavior. In the field of tourism, for instance, investigative efforts on individual's perceptions and attitudes towards nature have been prevailing for decades.

This chapter intends to further the current literature by exploring and comparing how tourists from China, South Korea and Japan relate to and connect with nature. In this chapter theoretical underpinning of the comparison rests on how changing cultural values also referred to as Neo Confucianism, are playing a role in influencing nature tourists from East Asia. Owing to the essential ingredient of Confucianism i.e., 'organic holism' (Tucker, 1991: 62), which explicates that the East Asian worldview of nature is one comprising of unity, and is holistic and interrelated. In this sense, studying relatedness and connectedness to nature in these three East Asian countries may seem to be a straightforward and simple task to undertake. It may appear so until one confronts the complex evolving, enduring and dynamic nature of the cultural and religious philosophy of Confucianism. Together with this complex dynamic, the very essence of tourism, its multidimensionality, adds to the width and depth of the scope of the question.

Three important motives have driven this planned enquiry. Firstly, as the visitor market of nature tourism is on the rise at a rapid pace (Balmford, Beresford, Green, Naidoo, Walpole & Manica, 2009; Mehmetoglu, 2007), better understanding of the phenomenon under investigation is vital for the tourism industry and academia. Secondly, revealing the East Asian tourists' relatedness and connectedness to nature offers a valuable platform to explain tourists' trip experiences in one of the world's fastest growing tourist markets with the highest expenditure patterns (UNWTO, 2015). Thirdly, scholars such as Mayer and Franz (2004) show that connection with nature is a defining predictor of ecological behavior and subjective wellbeing. They claim that scales such as people's connectedness to nature promises to be a useful empirical tool for research on the relationship between humans and the natural world. Therefore, testing the scale in a tourism context permits tourism managers and marketers to develop a tailored instrument measuring nature connectedness so that they can streamline their nature-related experiential offerings and target the right customer segments.

The chapter is organized in three main sections. Firstly, it reviews relevant literature on East Asian, specifically on Neo-Confucian cultural dimensions of Chinese, South Korean and Japanese in relation to relatedness and connectedness to nature. Secondly, it exhibits the study method, the study population, data collection process and the analytical process. Finally, it discusses the study results along with the limitations and future research recommendations.

Neo-Confucianism and Nature

Confucianism as the fundamental philosophical backbone amongst East Asians has been studied in connection with the region's economic growth and modernization (Hofstede & Bond, 1988; Dai, 1989) but relatively little research has been invested in the relationship between Confucianism and nature. Studies show that the education philosophy under Confucianism has been the foundation for not only educating young generations but also for providing guidelines, through which people in the society cultivate themselves as social members and relate themselves to other beings in the universe appropriately. As the overarching cultural philosophy along with Daoism and Zen Buddhism, Confucianism has a clear position when it comes to conceptualizing nature. Lee and Prebensen (2013) suggested a cultural knowledge framework of East Asia for nature-based tourism, illustrating overlapping and unique characteristics of the three cultural values in nature and learning. The highlighted elements of Confucian nature are Oneness, Organismic relation and Creative transformation (2013: 256). The study does not provide any unique traits for different countries that uphold the Confucius value. For the benefit of the current study, the following section provides shared and unique Confucian traits among China, South Korea and Japan. The unique characteristics of Confucianism for the three countries can be attributed to the constantly evolving social and political environments that have been experienced during the region's modernization journey.

Chinese neo-Confucianism and Nature

Confucianism originated in China more than 2,000 years ago, primarily as an education ethos. Its founder Confucius (551–479 B.C.) taught his pupils to become a governor of the people with wisdom and benevolence (Yao, 2000). The philosophy has nourished and influenced modern-day Chinese and East Asian societies. Given the origin of the philosophy, it is appropriate to first review how the evolving neo-Confucianism in China is connected to the concept of nature.

Suggesting the relevance of neo-Confucianism to today's environmental issues, Tucker (1991) draws attention to the central position of Chinese Neo-Confucians.

Comparing it to the ideas of Christianity-based Western part of the world, Tucker (1991) highlights the neo-Confucian perception of 'ongoing reality of a self-generating, interconnected universe' (1991: 63). This is in line with the identified characteristics of nature under Confucian values (Lee & Prebensen, 2013), namely Oneness and organismic relation. This position of neo-Confucianism makes relatedness and connectedness to nature seems obvious, since neo-Confucian values assert Oneness of nature and human. Therefore, trying to measure whether the neo-Confucian backgrounded Chinese people may identify themselves as being one entity with nature might not appear to be a necessary task.

However, there is criticism over the way the Chinese have gone on to develop the infrastructure and industries of the society, including tourism. In particular, Li (2008) argues that anthropocentrism is apparent in China, placing human comfort above nature. If neo-Confucianism, viewing nature and human as one entity, provide the overarching values in the changing and developing Chinese society, there should not be anthropocentric use of nature by the Chinese people.

Tu (1985, cited in Tucker, 2008) provides the relevant neo-Confucian notion of nature that might be misinterpreted as similar to anthropocentrism in the minds of the West: creative transformation. With the concept of creative transformation, he explicates that the fundamental position of Confucian values of unity between nature and human is different from the base position of anthropocentrism where imposition of humanity over nature is the underlying premise. The current state of our understanding of the Chinese neo-Confucianism and the concept of nature necessitate a closer inspection into relatedness and connectedness to nature in China.

South Korean neo-Confucianism

Literature on neo-Confucianism pays little attention to South Korea-specific versions of nature affected by the ideology, hence delineating a comparative concept of nature to that of China does not appear to be viable. However, although not specifically on the concept of nature, existing works highlight that neo-Confucianism in South Korea has been developing with its unique characteristics in comparison to China. One of the most distinctively Korean traits of neo-Confucianism compared to China is lineage in the society. Lineage in Korean society is built on a much more narrowly defined line of first the son of a family. This brought about adverse consequences for women and the second and subsequent sons of a family (Deuchler, 1992). Also, Japan's imperial rule over Korea between 1910 and 1945 affected the neo-Confucian traits in Korea. When compared to Chinese neo-Confucianism, Korean neo-Confucianism is described as filial, i.e., regional, while Chinese is national. Influencing Korean society even before the official annexation, colonial rule brought a split Confucian personality that is filial for older generations while national for younger generations (Kang, 1977). Though not concentrated on nature, neo-Confucianism in modernizing Korean society cannot be said to be identical to the Chinese.

Japanese neo-Confucianism

Similar to the case in Korea, neo-Confucianism research pays little attention and specifically aims to delineate a Japan-specific concept of nature. This reflects some issues in the approach to Confucianism studies. Critically assessing Confucian capitalism hypotheses, Watanabe (1996) points out that research into Confucianism has failed to investigate the differences among East Asian societies; that is their versions of Confucianism. At the same time, focuses have been put on the differences between East Asia and West. Nevertheless, it is unclear whether or not Confucianism is a social agent propelling economic growth, that is, whether the economic growth in East Asia exists despite Confucianism or because of Confucianism. Further, Watanabe (1996) articulates that the family unit as the base of the social unit is comparatively different within East Asian societies of China, Korea and Japan. The family unit, while considered as the essential unit of society in all three countries, has different degrees of significance in terms of lineage in Japan.

This literature review provides an overall concept of nature under neo-Confucian values as well as Chinese's specific notion of nature. However, Korean- or Japanese-specific concepts of nature do not appear to be apparent. Oneness between nature and human is the established and accepted concept of nature of the neo-Confucian East Asian societies. The current study, thus, compares the tourists from these three countries in response to nature relatedness (NR) and connectedness to nature (CN). This attempt serves as a departure point for measuring neo-Confucian's Oneness concept of nature and human.

Measuring Oneness between Nature and Human: Connectedness and Relatedness to Nature

Researchers have been actively trying to understand the degrees to which individuals identify themselves with nature or feelings of Oneness with nature. This is due to the relationships between people's feelings of connectedness to nature and their tendencies to participate in environmentally responsible behavior (Fisher, 2002; Mayer & Frantz, 2004; Roszak, Gomes & Kanner, 1995; Roszak, 2001). There are various sets of developed scales to measure individuals' Oneness with nature, such as a commitment to nature, connectivity with nature, emotional affinity toward nature, environmental identity, inclusion of nature in self, nature relatedness and connectedness to nature. Evaluating these sets, Tam (2013) finds that they have a commonly shared central idea, making it viable to use the sets as transferrable and compatible scales. The transferability is recommended with the caution that some unique traits of individual scales be noted in the application of them. In the current study, two specific scales of nature relatedness (NR) and connectedness to nature (CN) are taken up in order to examine the similarities and differences among tourists from the three East Asian countries in the way they feel Oneness with nature.

In order to study people's sense of connectedness with nature, Schultz (2002) suggests a scale that includes both affective and cognitive experiences with nature, the connectedness to nature scale. Schultz bases his scale on previous work, e.g., Dunlap, Van Liere, Mertig and Jones (2000) who aim to measure individuals' beliefs concerning their relationship to the natural world through the new environmental paradigm (NEP). The foundational idea of the NEP scale is to measure individuals' beliefs concerning their relationship to the natural world. The idea is that the individuals includes nature within their cognitive representation of the self. Mayer and Frantz (2004) built on Schultz (2002) and include affective experience to the NEP scale including individual's experiential connection to nature (Mayer and Frantz, 2004). They support the CN scale by examining its validity and reliability through five different tests.

Nisbet et al. (2008) recommend the Nature Relatedness (NR) scale in order to acknowledge human relatedness to nature that is the individual level of connectedness with the natural world. In a similar fashion as the CN scale, the NR scale includes the individual perception of nature as part of one self. Additionally, the NR scale includes one's gratitude for and acknowledgment of the interconnectedness with all other living elements on the earth and our understanding of the importance of all aspects of nature (Nisbet et al., 2008).

The CN and the NR scales show some similarities; however, while the CN scale focuses on the psychological aspect with nature, the NR scale involves the physical aspect of the human–nature relationship. Mayer and Franz (2004) test the CN scale across five different studies and reveal high validity and reliability in the scale.

It is apparent that people from the three East Asian counties embrace Oneness with nature in one form or another. Yet, it remains unknown what the differences among those from the three counties are when it comes to a neo-Confucianism-inspired concept of nature. In this regard, the present research adopts the aforementioned scales concerning connectedness and relatedness, although they are developed in the West, to measure Oneness with nature among Chinese, Korean and Japanese tourists.

Method

Study Population

Three countries in East Asia were chosen as study sites: (1) China, (2) South Korea and (3) Japan. Tourists visiting nature-based attractions near metropolitan cities participated in the survey. City residents throughout the year patronized these tourism spots.

The study involved 156 Japanese visitors (30 percent males, 70 percent females), 427 South Korean visitors (50 percent males and 50 percent females) and 400 Chinese tourists (55 percent males, 45 percent females) completed the questionnaire. With regards to the educational background, 25 percent of all respondents (all three countries) had secondary school, 26 percent had vocational training after secondary school, 16 percent had secondary education, 12 percent had primary education, 7 percent had tertiary education, 9 percent had postgraduate education and 5 percent did not participate. In the collected data, the majority of the Chinese respondents were under 24 years of age, while the Japanese respondents were in the group between 25 and 44 years of age, and majority of Korean respondents were between 55 and 64 years of age.

Procedure

The survey was tested in a pilot study. First, the original scales were adjusted to a nature tourism setting. Scholars working with nature tourism were then asked to screen the questionnaire. Based on feedback from the scholars, some questions were removed and some were somewhat altered.

As the main survey mechanism, an online survey was performed for Chinese and South Korean subjects. For the Japanese, a printed survey was conducted in Tokyo. Potential Japanese participants were approached by trained research assistants, provided with a general verbal introduction to the study, and were asked to complete the survey. Those who agreed to participate completed a questionnaire anonymously. They supplied basic demographic information, including age, gender, education level and the type of environment in which they were brought up. In addition, all participants were asked to complete the following sets of scale-related questions regarding nature connectedness and nature relatedness.

Tourist Connectedness to Nature (TCN) Scale

The scale entailing 17 items is mirrored from Mayer and Frantz (2004) and further expanded via a process involving the researchers and psychology scholars. In order to utilize the TCN scale, a modification process was carried out that invites suggestions from tourism researchers for the most appropriate wording to measure each item. The initial scale was further reviewed by different researchers and potential tourists. Finally, 14 items were included in the scale to explain tourist's connectedness to nature.

Tourist Nature Relatedness (TNR) Scale

This scale is inspired by the work of Nisbet et al. (2008) that entails the affective, cognitive and experiential aspects of individuals' connection to nature. It includes three dimensions: nature relatedness to self (NR-Self), nature relatedness to perspective (NR-Perspective) and nature relatedness to experience (NR-Experience).

Nature relatedness to self is often referred to as an individual's ecological identity and is considered imperative in order to understand human behavior as part of the planet and ecosystem (Conn, 1998; Næss, 1973). Damage to nature is viewed as a way of harming the self as researchers have studied the environmental self-concept, linking environmental self-definition with self-reports of environmental attitudes and behavior.

NR-Self signifies an internalized identification with nature. NR-Self describes feelings and thoughts about one's personal connection to nature, such as 'My connection to nature and the environment is part of my spirituality', and 'My relationship to nature is an important part of who I am'.

NR-Perspective mirrors an external, nature-related worldview. This dimension includes a sense of individual human actions and their impact on all living aspects, for example, 'Humans have the right to use natural resources the way they want', and 'Conservation is unnecessary because nature is strong enough to recover from any human impact'.

NR-Experience reveals a physical awareness of the natural world, the level of comfort with and desire to be out in nature and includes items such as 'The thought of being deep in the woods, away from civilization, is frightening', 'My ideal vacation spot would be a remote, wilderness area' and 'I enjoy being outdoors, even in unpleasant weather'.

A total of 21 items were used in a tourist's relatedness to nature scale.

Findings and Discussions

In order to examine the dimensionality of the constructs and to assess the discriminant validity of the scales, i.e., tourist relatedness and connectedness to nature, exploratory factor analysis were conducted. Exploratory factor analysis is chosen because the intention is to examine whether a set of indicators can be reduced to a more limited set of underlying dimensions. It should be noted that exploratory factor analysis is performed to test whether the original relatedness and connectedness scales are appropriate in a tourism context. First, an un-rotated factor analysis is performed in order to decide the number of factors. Varimax rotation are conducted for both scales, and four relatedness factors and two connectedness factors are extracted.

The factor analysis of the 27 relatedness-to-nature items shows 58.7 percent explained variances. In a purification process, this study first removes three items with a low correlation and then conducts a new factor analysis on the remaining 24 relatedness items. Based on the correlations, the four factors are given the following names: 'personal relatedness', 'environmental relatedness,' 'man above animal' and 'active in nature'. The factor analysis of the 13 connectedness to nature items results in two factors, explaining 57.4 percent of the variances. These factors are labelled as 'engaged connectedness to nature' and 'remote connectedness to nature'. In Table 6.1, the findings reveal that both the relatedness and connectedness to nature differ among the three study populations except for the factor of 'active in nature' which belongs to the relatedness-to-nature scale.

The current chapter is an exploratory attempt to understand if Confucianism-inspired concepts of nature can be measured and compared. The reviewed literature provides a Chinese neo-Confucianism-based concept of nature; however, there is a paucity of literature on Korean and Japanese notions of nature.

The factor analysis proposes four nature relatedness factors and two connectedness to nature factors. Compared with the original scales (Nisbet et al., 2008; Schultz, 2002) the data reveal somewhat different results when it comes to tourism. However, based on explained variances and the correlations the study

Table 6.1 Mean Scores for Nature Relatedness and Connectedness in Tourism

Nationality	Relatedness: Personal	Relatedness: Environmental Importance	Relatedness: Man above animal	Relatedness: Activity in Nature	Connectedness: personal connected	Connectedness: Disconnected and Distant
Japan (n = 156)	4.1	4.0	2.8	4.0	4.2	2.9
Korea (n = 427)	4.1	4.4	3.3	3.7	4.5	4.3
China (n = 400)	5.1	4.7	3.1	3.9	5.6	2.5
Total (N = 983)	4.5	4.5	3.1	3.8	4.9	3.4

findswthat the scales could evolve into an effective assessment tool measuring tourist's connectedness and relatedness to nature.

The respondents from the three studied countries reveal similar attitudes when it comes to their connectedness and relatedness to nature. The factor 'man above animal' shows the lowest scores for all nationalities. This result suggests that East-Asian tourists are more connected to nature than disconnected to nature. Interestingly, while China and Japan rate 'disconnectedness with nature' as very low, South Korea rate it high.

Differences among the countries do exist. The Chinese respondents score stronger on personal relatedness and environmental importance—as compared to the respondents from the other two countries. Chinese identify themselves as being one entity with nature as an obvious fact of life, more strongly than the Koreans and the Japanese.

South Korean domestic tourists score stronger on 'man above animal' and 'remote connectedness to nature'. Based on these results, it may be suggested that the South Koreans feel less connected and related to nature than the other studied nationalities. One possible explanation of the result can be the society's modernization pathway, which reflects the historical influences of Japanese colonial rule. Indeed, the colonial modernization in Korea (Robinson & Shin, 2001) has somewhat altered even the characteristics of the society's philosophical backbone, Confucian values. Detailing the many phases of the colonial rule's policy implementation, Kang (1977: 22) shows that 'orientation of love' (*jen* in Chinese) formed the binding philosophical base in the pre-colonial society, creating the social bonding similar to a father–son relationship. The implementation of colonial policy, however, transformed the base for the bonding of the society to a 'sense of imperative' (*i* in Chinese), moving to a social bonding similar to that of an emperor-subject. However, due to the exploratory nature of the current study, this suggestion needs further investigation.

Japanese tourists score somewhat higher on 'active in nature'. The result points however to what Watanabe (1996) discusses as caused by Confucian capitalism. Being active in nature may reflect modernity as people need to get away from everyday life and stress (e.g., Dann, 1981). It is therefore expected that 'active in nature' will increase in China and South Korea as modernism calls for new lifestyles.

Conclusion

The current study identified a concept of Oneness between nature and human in neo-Confucian valued societies of China, Korea and Japan. Existing literature mostly highlights the shared cultural traits of neo-Confucianism instead of identifying differences among the values and practices of neo-Confucian-influenced Oneness concepts of nature and human. The results of the current research need to be taken with two points of limitation. First, the data collection for Chinese and Korean participations were via an online survey, the Japanese, through a face-to-face survey method. Secondly, the adopted scales for study reflect the viewpoints from Western countries. Thus, a new scale needs to be developed, illuminating the value constructs of East Asian culture and their sentiment for nature. Further, while recognizing the Oneness between nature and human, the difference in the fundamental starting points must be recognized. As Tu (1985) points out, Oneness between nature and humanity in neo-Confucian values can even be misinterpreted as anthropocentrism in the West, which is at the stark opposite end of the spectrum in the debate of environmentalism and its values.

The study has its own limitations. Two of the surveys were performed online, while one survey was performed on site. The online respondents were instructed to imagine their last visit to a nature-based spot. We, however, recognize possible shortfalls in perfectly capturing the respondents' feelings at the time of their responses due to the time lag. Furthermore, the respondents show demographical differences, which should be taken into consideration. For instance, age differences in the three datasets were substantial and might affect the study result. These issues should be controlled in further research.

References

Balmford, A., Beresford, J., Green, J., Naidoo, R., Walpole, M. & Manica, A. (2009). A global perspective on trends in nature-based tourism. *PLoS Biology*, 7(6), 1229.

Conn, S. (1998). Living in the earth: Ecopsychology, health and psychotherapy. *The Humanistic Psychologist*, 26, 179–198.

Dai, H. (Ed.) (1989). *Confucianism and Economic Development: An Oriental Alternative?* Washington, DC: Washington Institute Press.

Dann, G. M. (1981). Tourist motivation an appraisal. *Annals of Tourism Research*, 8(2), 187–219.

Deuchler, M. (1992). *The Confucian transformation of Korea: A study of society and ideology* (No. 36). Cambridge, MA: Harvard University Asia Center.

Dunlap, R. E., Van Liere, K. D., Mertig, A. G., & Jones, R. E. (2000). New trends in measuring environmental attitudes: Measuring endorsement of the new ecological paradigm – a revised NEP scale. *Journal of Social Issues*, 56(3), 425–442.

Fisher, A. (2002). *Radical ecopsychology: Psychology in the service of life*. New York: University of New York Press.

Hiroshi, W. (1996). 'They are Almost the Same as the Ancient Three Dynasties': The West as Seen Through Confucian Eyes in Nineteenth-Century Japan. In: W. Tu (Ed.), *Confucian traditions in East Asian modernity* (pp. 119–131). Cambridge, MA: Harvard University Press.

Hofstede, G., & Bond, M. H. (1988). The Confucius connection: From cultural roots to economic growth. *Organizational Dynamics*, 16(4), 5–21.

Kang, T. H. (1977). The changing nature of Korean Confucian personality under Japanese rule. *Korea Journal*, 17(3), 22–36.

Lee, Y. S., & Prebensen, N. K. (2014). Value creation and co-creation in tourist experiences: An East Asian cultural knowledge framework approach. *Creating Experience Value in Tourism*, 248.

Li, S. F. M. (2008). Culture as a major determinant in tourism development of China. *Current Issues in Tourism*, 11(6), 492–513.

Mayer, F. S., & Frantz, C. M. (2004). The connectedness to nature scale: A measure of individuals' feeling in community with nature. *Journal of Environmental Psychology*, 24(4), 503–515.

Mehmetoglu, M. (2007). Typologising nature-based tourists by activity: Theoretical and practical implications. *Tourism management*, 28(3), 651–660.

Næss, A. (1973). The shallow and the deep ecology movements. *Inquiry*, 16, 95–100.

Nisbet, E. K., Zelenski, J. M., & Murphy, S. A. (2008). The nature relatedness scale: Linking individuals' connection with nature to environmental concern and behavior. *Environment and Behavior*, 41, 715–740.

Robinson, M. E. & Shin, G. W. (2001). *Colonial modernity in Korea* (Vol. 184). Cambridge, MA: Harvard University Asia Center.

Roszak, T. (2001). *The voice of the earth: An exploration of ecopsychology*. Grand Rapids, MI: Phanes Press.

Schmuck, & Schultz, W. P. (Eds.), *Psychology of sustainable development*. Dordrecht: Kluwer Academic Publishers.

Schultz, P. W. (2002). Inclusion with nature: The psychology of human-nature relations. In P.

Tam, K. P. (2013). Concepts and measures related to connection to nature: Similarities and differences. *Journal of Environmental Psychology*, 34, 64–78.

Tucker, M. E. (1989). *Moral and Spiritual Cultivation in Japanese Neo-Confucianism: The Life and Thought of Kaibara Ekken (1630-1714)*. SUNY Press.

Tucker, M. E. (1991). The relevance of Chinese Neo-Confucianism for the reverence of nature. *Environmental History Review*, 15(2), 55–69.

Tu, W.-M. (1985). *Confucian Thought: Selfhood as Creative Transformation*. New York: SUNY Press.

UNWTO (2015). Tourism highlights. Accessed December 30, 2015, from www.e-unwto. org/doi/pdf/10.18111/9789284416899

The West as Seen Through Confucian Eyes in Nineteenth-Century Japan. In *Confucian Traditions in East Asian Modernity: Moral Education and Economic Culture in Japan and the Four Mini-Dragons*, edited by T. Wei-Ming, 119–131. Cambridge, MA: Harvard University Press.

Yao, X. (2000). *An Introduction to Confucianism*. Cambridge: Cambridge University Press.

7 How Local Traditions and Way of Living Influence Tourism

Basecamp Explorer in Maasai Mara, Kenya and Svalbard, Norway

*Øystein Jensen, Frank Lindberg,
Damiannah M. Kieti, Bjørn Willy Åmo, and
James S. Nampushi*

Introduction and Perspectives

As nature-based tourism relies on the natural environment as the main source of tourism, many natural areas exposed to tourism are or have been populated by local people having developed tacit knowledge and skills over generations to be able to survive frequently harsh environmental conditions. This way of living might have resulted in practices, traditions, and norms that even today can be of great value for tourists visiting such areas, and for the enhancement of their experience of being amidst nature, and can be regarded as an integrative part of the natural areas from an ecotourism perspective (Allcock, Jones, et al. 1994, Weaver 2008). Ecotourism is widely recognized as a more benign alternative to *laissez-faire* mass tourism, due to its purported emphasis on nature-based attractions, learning opportunities, and management practices that adhere to the principles of ecological, socio-cultural, and economic sustainability (Fennell 1999). In totality, ecotourism is viewed as a sustainable form of natural resource-based tourism that focuses primarily on experiencing and learning about nature, and which is ethically managed to be low-impact, non-consumptive, and locally oriented in terms of control, benefits, and scale (Fennell 1999). Ecotourism contributes to the preservation of the environment through a contribution to conservation and/or indirectly by providing revenue to the local community sufficient for local people to value, and therefore protects their natural heritage area as a source of income (Goodwin 1996). As the idea that ecotourism can be locally beneficial has been promoted within tourism research it has moreover been argued that the involvement of local communities in ecotourism operations additionally can contribute to improving the quality of tourist experience, such as by the provision of knowledge and services (Newsome, Moore, et al. 2002). For tourists the appreciation of such local skills and attitudes to nature can similarly be perceived as an extension of their nature-based experiences. This can take place, for example, through the interaction with trained local guides who combine professional skills with their local traditional knowledge and philosophy that enable the tourists access to dimensions of a natural and spiritual world that they otherwise would not have been aware of.

The social encounters between Western tourists and developing world tribal communities, for example in some African and Asian countries, have frequently been looked at quite critically in the literature on mass tourism (Bruner 2001, Scheyvens 2002, Salazar 2006). Various perspectives on the role of tourist guides have been described and discussed by several authors (Cohen 1985, Smith 1989, Pond 1993, Weiler and Ham 2001, 2002, Cohen, Ifergan, et al. 2002, Scherle and Nonnenmann 2008, Jensen 2010). As, on the one hand, a local guide can play the role of a mediator (Cohen 1985) in the encounter between the cultures of the hosts and the visitors (Nettekoven 1979, Jensen 2010) she/he can also, on the other hand, serve as a mediator of meanings and experience-dimensions of the natural environment and the visitor. Acknowledging the dilemmas of host–guest encounters (Smith 1989, Robinson 1999), especially related to mass tourism, this issue is, however, not in main focus within this case description.

This case description of the multi award-winning Basecamp Explorer (BCE) offers illumination of the way indigenous people can play a key role in nature-based tourism and especially in the forming of the tourist experience. Moreover, it illustrates how traditions of dealing with wilderness and extreme environment can increase the tourists' physical and spiritual access to such areas, even in case of traditions from past settlements. The case descriptions offer in particular illustrations of the way the Maasai people have been deeply involved in the Basecamp Masai Mara tourism experience, but it also offers insight into the significance of past settlement traditions in the case of Basecamp Spitsbergen in the Arctic.

An in-depth exploration of the involvement of the local Maasai traditions and way of living in adding value to nature-based tourism experience was undertaken in March 2016. Unstructured interviews with the local "Maasai" (elders, women, and youth), management, and staff of Basecamp Maasai Mara were used to derive thick qualitative data. The research participants were interviewed at various places including: at the Basecamp, cultural manyattas (special homesteads where the local culture is displayed) at Talek and Sekenani, and at tourist facilities, including Sekenani camp.

In Basecamp Spitsbergen, the data was collected through a) secondary information about activities, firms, and sociocultural contexts, b) interviews with management and staff c) participant observations at the Trapper's Hotel and of various tourist activities that were offered by Basecamp, and d) partly structured interviews with tourists. The tourist activities in focus were the boat safari to Icefjord Radio Station (Arctic hiking, glacier trip, and whale watching), dog sledding from Trapper's station to the "ship in the ice", and mountain hiking. The focus during the data collection was on substantial and communicative staging (Arnould 2007) from micro (e.g., tourists), meso (e.g., Basecamp) and macro (e.g., cultural-historical traditions) perspectives. The researchers stayed for one week in August 2011 and in March 2012 and 2013.

The data collection at both locations was designed to develop a rich understanding of the involvement of local traditions and way of living in nature-based tourism by identifying the tacit knowledge and skills that have enabled the local Maasai, trappers, miners, and explorers to endure harsh environmental conditions and live harmoniously with nature. The local traditions, practices, and norms, which could be of great value for tourists engaging in nature-based tourism were then identified, before exploring how such local traditions and way of living can add value to tourists' experience.

The Case of Basecamp Masai Mara

Description of Basecamp Masai Mara

Started in 1998 and located in Koiyaki group ranch adjacent to Maasai Mara National Reserve, Basecamp Maasai Mara is part of Basecamp Explorer, a tourism company that operates in several destinations throughout the world. The camp lies on 6 hectares of land and provides 12 spacious and magnificent tents, all built along the banks of Talek river, which forms the Maasai Mara National Reserve's north-east boundary. Raised from wooden platforms, all the 12 guest tents are built using canvas with the interior and exterior design fashioned from clay, deadwood, and grass-thatched roofs, thereby blending excellently with the natural environment. While the camp is 95 percent staffed by permanent employees from the local area, casual job opportunities are exclusively given to the local people. Through scheduled in-house training, the staff acquire knowledge and requisite skills in environmental management issues, including water, energy, and waste management.

The tourism operations within the Basecamp Maasai Mara are primed by the concept of 3Ps: People, Planet, and Profit, with the main goal of improving the local community livelihoods and generating income through eco-friendly activities in order to conserve wildlife and its habitat, uphold the Maasai culture, and develop local communities. Specifically, Basecamp approaches involve responding to and investing in people and the planet by empowering local people through training, education, and employment, sharing benefits, conservation of biodiversity, restoration of environmental values, minimum impact from tourist activities, innovations in cultural conservation, and visitor transformation. The main activities and experiences offered to tourists in the camp include: game drives in the Maasai Mara National Reserve, hot air balloon safaris over the Maasai Mara plains, local Maasai-guided nature walks, and cocktails from picturesque viewpoints.

The camp has applied various eco-friendly and sustainable tourism measures. These include: (i) extensive use of local materials for example, deadwood for construction; (ii) use of tree-top wildlife viewing and low impact activities, such as nature walks, bird watching, and authentic village visits to sensitize visitors about the environment, as well as minimize the need for game drive; (iii) planting of approximately 70,000 trees since the year 2000, as part of restoring vegetation along the river near the camp and reducing the carbon footprint; (iv) use of a solar cooker at its kitchen, as a demonstration to the local community of energy-efficient technologies, as well as the use of ISO-certified solar water heaters and energy saving bulbs (Munyoro 2011); (v) partnering with 500 Maasai landowners to establish Naboisho Wildlife Conservancy, where each of the landowners earns a monthly income paid as rent for setting aside part of the land for conservation. Presently, several community conservancies are being modelled along the tenets of Naboisho conservancy; (vi) remitting conservancy, lease and bed night fees to Naboisho conservancy, most of which is used to fund local community wellbeing projects; (vii) establishing Basecamp Maasai Brand (BMB) whose aim is to use traditional beading practices to empower and improve the local Maasai women's financial freedom, as well as encourage them to conserve their culture; and (viii) working closely with Koiyaki Guiding School (KGS) to enhance the employability of young Maasai. The camp sponsors two students every year to join KGS, offers work experience placement opportunities for a number of students, and helps the school to fundraise for additional scholarships. Currently, three of the Basecamp driver guides are graduates of KGS.

Basecamp Maasai Mara has won several prestigious awards, including the Eco-warrior award in 2005, First choice responsible tourism award in 2006, First gold eco-rating in Kenya award in 2007, and the Skål sustainable tourism award in the category of rural accommodation in 2015, among others. As a result, the camp has become a role model for upcoming eco-lodges throughout East Africa, particularly in the use of sustainable technologies, conserving the environment, promoting and conserving culture, enhancing quality of life of local people, and creating a unique tourism experience.

The Maasai People, Cultural Background and Their Traditional Relationship to Nature

The Maasai people are semi-nomadic pastoralists whose lives revolve around their cows, sheep, goats, donkeys, and camels (AWF 2005). The livelihoods, as well as the major source of income, is therefore livestock (mostly goats, sheep, and cattle), which is also an indicator of wealth and prestige. Presently, the nomadic way of living among the Maasai is slowly dying out. Instead, they are now becoming herdsmen who move with the livestock from one place to another in search of water and grass, leaving the rest of the family members behind (Nyariki, Mwang'ombe, et al. 2009). However, they still cherish and retain the customs and ceremonies of their forebears (Kieti, Jones, et al. 2008). Their society has over time been glued together by their prevailing cultures that they still find it hard to change to a more limited lifestyle (AWF 2005). The Maasai live in either small mud-plastered huts or under hides and grass mats stretched over a frame of poles, surrounded by a fence of thorny branches. They depend on milk for their main stay, sometimes mixed with blood, while meat is normally eaten only at special occasions. Occasionally, they make soups from roots and barks and they do not eat or hunt any game for food. There are clearly defined roles for each member of a family. For instance, adult men care for the grazing cattle, sheep, goats, and camels, which are the major source of livelihood, whereas women take charge of maintaining the portable huts, milking cows, fetching

Figure 7.1 Maasai Preparing the Bonfire, by Øystein Jensen

water, and gathering firewood, and the young boys herd cattle and goats, learning to defend their flocks (see also Jenkins 1997). Their knowledge of nature does not rely on formal education but on real life education and experiences from home, in their community, and through their own practice. This knowledge of nature can also be formed by storytelling in their village, especially by bonfires in the evenings where men gather to communicate and discuss. Generally, the Maasai traditionally consider the savannas as their territory, with an exclusive right to own cows. In this sense, they could be perceived as territorial hosts for tourists visiting Maasai Mara.

The BCM Maasai Staff's Influence During Interface with the Tourists and the Intended Influence on the Tourist Experiences

The Maasai staff's interface with the tourists take place on most service point levels at Basecamp Masai Mara (BCM). Within the natural setting it especially takes place through the Maasai guides, such as within the contexts of game drives (for example, a whole day in the reserve with smaller or bigger groups), walking safaris (day or night), and a combination of tours or trekking that can last for several days. Playing the classical role of local guides (Cohen 1985), the Maasai's fundamental link and skills in relation to life on the savannah, combined with challenging and dynamic environmental conditions, offer them a position of influence over the tourists' experience through interpretation and social contacts. This is basically not produced by formal education but is essentially rooted in traditions and in primarily sustainable practices that have taken place over generations. Indeed, most tour guides utilize their vast experience and repertoire of local knowledge to guide, interpret, and disseminate

Figure 7.2 Maasai Guide from Sekenany Camp and Tourist on Walking Safari, by
       Øystein Jensen

information to tourists. Within a tourism business, the intended contribution
to the visitors' nature-based experiences would be to be able to experience the
nature "through the eyes and the minds of the Maasais" and by this open the
minds of tourists to the amazing hidden treasures of the natural environment and
add to the nature-based experience in a particular direction. The Maasai people
have over time developed and evolved intricate traditional knowledge, skills,
and natural resource management practices, and cultural ritual derived from
interaction with nature. However, as reported from Uganda (Victurne 2000)
it was necessary to provide targeted in-house training for the Maasai staff in
order to comply with the guest's expectations. Additionally, Muriithi (2007)
observes that several eco-rated lodges in the Maasai Mara provide interpretative
programs involving environmental and cultural conservation using tour guides
professionally trained locally by the Mara Basecamp Foundation at Koiyaki
Guding School in Maasai Mara. Over the years, the Maasai have continued
to improve unique knowledge, life skills, and practices in the management of
natural resources and their total environment. It should still not be ignored that
beside professional training and education, including at Koyaki Guiding School,
modernization processes have contributed to a change of attitudes and lifestyles
of the younger generations as is the case of many other tribal societies, and
staged cultural performance and host–guest encounters take place (MacCannell
1976; Smith 1989). This discussion exceeds, however, the limitations of this
brief case description.

  According to Masau and Prideaux (2003), there is a willingness among
tourist to pay a premium for environmentally friendly and differentiated products and services. Tourists want to learn about the environment they visit and
to understand the connections with a broader natural and cultural environment.

When interpretation succeeds in provoking a tourist to have personal thoughts and to make personal meanings about a place or thing, it helps to shape that tourist's experience with the place or thing if these thoughts are pleasing or gratifying, thereby enhancing a person's experience (Ham and Sandberg 2012). By taking the cultural influencing approach to the nature-based experiences the point of departure would be a "Maasai" approach to the meditation of the nature-based experience that relies on a collective "Maasai way" of dealing with the natural environment, both as survival practice and as expressed through their attitude to nature. Referring to examples from the interviews reflecting wildlife, each animal has a particular significance and way of behavior depending on situations, such as season, time of the day, weather conditions, etc. The dynamic co-existence among different species within the Mara ecosystem adds to this picture alongside the observable interactions between them, such as between predators and prey, that tend to be the most exiting forms targeted by tourists. The way such events are accessed, the way they are explained by factual information and narratives told by the Maasai guide, can thus be regarded as frames or perceptional glasses through which wildlife can be experienced. This will frequently also be enforced by dramas from storytelling. For example, the most "popular" figure tends to be the lion, and heroic stories about encounters with lions among Maasai are frequently told and requested. Other animals have also earned their particular positions, for example, a Maasai camp's security staff member told a story from his own childhood about how they were hiding among their herd of goats to detect and track a leopard attacking them and later how it was killed. However, now the leopard has a value for the community when alive due to tourism, so talking about it and its particular characteristics as compared with other animals would be more beneficial. The Maasai consider the Wildebeest to be "the most loved by God" because all other animals can give birth during the dry season but not a wildebeest. In his study, Goldman (2007) established a

Figure 7.3 Lions Resting in the Shadow, by Øystein Jensen

close observation of the movement of wildebeest, known to follow the rain, as an important animal husbandry strategy for the Maasai. Arguably, the Maasai identity may be considered to be exclusively intertwined with land, nature, and livestock, which ultimately inform their traditional expressions, knowledge, skills, and practice.

Our interviews indicated moreover, that as shorter encounters with tourists offered limited opportunities of communicating on a deeper level, longer trips, especially for several days that included walking in small groups, created closer contact between the guides and the visitors, and thereby offered opportunities of obtaining a deeper insight into the Maasai culture and their tacit knowledge of nature. Gathering around the bonfire occurred as a frequently used technique of creating an atmosphere for interaction reflecting a traditional social setting for communication between Maasai males. Tourists gathering around the bonfire coupled with storytelling enables them to enjoy the freedom and spontaneity that being on holiday affords them. However, it is important to mention that the pre-paredness of the visitors to open up was also mentioned as a critical condition for the mediation processes. The danger of "staging" would be greater by tourists staying only for a short time and by tourists with limited preparedness for receiving traditional knowledge in comparison with longer trips with more time for personal contact.

The idea of the Maasai people as the actual hosts of the Mara—not the Basecamp as a company or site—remains the founding principle of the camp. As expressed by the founder of BCE and BCM, Svein Wilhelmsen, as most people come for the wildlife experience, for example symbolized by "The big five", it is normally the encounters with the Maasai and their culture that frequently leave the strongest impact and thus can create memorable experiences (Tung and Ritchie 2011). This also generates opportunities for adding a "Maasai perspective" to the tourists' nature-based experiences thereby stimulating and encouraging enjoyment, understanding, and appreciation of nature.

Figure 7.4 Walking with Maasai Guides, by Øystein Jensen

The Case of Basecamp Spitsbergen

Since the Norwegian Government opened up for tourism in the beginning of the 1990s the Arctic Svalbard has changed from being an isolated place that mainly attracts explorers, hunters, and miners to becoming a destination for people with dreams of holidaying at the northern-most settled place on earth. The average temperature in summer is 5 degrees Celsius and during winter the temperature can drop to below –30 degrees Celsius, and 60 percent of the land is covered by ice and snow all year around. The midnight sun lasts from April until August, and the polar night from October to February (Governor of Svalbard, sysselman-nen.no). About 2,500 people live in Svalbard, at four different locations, with Longyear City where Basecamp Spitsbergen is located the most populated place. Most of the people living there come from the mainland of Norway and no roads exist between various areas and all transport is done by boat, plane, helicopter, or snowmobile. According to the Governor of Svalbard, 75,000 passengers arrived at Svalbard airport in 2013, and the number of guest nights in Longyearbyen rose from just over 43,000 in 1999 to 119,000 in 2014.

Basecamp Spitsbergen (BCS) consists of the Trappers hotel, the Svalbard radio hotel, cabins, and a variety of tourist products. Like in BCM, the ideology is based on generating income through eco-friendly activities in order to conserve wildlife and the habitat. The small 16-room hotel has a remarkable design covered with driftwood, sealskins, maps, pictures, and objects that tell stories of the past life of trappers, miners, and polar expeditions in the Arctic. In all the rooms there are comfortable beds, private bathrooms with showers, and even wireless Internet connection. The hotel constitutes the base camp for tourists' "expeditions" in Svalbard, and its location in downtown Longyear city makes it easy to walk around this small town and visit museums, cultural houses, pubs, restaurants, and shops.

Figure 7.5 With the Dog-Sledges by Trapper's Hut, by Frank Lindberg

Figure 7.6 On the Way with the Dogs, by Frank Lindberg

The tourists that come to BCS join organized trips, such as glacier crossing, boat trips, safaris, and dog sledding. Traveling there is not without risk, and accidents and deaths among tourists have raised debates about safety and risk management. The Svalbard Environmental Protection Act regulates tourism, and tourists are always picked up at the Trappers hotel by a guide when joining tourist treks. Tourists must sign a "declaration of conduct" in which they agree to act according to guides' instructions, mainly due to the polar bear threat, and then they receive information and equipment (e.g., survival suits) that prepare them for the upcoming trip.

Tourists traveling to BCS receive "communicative staging" (Arnould 2007) through thematized experiences and storytelling. For example, the thematized Trappers hotel and the Trapper's station, a replica of an original hunting community with a dog yard, help the tourists transform into an Arctic tourist role. Basecamp have constructed trips following an ideal of authentic symbolic staging where stories of Arctic wildlife and socio-historical traditions of polar expeditions and trapper life permeate the experiences. It is even possible for tourists to "live" as miners by going to one of the abandoned mining communities. There they eat in the cantina and stay in small rooms in the barracks just like the miners did. Another popular adventure is dog sledding to the "Ship in the ice", where the tourists may "Spend a night onboard the only ice-bound hotel ship in the world, and join the exclusive club of Arctic explorers like Nansen, Amundsen and Shackleton" (http://basecampexplorer.com, April 2016). As, however, no native settlement exists, i.e., there are no miners or trappers involved in tourism, the magical experiences depend on communicative staging; knowledge about the wild Arctic (e.g., polar bears) and stories of former trapper settlements and polar expeditions are presented and interpreted by experts (e.g., web) and guides at BCS.

Figure 7.7 Ship Frozen in the Ice, by Per Østergaard

Conclusions

This case has demonstrated how nature-based tourism can take place and can be mediated in an institutionalized way by an indirect approach to nature. Basecamp Explorer concepts of nature preservation "through the eyes of the Maasais" and the focus on Arctic exploration and traditions can be argued to be illustrations of this approach.

As regarded from the tourist perspective, the Maasai culture and efforts in encouraging the tourist to take part in experiencing the nature-based wonders of Maasai Mara bring additional value to the visiting tourist. By combining both environmental and socio-cultural components, BCM is able to frame their attractions based on local Maasai perception and practices of the living man–nature interaction in a particular direction where tourists inhabit the scenery. Our case material indicates moreover that the framing of nature-based experiences in the Mara may go beyond the level of superficial staging as described in the tourism literature (Bruner 2001, Salazar 2006). This is supported by the comprehensive politics of management in offering the Maasai opportunities and incentives to make maximum use of their traditions and cultural heritage in their involvement with visitors in parallel with professional training, education, and involvement of local communities. This has also been combined with a profound goal of protecting the wildlife of the Mara where the participation and involvement of the Maasai represents an imperative condition. Thus, the communicated principles and practices of ecological preservation are primarily drawn from the perspective of the Maasai, and not from the market.

The tourism experiences offered by BCS follow the core principle of ecotourism but with different framing than in Kenya. In the Arctic Svalbard there is no indigenous population, but a rich socio-historical culture of polar expeditions, trappers, and mining. These are the fundamentals for narrating and staging Arctic living, and Basecamp have built a sustainable focus through the Trappers hotel, Trappers station (dog yard) and the various polar activities (dog sledding, hiking, adventures) that tourists must actively engage in. While the Maasai community is directly involved in the BCK business model, leaving the substantial staging a focal advantage, the symbolic staging is vital for the tourist attraction of BCS since they rely on tourist immersion into an imagined role of trappers, miners and explorers.

It has been argued that there is an over-reliance on western social and environmental values in the promotion and substantiating of tourism (Akama 1996: 567), and critical voices have been raised regarding the consequences of the push/pull factor of mass tourism (Dann 2014) and "gazing" behavior (Urry and Larsen 2011). The ecotourism of Basecamp Explorer is thus not without challenges. For example, how can BCM promote its commitment, including the local people as employees, hence its facilitation of tourist/local culture interaction, in a better way? Which elements of the Maasai culture represent an under-explored source for nature-based tourism that has the potential of adding value to the tourist experience? How can young Maasai maintain their enthusiasm for their own traditions and their tacit knowledge and skills of dealing with hash environmental conditions within the modernization process of contemporary society? How can BCS dramatize the symbolic core so that tourists may enter an embodied Arctic life in a secure manner? To what extent can Basecamp Explorer continue to develop ecotourism in destinations that are also threatened by mass tourism, competitors with less responsible practices and tourists merely seeking enjoyment?

The cases presented in this chapter generally demonstrate a basic wish by the management of running a tourism business by simultaneously enriching the nature-based experiences of the tourists in trying to incorporate local socio-cultural aspects and history into the visitation experience. As this, on the one hand, can be regarded as a way or an effort of framing the nature-based experience, it can, on the other, be perceived as a means of promoting environmental and local cultural values that, without those efforts, otherwise would not have been accessed by the visitors. These efforts do thus have potential for widening environmental awareness among tourists as well as nature-based experiences. The balance between framing, care for authenticity, and promotion of environmental values remain, however, a continuous, intricate challenge within a destination area that also is subject to strong internal and international competition and capacity restraints.

Acknowledgement

The authors would express their gratitude to Svein Wilhelmsen for generously permitting us research access to Basecamp Explorer.

References

Akama, J. S. (1996). Western environmental values and nature-based tourism in Kenya. *Tourism Management* 17(8), 567–574.

Alcock, A., Jones, B., Lane, S., & Grant, J. (1994). *National ecotourism strategy*. Canberra: Commonwealth Department of Tourism, Australian Government Publishing Service.

Arnould, E. J. (2007). Consuming Experience: Retrospective and Prospects. In A. Carù & B. Cova (Eds.), *Consuming Experience* (pp. 185–194). London: Routledge.

AWF (2005). *Samburu: The heartland of Kenya*. Available from: www.AWF Samburu the Heart of Kenya.htm

Bruner, E. M. (2001). The Maasai and the Lion King: Authenticity, nationalism, and globalization in African tourism. *American Ethnologist* 28(4), 881–908.

Cohen, E. (1985). The tourist guide. The origins, structure and dynamics of a role. *Annals of Tourism Research* 12, 5–29.

Cohen, E. H., Ifergan, M., & Cohen, E. (2002). A new paradigm in guiding: The madrich as a role model. *Annals of Tourism Research* 29(4), 919–932.

Dann, G. M. S. (2014). Why, oh Why, oh Why, Do People Travel Abroad? In N. K. Prebensen, J. S. Chen & M. Uysal (Eds.), *Creating Experience Value in Tourism* (pp. 48–62). London, UK: CABI.

Fennell, D. A. (1999). *Ecotourism: An Introduction*. Routledge: London.

Goldman, M. (2007). Tracking wildebeest, locating knowledge: Maasai and conservation biology – Understanding of Wildebeest behaviour in Northern Tanzania. *Environment and Planning* 25, 307–331.

Goodwin, H. (1996). In pursuit of ecotourism. *Biodiversity and Conservation* 5(3), 277–291.

Ham, S. H., & Sandberg, E. K. (2012). Interpretation as Strategic Communication in Protected Area Management. In P. Fredman, M. Stenseke, H. Liljendahl, A. Mossing, & L. Daniel (Eds.), *The 6th International Conference on Monitoring and Management of Visitors in Recreational and Protected Areas*, 6, 132–133. Stockholm, Sweden.

Jenkins, B. O. (1997). *People profile: The Samburu*. Available from: www.Profile of the Samburu people of Kenya.htm

Jensen, Ø. (2010). Social meditation in remote developing world tourism locations: The significance of social ties between local guides and host communities in sustainable tourism development. *Journal of sustainable Tourism* 18(5), 615–633.

Kieti, D. M., Jones, E., & Wishitemi, B. (2008). Alternative models of community tourism: Balancing economic development and the aspirations of the poor. *Tourism Review International* 12(3–4), 275–290.

MacCannell, D. (1976). *The tourist: A new theory of the leisure class*. New York: Schocken Books.

Masau, P., & Prideaux, B. (2003). Sustainable tourism: A role for Kenya's hotel industry. *Current Issues in Tourism* 6(3), 197–208.

Munyoro, P. (2011). Eco-rating. Ecotourism, Nairobi, Kenya.

Muriithi, J. K. (2007). Continuity and Change in Kenyan Ecotourism Practices. *MAMBO! The Newsletter of the French Institute for Research in Africa 2*. Nairobi, Kenya: French Institute for Research in Africa.

Nettekoven, L. (1979). Mechanisms of intercultural interaction. In: de Kadt, E. (ed.) *Tourism Passport to Development? Perspectives on the Social and Cultural Effects of Tourism in Developing Countries*, 135–145. Published for the World Bank and Unesco by Oxford University Press.

Newsome, D., Moore, S. A., & Dowling, R. K. (2002). *Natural area tourism: Ecology, impacts and management*. Clevedon, UK: Channel View Publications.

Nyariki, D. M., Mwang'ombe A. W., & Thompson, D. M. (2009). Land-use change and livestock production challenges in an integrated system: The Masai-Mara ecosystem, Kenya. *Journal of Human Ecology* 26(3), 163–173.

Pond, K. L. (1993). *The Professional Guide: Dynamics of Tour Guiding*. New York: Van Nostrand Reinhold.

Robinson, M. (1999). Cultural Conflicts in Tourism: Inevitability and Inequality. In M. Robinson & P. Boniface (Eds.), *Tourism and Cultural Conflicts* (pp. 1–32). Wallingford, UK: CAB International.

Salazar, N. B. (2006). Touristifying Tanzania: Local guides, global discourse. *Annals of Tourism Research* 33, 833–852.

Scherle, N., & Nonnenmann, A. (2008). Swimming in cultural flows: Conceptualising tour guides as intercultural mediators and cosmopolitans. *Journal of Tourism and Cultural Change* 6(2), 120–137.

Scheyvens, R. (2002). Tourism for development: Empowering communities. Essex: Pearson Education Limited.

Smith, V. J. (Ed) (1989). Host and guests: The anthropology of tourism. Philadelphia: University of Pennsylvania Press.

Tung, V. W. S., & Ritchie, J. (2011). Exploring the essence of memorable tourism experiences. *Annals of Tourism Research* 38(4), 1367–1386.

Urry, J., & Larsen, J. (2011). *The Tourist Gaze 3.0* (3rd ed.). London: Sage Publisher.

Victurne, R. (2000). Building tourism excellence at the community level: Capacity building for community-based entrepreneurs in Uganda. *Journal of Travel Research* 38(3), 221–229.

Weaver, D. (2008). *Ecotourism*. Sidney: John Wiley & Sons.

Weiler, B., & Ham S. H. (2001). Tour guides and interpretation. In D. Weaver (Ed.), *Encyclopedia of Ecotourism* (pp. 549–564). Wallingford: CABI Publishing.

Weiler, B., & Ham S. H. (2002). Tour guide training: A model for sustainable capacity building an developing countries. *Journal of sustainable Tourism* 10(1), 52–69.

8 Impact of Climate Change on Tourism in World Heritage Sites

A Case Study from the Wet Tropics Region of Australia

Bruce Prideaux and Michelle Thompson

In a process that commenced with the 1997 Kyoto Protocol on Climate Change, the agreements that emanated from the 2015 United Nations Climate Change Conference indicate that for the first time there is global recognition at government level that climate change poses a serious threat to humanity. The success of international efforts to mitigate the adverse impacts of climate change, and the ability of the destinations that rely on the continuing health of ecosystems they promote to adapt to predicted changes, will have a significant effect on the long term viability of many destinations. The urgency of this issue has become apparent in recent years at the macro scale with persistent reports of declining sea ice cover in the Artic, rapid melting of glaciers in many areas, coral bleaching, and more recently, of monthly temperatures that were the hottest ever recorded. On a micro scale, many ecosystems are likely to become less stable as temperature, wind, and precipitation patterns begin to change. Changes at both the macro and micro scales will affect the desirability of many protected areas and the destinations they support (Becken & Hay 2007).

As global temperatures increase, species that are either temperature dependent or rely on food sources that are weather dependent (this might include temperature and precipitation), may migrate vertically up mountain slopes or horizontally through the landscape to occupy ecosystems that match their climatic requirements. Via this mechanism, out-migrating organisms assume the role of invaders in the new ecosystems they occupy. The potential impact of invasive species is illustrated by the impact of the king crab (Neolithodes yaldwyni) which has moved south of its usual range in the Antarctic in response to a rise in water temperature from 1.20 degrees Celsius in 1989 to 1.47 degrees Celsius in 2010 below the 800-meter level (Smith et al. 2011). The arrival of the king crab in the Palmer Deep (a basin on the Antarctic Peninsular continental shelf) has resulted in a significant reduction in species richness with the disappearance of echinoderms, sea urchins, sea lilies, sea cucumbers, and star fish in areas where the king crab has colonized.

Other species may face extinction because their food sources are depleted due to temperature related changes in flora and fauna or to changes in sea levels. Recent research (Metcalf et al. 2016) into the extinction of megafauna in the Patagonia region of South America over a 300-year period that ended about

12,280 BC points to the cause being a change in forest cover that occurred as global temperatures increased at the end of the last ice age. In a more recent example of an extinction event, rising sea levels appear to have led to the extinction of the Bramble Cay melomy, a small rat-like animal. Inundation of the low-lying cay led to loss of habitat and ultimately extinction (Whigham & AFP 2016). Multiple micro level changes such as that occurring in the Palmer Deep and larger scale extension of South American megafauna on a global scale give some idea of the type of change that is beginning to occur and the impact that it will cause can already be seen.

In many terrestrial and marine ecosystems, invasive species are likely to have adverse impacts on ecosystem stability with some resident species either migrating out in search of more preferable habitats or in the worst case simply heading towards extinction (Beier & Noss 1998). Against this backdrop of climate change-generated change to ecosystems is the growing demand for recreation by local communities and tourists in protected areas. To examine some of the possible impacts of climate change on protected areas that are promoted as key tourism drawcards, this chapter adopts a case study approach using the World Heritage-listed Great Barrier Reef Marine Park (GBRMP) and the World Heritage-listed Wet Tropics Rainforests (WTR) located in the Wet Tropics region of north Queensland, Australia. The chapter commences with a brief review of the status of research into climate change-related issues, outlines the role of tourism in the Wet Tropics region, examines how climate change is expected to affect the World Heritage Areas (WHAs) located in the Wet Tropics, then suggests a number of strategies that may be used to prepare the study region's natural area-dependent tourism industry for the possible impacts of climate change.

Previous Research

The science of climate change has been extensively documented elsewhere (see IPCC reports published in 2007 and 2014) and will not be repeated in this chapter. It is important however to look at both the process of change that will occur and how natural area-dependent regions may be affected. Figure 8.1 illustrates the linkages between the effects (changes in temperature, sea levels, wind speed, fire, and precipitation) of climate change, the physical and biological impacts that are caused at ecosystem level (loss of biodiversity, ecosystem changes, physical changes, and reduced sustainability), the potential scale of impacts on the tourism sector, and the potential response by the tourism system. An understanding of the backward linkages between changes in tourism demand in a climate change-affected destination and the scientific understanding of the effects of climate change on ecosystems is essential if the tourism industry is to develop workable adaptation strategies. This chapter is particularly concerned with potential impacts on the tourism system and response strategies.

Scientifically, there is almost unanimous agreement that the threat posed by climate change is real, that many areas of the tourism industry will suffer the impact of climate change, and that the industry is both part of the problem and

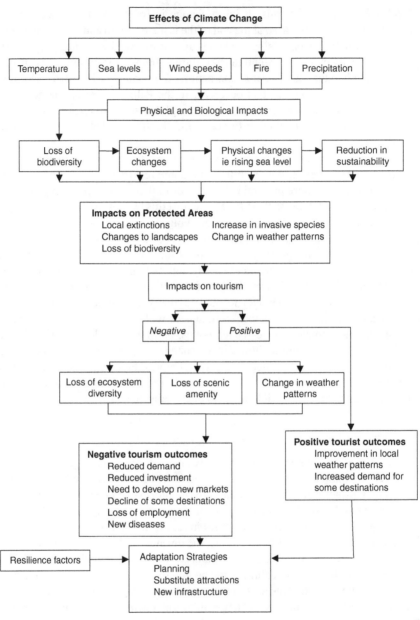

Figure 8.1 Flow Diagram Illustrating the Impact of Climate Change on a Protected Area and How it Can Be Responded to by the Tourism Industry

part of the solution. The academic literature has responded with an increasing number of publications on issues such as the causes of climate change (the IPCC series of reports are arguably the most authoritative) and the impact of climate change on ecosystems (Becken & Hay 2007; Burki, Elasser, Abegg, & Koening 2007; Elsasser & Bürki 2002; Gossling & Scott 2008; McKercher, Prideaux, Cheung, & Law 2010; Stern 2006;). There are a growing number of commentaries on the impact of climate change including how tourism has contributed to climate change (Buzinde, Manuel-Navarrete, Yoo, & Morais 2010), the impact of climate change on ecosystems that are popular with tourists (Hall & Higham 2005; Ramis & Prideaux 2013; Scott, Jones, & Konopek 2007) and on how sections of the tourism industry may be able to respond to the challenges created by climate change (Prideaux 2015; Richardson & Loomis 2004; Scott et al. 2007). Not all impacts are potentially negative as Scott et al. (2007) noted and in some areas warming may make destinations more attractive for tourism activity.

Recent reports on rising global temperature levels indicate the magnitude of the climate change problem that is about to confront the study region and on a wider scale, all destinations. Preliminary results of monthly measurements of global temperature by the National Oceanic and Atmospheric Administration (NOAA) indicate that the average global temperature in the 11 months to March 2016 were the highest since records commenced in 1880 (NOAA 2016). Of particular concern is the February 2016 temperature which was 1.35 degrees Celsius hotter than the long-term average. Continuing increases in temperature increase the likelihood of environmental tipping being reached where irreversible change begins to occur to ecosystems such as the Great Barrier Reef (GBR).

Tourism in the Wet Tropics Region

From a destination perspective the Wet Tropics region mirrors the extent of the Wet Tropics Rainforests (WTR). In 2015 an estimated 2.8 million tourists visited the region spending about AU$3 billion (TEQ 2015). The city of Cairns is the aviation gateway to the region with an estimated 60 percent of all tourists travelling to the region arriving by either domestic or international flights (TEQ 2013). Apart from its role as an aviation gateway, Cairns is also an activity gateway to the Great Barrier Reef and the Wet Tropics Rainforests. Nearby Port Douglas is also a popular tourist destination and acts as a complementary destination to Cairns.

Commercial tours to the GBR include day trips to permanent pontoons moored on the reef, day trips to nearby islands, day diving trips, fishing trips, overnight diving expeditions, and in the winter months, whale watching trips. In a similar pattern, most trips to the Wet Tropics Rainforests are undertaken on a day basis either via commercial tour operators or by self-drive trips into the rainforest. Unlike the limited dispersal pattern of GBR visitors, there are more opportunities for tourists to find accommodation in nearby rainforest areas such as the Atherton Tablelands, Mission Beach, and Cape Tribulation.

A recent survey of departing tourists conducted at Cairns International Airport indicates the importance of both the Great Barrier Reef and the Wet Tropics

Rainforests to the region's tourism industry (Prideaux & Thompson 2016a, 2016b). Respondents ranked the opportunity to visit the Great Barrier Reef as the most significant motive (mean = 4.36) for visiting the region followed in third place by the Wet Tropics Rainforests (mean = 3.88). The popularity of both WHAs is reflected in estimates made about the economic contribution of these areas to the national economy. A recent report funded by the Wet Tropics Management Authority (WTMA) estimated that the WTWHA generated an estimated AU\$2.6 billion of economic value (WTMA 2015). In relation to the contribution of the GBR to the Australian economy, Access Economics (2007) reported a contribution of AU\$6.9 billion. Given that the total estimated expenditure of tourists in the Cairns region in 2015 was AU\$3 billion (TEQ 2015) these figures appear very inflated even when the multiplier effect is taken into account. However, these figures do give some indication of the value of these WHAs to the regional and national economy.

The Wet Tropics Rainforests

Proclaimed as a World Heritage site in 1988 the Wet Tropics stretches along the north-east coast of Queensland for about 450 kilometers and encompasses an area of 894,420 hectares. Much of the region contained in the Wet Tropics is mountainous, with the majority of the region's lowland rainforest having been cleared for farming and settlement in the first half of the 20th Century. The remaining rainforest is bounded by low rainfall areas to the west and south. The region contains relics of the Gondwanan forests that extended over much of Australia and Antarctica between 50 and 100 million years ago. The area has significant biodiversity and is claimed to contain the oldest continually surviving tropical rainforests on Earth (WTMA, n.d.). The flora of the WTR includes over 3,000 vascular plants in 224 families and includes 576 species which are endemic. The area also has high vertebrate diversity and endemism with 107 mammal species including 11 that are endemic. In addition, the region has 368 bird and 113 reptile species. An estimated 5 million visits are made to the area each year by tourists and local residents (WTMA 2015). According to the management authority (WTMA 2008) the main dangers faced by the WTWHA include invasive species, fragmentation, encroachment by settlement, altered fire and hydrological regimes, and in the near future, the problems that will be generated by temperature increases that are associated with climate change.

The impact of climate change on the rainforest is likely to include changes to the structure of the forest and changes in the diversity of flora and fauna found in the forest. As temperatures increase, the cool-adapted upland forests will be lost as will the fauna that are endemic to these forests. Species are not able to out-migrate because the WTWHA is bounded by low rainfall areas and the ocean to the east. According to Wilson (2014) longer and warmer dry seasons will increase the risk of fires (Williams, Karoly, & Tapper 2001) damaging habitats, and see the rainforest change to drier woodlands. An increase in the number of fires along the boundary between the sclerophyll forest elements of the region and the rainforest elements can be expected to place further pressure on ecosystems that are beginning to be weakened by the impacts of climate change (Williams et al. 2001). Moreover, tropical biota have a fairly narrow thermal-tolerance range (Colwell et al. 2008) which will affect most of the region's endemic upland mammals, reptiles and birds. Research undertaken into the impact of the species richness of endemic fauna by Williams, Bolitho, and Fox (2003) indicates the extent of impacts likely to be experienced by the Wet Tropics rainforests as global temperatures climb. A 2 degrees Celsius increase in temperature will reduce the range of endemic species but if the temperature increases to 3.5 degrees Celsius almost all endemic species will have been lost with the remaining species restricted to a small refuge in the northern section of the WTWHA.

The region's flora and fauna will also face other climate change-related threats including the potential introduction of new pathogens and predators (Dukes 2003), competition from invasive species, and introduction of diseases to which they have no natural defence (WTMA 2008).

Current tourism activity in the Wet Tropics is centred on the area's scenic qualities including waterfalls and mountain vistas as well as hiking and a number of commercial ventures that include interpretive activities, rainforest adventure activities such as abseiling and white water rafting, and animal spotting tours. Research undertaken by Prideaux and Falco-Mammone (2010), after a major cyclone event in 2006 in the Mission Beach area of the Wet Tropics, indicated the type of response that may be expected from tourists and also provides some insights into how changes in the structure of the forest may be handled by the tourism industry. With recorded wind gusts of 294 kilometres per hour, Category 5 Tropical Cyclone Larry caused significant damage to the rainforest, stripping leaves from and felling large numbers of trees. Visually, the forest looked devastated although within 12 months the leaf cover on most remaining trees had returned. Surveys of tourists undertaken 3 months and 15 months after the event give some clues to the manner in which tourists who are unfamiliar with what can be classed as a normal rainforest, can be expected to respond to a future climate change-affected forest. Just over half the tourists surveyed 3 months after the event reported noticing significant damage to the forest. However, 15 months after the event less than 6 percent of respondents (of a total of 272) reported that they noticed damage to the forest. The apparent lack of concern that the tourist experience would be compromised by cyclone damage was a product of the 'crisis memory' effect described as the propensity of tourists to forget about the impact of past crises in a particular destination over time providing that the crisis is a one-off event rather than a series of events. These findings indicate that if the rate of change in the structure of the forest is slow, as anticipated, the vast majority of tourists will not be aware of the relatively slow change process that the forest is undergoing and unlikely to suffer a reduction in satisfaction.

The potential loss of many of the region's endemic wildlife predicted by Williams et al. (2003) is of particular concern but need not be a major concern for the tourism industry. Most rainforest animals are small and many are nocturnal feeders making them difficult to observe in their natural setting. For this reason, the majority of animal viewing activity in the Cairns area is in a captive situation (Coghlan & Prideaux 2008) with only a small number of tours that focus on wildlife viewing. Many of the animals that are expected to experience significant population declines are difficult to observe in their natural habitats and unlikely to be seen by tourists unless they visit a zoo. The problems encountered with viewing wildlife in natural settings has been partially offset by zoos and this can be expected to continue in the future, although zoos will face increasing problems in maintaining populations of endemic animals that have become extinct in the wild.

One problem that will need to be addressed by park managers and the tourism industry is that ecosystems will begin to change at an accelerated rate as species migrate in and out of the area in response to climate change. The example of the king crab given earlier is only one of a growing number of examples of the impacts that invasive, or out-migrating species, may have on the ecosystems they migrate into. One outcome may be changes that leave the ecosystem less resilient and hence more fragile to the pressures generated by tourism use. From a tourism perspective this will necessitate adjustments to infrastructure to reduce pressure on the ecosystem, using increased entry fees as a rationing device to reduce demand or in some cases, closing protected areas to tourism.

Great Barrier Reef

Australia's Great Barrier Reef is the world's largest reef system stretching 2,300 kilometres along the Queensland coast and covering an area of 344,400 kilometres squared and includes 3,000 coral reefs, 300 coral cays and 600 continental islands (GBRMPA, n.d. a). There are 70 bioregions (broad scale habitats) comprising 30 reef bioregions and 40 non-reef bioregions with the latter containing over 2,000 kilometres squared of mangrove forest that represents 54 percent of the world's mangrove diversity and about 6,000 kilometres of seagrass beds. In area, the GBR is about the same size as Italy or Germany. The GBR has a very diverse ecosystem that includes 600 species of soft and hard corals, over 3,000 varieties of molluscs, over 100 species of jelly fish, 1,635 species of fish, more than 30 species of whales and dolphins, and six of the world's seven species of turtles (GBRMPA n.d. a). The GBR was listed as a World Heritage Area in 1981 and is administered by the Great Barrier Reef Marine Park Authority (GBRMPA). From a tourism perspective the GBR is the main attraction for many destinations located in the region.

Climate change poses a number of threats to the GBR including coral bleaching, increased acidity of sea water, and the increased number and severity of wind storms (cyclones). In response to this threat the GBRMPA (2013) has developed a coral bleaching risk and assessment plan and both the Queensland State Government and the Australian Federal Government have agreed to jointly fund a number of schemes to protect the reef as well as launch the Reef 2050 Long-term Sustainability Plan (GBRMPA 2016) which is underwritten by an AU$2 billion investment in the coming decade.

Coral bleaching describes the reaction of coral to stress such as during long periods of heightened water temperature. Corals live in a symbiotic relationship with microscopic marine algae (zooxanthellae) that live within the coral polyp's tissue (GBRMPA n.d. b). These algae not only provide most of the energy corals need to grow but also give corals their colour. When water temperatures rise, or corals are stressed in other ways, the zooxanthellae are expelled, giving the coral a white or bleached appearance. Coral can recover and take back the expelled algae if the temperature falls before stage 4 bleaching (coral death) occurs. Global scale bleaching events occurred in 1998 and 2002. During the 1998 event an estimated 50 percent of coral reefs in south Asia and the Indian Ocean lost much of their coral cover (Fabricius, Hoegh-Guldberg, Johnson, McCook, & Lough 2007). A third global coral bleaching event occurred in early 2016 when water temperatures rose to 33 degrees Celsius, 2 degrees Celsius above the usual summer maximum. The danger for reef systems is that as bleaching becomes more severe and occurs at intervals less than the time taken for coral recovery, the cumulative effect is likely to be a long term decline in coral cover and biodiversity. Initial estimates by coral reef scientists of the damage caused by the 2016 coral bleaching event were widely reported during the event with some claims indicating almost total loss of large areas of coral. One eminent coral reef researcher claimed that based on an aerial assessment, 95 percent of the northern section of the GBR (Cairns north to the Torres Strait) had experienced significant coral bleaching, and is reported as saying,

It's too early to tell precisely how many of the bleached coral will die, but judging from the extreme level even the most robust corals are snow white, I'd expect to see about half of those corals die in the coming month or so.

McCutcheon 2016

This initial assessment proved to be inaccurate and a later in-water survey (Reef and Rainforest Research Centre and Association of Marine Park Tourism Operators 2016) found that as of April 2016, 29 percent of corals in the northern section of the GBR showed no evidence of bleaching, 4.6 percent showed some evidence of minor bleaching, 43.3 percent were stressed but still maintained part of their photosynthetic bacteria, and 2.5 percent were dead. The initial concerns reported in McCutcheon (2016) were inaccurate and appear to have been based on emotion rather science. Unfortunately, global media coverage and the resulting concern has damaged the credibility of science as a neutral observer and as a source of accurate assessment free of the 'spin' observed when special interest groups use events of this type to push their cause or ideology. The reporting also caused considerable concern to tourists planning to visit the GBR during their holiday. These initial reports were inaccurate and overstated the extent of bleaching. Because of these reports the destination marketing organisation and marine tour operators received a large number of enquiries about the impact of the coral bleaching event indicating a possible future decline in visitors over fears that the destination's major natural attraction had been seriously damaged. Fortunately, as the results of Prideaux and Falco-Mammone's (2010) earlier work on the length of visitors 'crisis memory' show, the initial level of visitor concern is likely to dissipate over time as long as a further bleaching event does not reoccur in the short term.

In a recent discussion on management strategies that build the resilience of coral reefs to climate change, Fabricius et al. (2007) stressed the need for protection of water quality, protection of coastal habitats and protection of biodiversity. Water quality in this case includes reduced inflows of chemicals and silting from farming and sewerage and reduction of dredging. Other interventionist approaches suggested include shading of water at specific reefs and transplantations of temperature-adapted corals from the northern sector of the GBR to the southern GBR. In the long term, the fate of the GBR will be determined by the ultimate level of global warming. At this juncture it is not possible to determine at what level temperatures will eventually level out or when. Unfortunately, at the time of writing the long-term outlook for coral reefs is poor. Destinations that depend on coral reef tourism must therefore look for other attractions to replace coral reef-focused tourism.

Discussion and Conclusion

A growing number of scholars (Beck & Hay 2007; Gossling & Scott 2008; McKercher et al. 2010) have expressed concerns about how the tourism industry will deal with the impact of climate change. From a destination perspective, there is little that can be done to mitigate the processes that are causing global warming. Strategies are required on a global level and the progress made towards this, at the 2015 United Nations Climate Change Conference, holds some promise that appropriate action will be taken in the near future.

There are a number of unknowns about climate change that make the process of adaption difficult. These include the rate at which global temperatures will increase, the ultimate level at which temperatures will cease rising, and when various 'tipping points' will occur. From a tourism perspective there is also concern about how a possible reduction in the attractiveness of key natural attractions such as the GBR will affect future visitor numbers.

At the destination level the most effective action is adopting strategies that assist in adaptation of destinations to climate change over time. In the short term where degrading of natural resources has commenced but the resource (such as the GBR) still retains a high level of attractiveness, intense media campaigns may be required to reassure potential visitors. In the long term however as decline in quality increases, other strategies will need to be considered. This may include developing substitute attractions that continue to focus on some aspect of nature (coral reef aquariums for example) or built attractions. As Figure 8.1 highlights, destinations will need to be pragmatic and where climate change is likely to have a negative impact, plan for reduced demand in the nature-based segment of their markets. Concurrently, destinations will need to develop market recovery strategies when events such as coral bleaching occur. Destinations also need to actively search for new experiences and attractions to promote to new market sectors and attract the investors required to build these experiences. Failure to adopt a forward looking, pragmatic view of this type may result in a declining tourism sector.

From a destination perspective the most significant factors likely to determine the level of impact caused by climate change are:

- the speed and extent of change;
- the form that change will take;
- the level of both ecosystem and human community resilience;
- the success of adaptation strategies implemented by destinations;
- the extent to which adverse media reports influence tourists to avoid areas suffering the adverse impacts of climate change;
- the success of plans by management agencies to combat the impact of climate change;
- the ability of the tourism sector to offer substitute experiences;
- the level of support that the public sector gives the tourism industry.

As the previous discussion indicated, not all tourists will notice subtle changes in landscapes particularly where change is slow. For example, the change from rainforest to sclerophyll forest is likely to be slow and largely unnoticed in the short term. In relation to the GBR, the rate of decline will depend on the success of strategies to improve the water quality, the rate at which coral species adapted to warm waters can migrate southward and ultimately, the rate at which global temperatures increase.

Tourism demand is constantly evolving, driven by innovation, a thirst for novelty, and new experiences. Harnessing these trends provides destinations such as Cairns with the opportunity to adapt, evolve, and introduce new experiences. This may require de-emphasizing nature and refocusing on other forms of tourism such as adventure and lifestyle tourism. A shift of this type is in reality an acknowledgement of the urban origin of most domestic and international tourists. Embracing urban lifestyle themes such as indulgence, café culture, gastronomy, entertainment, and shopping provides an opportunity to adapt to the reality of a climate changed future. Beyond the urban environment, numerous opportunities remain to develop recreational activities such as mountain bike riding, horse riding, as well as soft adventure activities such as paddle boarding, jet skiing, sailing, etc. Failure to accept the reality of a climate changed future where the current tourism drawcards provided by nature have been degraded will doom destinations such as Cairns to a long slide towards obscurity.

References

Access Economics. (2007). *Measuring the economic and financial value of the Great Barrier Reef Marine Park 2005/06*. Townsville, Australia: GBRMPA.

Becken, S., & Hay, J. (2007). *Tourism and climate change: risks and opportunities*. Clevedon: Channel View Publications.

Beier, P., & Noss, R. (1998). Do habitat corridors provide connectivity? *Conservation Biology*, *12*(6), 1241–1252.

Burki, R., Elsasser, H., Abegg, B., & Koenig, U. (2007) Climate change and tourism in the Swiss Alps. In C.M. Hall, & J. Higham (Eds.), *Tourism, recreation and climate change* (pp. 155–163). Clevedon: Channel View Publications.

Buzinde, C., Manuel-Navarrete, D., Yoo, E., & Morais, D. (2010). Tourists' perceptions in a climate of change: eroding destinations. *Annals of Tourism Research*, *37*, 333–354.

Coghlan, A., & Prideaux, B. (2008). Encounters with wildlife in Cairns, Australia: where, what, who…? *Journal of Ecotourism*, *7*(1), 68–76.

Colwell, R., Brehm, G., Cardelus, C., Gilman, A., & Longino, J. (2008). Global warming, elevational range shifts, and lowland biotic attrition in the wet tropics. *Science*, *322*, 258–261.

Dukes, J. (2003). Hotter and weedier? Effects of climate change on the success of invasive species. In R. Green, M. Harley, L. Miles, J. Scharlemann, A. Watkinson, & O. Watts (Eds.), *Global climate change and biodiversity*. Norwich: The Tyndall Centre for Climate Change Research.

Elsasser, H., & Bürki, R. (2002). Climate change as a threat to tourism in the Alps. *Climatic Research*, *20*, 253–257.

Fabricius, K., Hoegh-Guldberg, O., Johnson, J., McCook, L., & Lough, J. (2007). Vulnerability of coral reefs of the Great Barrier Reef to climate change. In J. E. Johnson, & P. A. Marshall (Eds.), *Climate change and the Great Barrier Reef*. Australia: Great Barrier Marine Park Authority and Australian Greenhouse Office.

GBRMPA (n.d. a). *Facts about the Barrier Reef*. Retrieved from www.gbrmpa.gov.au/about-the-reef/facts-about-the-great-barrier-reef

GBRMPA (n.d. b). *Coral bleaching fact sheet*. Retrieved from www.gbrmpa.gov.au/data/assets/pdf_file/0008/241793/Coral-Bleaching-Fact-Sheet.pdf

GBRMPA (2013). *Coral bleaching risk and impact assessment plan*. Townsville: Author.

GBRMPA (2016). Reef 2050 long term sustainability plan. Retrieved from www.environment.gov.au/marine/gbr/publications/factsheet-reef-2050-long-term-sustainability-plan

Gossling, S., & Scott, D. (2008). Climate change and tourism: exploring destination vulnerability. *Tourism Review International*, *12*, 1–3.

Hall, C. M., & Higham, J. (2005). *Tourism, recreation and climate change*. Clevedon: Channel View Publications.

IPCC. (2007). Contribution of Working Groups I, II and III to the Fourth Assessment Report of the Intergovernmental Panel on Climate Change. Retrieved from http://www.ipcc.ch/publications_and_data/ar4/syr/en/contents.html

IPCC (2014). *Climate change 2014, synthesis reports summary for policymakers*. Retrieved from www.ipcc.ch/pdf/assessment-report/ar5/syr/AR5_SYR_FINAL_SPM.pdf

McCutcheon, P. (2016). Great Barrier Reef coral bleaching at 95 per cent in northern section, aerial survey reveals, *ABC News* (28 March, 2016). Retrieved from www.abc.net.au/news/2016-03-28/great-barrier-reef-coral-bleaching-95-per-cent-north-section/7279338 (accessed 10 June, 2016).

McKercher, B., Prideaux, B., Cheung, C., & Law, R. (2010). Achieving voluntary reductions in the carbon footprint of tourism and climate change. *Journal of Sustainable Tourism*, *18*(3), 297–317.

Metcalf, J., et al. (2016). Synergistic roles of climate change warming and human occupation in Patagonian megafauna extinctions during the last Deglaciation, *Science Advances*, *2*(6).

NOAA (April 23, 2016). *For 11th straight month, the globe was record warm.* Retrieved from www.noaa.gov/11th-straight-month-globe-was-record-warm

Prideaux, B. (2015). Climate change as a major crisis event: implications for a tropical nature based destination. In L. Ruhanen (Ed.), *Responding to climate change: tourism initiatives in Asia and the Pacific* (pp. 182–189). Madrid: UNWTO.

Prideaux, B., & Falco-Mannome, F. (2010). *The impacts of cyclone Larry on tourism in the Mission Beach, Tully and the Atherton Tablelands Region, One Year Later.* Cairns: James Cook University.

Prideaux, B., & Thompson, M. (2016a). *Cairns region visitor survey: October–December 2015 barometer.* Cairns: CQ University.

Prideaux, B., & Thompson, M. (2016b). *Cairns region visitor survey: January–March 2016 barometer.* Cairns: CQ University.

Prideaux, B., Coghlan, A., & McNamara, K. E. (2010). Assessing the impacts of climate change on mountain tourism destination using the climate change impact model, *Tourism Recreation Research, 35,* 187–200.

Ramis, M., & Prideaux, B. (2013). The importance of visitor perceptions in estimating how climate change will affect future tourists flows on the Great Barrier Reef. In M. Reddy & K. Wilkes (Eds.), *Tourism, climate change and sustainability* (pp. 173–188). London: Routledge.

Reef and Rainforest Research Centre and Association of Marine Park Tourism Operators (2016). *Coral bleaching assessment on key tourism sites between Lizard Island and Cairns.* Reef and Rainforest Research Centre Limited, Cairns.

Richardson, R.B., & Loomis, J.B. (2004). Adaptive recreation planning and climate change: a contingent visitation approach. *Ecological Economics, 50,* 83–99. doi: 10.1016/j.ecolecon.2004.02.010

Scott, D., Jones, B., & Konopek, J. (2007). Implications of climate and environmental change for nature-based tourism in the Canadian Rocky Mountains: a case study of Waterton Lakes National Park. *Tourism Management, 28,* 570–579.

Smith, C., Grange, L., Honig, D., Naudts, L., Huber, B., Guidi, L., & Domack, E. (2011). A large population of king crabs in Palmer Deep on the west Antarctic Peninsula shelf and potential invasive impacts. *Proceedings of the Royal Society B: Biological Sciences, 279*(1730), 1017–1026. doi: 10.1098/rspb.2011.1496

Stern, N. (2006). *Stern review report on the economics of climate change.* Cambridge: Cambridge University Press.

Tourism and Events Queensland (TEQ) (2013). *Cairns tourism profile: average annual data from your ending December 2009 to December 2012.* Retrieved from http://cdn.queensland.com/~/media/234FE2D7D91E4918B9CB9D27E7B6BB06.ashx?la=en-CA&vs=1&d=00010101T000000

Tourism and Events Queensland (TEQ) (2015). *Tropical North Queensland regional snapshot year ending September 2015.* Retrieved from http://cdn.queensland.com/~/media/DB2D0BCFC9C8484DBD2E2305A33E65A6.ashx?vs=1&d=20160218T175644

Wet Tropics Management Authority (WTMA) (2008). *State of the Wet Tropics report, 2007–2008.* Cairns: Author.

Wet Tropics Management Authority (WTMA) (2015). *State of Wet Tropics report 2014/15: economic value of the Wet Tropics World Heritage Area.* Cairns: Author.

Wet Tropics Management Authority (WTMA) (n.d.). *Outstanding universal value.* Retrieved from www.wettropics.gov.au/outstanding-universal-value

Whigham, N., & AFP (2016). Australian rodent the first mammal driven to extinction by climate change, researchers say, *News com.au* (14 June, 2006). Retrieved from www.news.com.au/technology/environment/climate-change/australian-rodent-the-first-mammal-driven-to-extinction-by-climate-change-researchers-say/news-story/eaab580b01aa7777bdfa64d5427c8b95

Williams, A., Karoly, D., & Tapper, N. (2001). The sensitivity of Australian fire danger to climate change. *Climate Change, 49*, 171–191.

Williams, S., Bolitho, E., & Fox, S. (2003). Climate change in Australian tropical rainforests: an impending environmental catastrophe. *Proceedings of the Royal Society of London Series B: Biological Sciences, 270*, 1887–1893.

Wilson, R. (2014). Climate change impacts and response strategies for rainforest tourism: Cairns case study. In B. Prideaux (Ed.), *Rainforest tourism, conservation and management challenges for sustainable development*. Oxon: Routledge.

9 Quality Perspectives in Managing Visitor Experiences

Lynn M. Jamieson

What does it take to ensure that the nature tourism experience is optimal? This chapter will identify the components of maximizing the visitor experience prior to, during, and after the visitor is exposed to the unique aspects of the natural environment. While quality is a consideration in all visitor experience, those who venture into a natural environment are engaging in a less controlled environment—one that is full of beauty, intrigue, and strangeness. Tourism professionals, who provide this experience, need to be aware of and plan for a visitor who is not used to the challenges of the natural environment. In addition, the respect for the environment must be paramount in decisions to provide opportunities for visitors to experience the natural environment and come away from that experience enriched and informed about the challenges and risks inherent in the experience and also the value of living according to sound sustainability principles.

The Message

Nature tourism is a very broad term encompassing everything from experiencing a short walk in a small park to recognizing the entire ecological system of the earth and leaving a minimal impact on the environment. Therefore, in planning for an experience in the natural environment, educating the visitor is, perhaps, the most important and responsible component of the experience. This section covers essential messages that ideally are delivered in a consistent way from the time a visitor seeks initial information to the time that the individual reflects on the experience.

The Importance of and Components for a Positive Visitor Experience

Anticipation—Envisioning

When a prospective visitor begins the process of selecting a place for a vacation, a barrage of online and print media is available. It is this information that forms lasting impressions of potential choices, and the prospective customer relies on accuracy and specificity of the proposed trip. In producing marketing information for natural environment experiences, it has been found that the message is not always accurate. For example, in a study of the state tourism literature in 49 states, Masberg and Jamieson (1999) found inaccuracies in most of the guides that included either insufficient information or no information about the location, characteristics, regulations, or risks of natural environments featured on the covers and in pictures within the document. The importance of delivering an accurate message to prospective customers may inadvertently predispose the visitor to a bad experience. Further, it is difficult for destination managers and tour guides to plan a trip that does not address regulations specific to size of group, minimal trace characteristics, dangers, and directions.

FEAR OF THE UNKNOWN

Prospective tourists may also enter into a prospective nature tourism trip with a certain amount of fear and trepidation. In many ways, a site may be not only very unfamiliar, but it also may be feared due to one's lack of experience in the wild. Many individuals may not have had a broad experience such as a hike in the woods, or a camping experience. Even though many nature tourism experiences have comfortable lodging, the daily exposure to the out-of-doors could be perplexing.

ABILITY

Individuals planning for this type of experience may also have real or imagined issues about being able to endure a hike or even a brief outing from a bus. There could be difficulties with the effects of being outdoors on their health if they suffer even the simplest of medical issues, from food and pollen allergies to problems with heat and cold. When an individual moves from a heavy reliance on creature comforts to that of the experiences often offered in a natural environment, even a short walk on a sunny day may be more challenging than a similar walk for the purpose of shopping or viewing a monument.

MEDICAL CONSTRAINTS

There also are those with more serious medical constraints that need to be anticipated for and adjusted, if necessary. The Americans with Disabilities Act (ADA) provides strong legislation to include all people regardless of their ability. Therefore, planners must be knowledgeable about people with identifiable medical conditions who wish to venture into a natural environment (Department of Justice, 2016).

CULTURAL COMPETENCE

The more remote an area is, the greater the chances are for interaction with residents of that particular environment. Tourism planners need to be familiar with local cultures and educate the tourist about positive ways to interact with local residents. This includes fostering an appreciation of the culture, language differences, colloquialisms, mores and folkways, and attitudes toward newcomers. Involving residents in portions of the trip experience may accomplish this so that the tourists grow appreciative of the full experience. This is particularly true of a nature experience on land and between flora and fauna that are revered by local residents. Any damage to the natural environment may cause tensions and resistance to the tourists, thus affecting the overall tourist experience.

ENGAGEMENT—INTERACTING

The next phase of the tourist experience is the actual involvement in the trip. At this point, it should be assumed that tourists have become well prepared for the environmental challenges of the natural experience. Three major areas of preparation are particularly important in a natural environment: mental outlook, comfort, and challenge. These are in addition to the general preparation a tourist needs for travel—the nature experience may require greater consideration for clothing, weather, and event preparation.

MENTAL PREPARATION

It is difficult for a prospective tourist to envision the natural environment if pictures are not shared ahead of the trip. The sheer size and scope of an environment may be hard to adequately prepare for without some visual reference. Therefore, trip planners should be able to provide extensive information about the type of area that will be visited, prevailing weather conditions for the time of year, level of activity to prepare for, and proper clothing, food, and protection to bring. Environmental restrictions in terms of regulations to stay on pathways, feeding animals, hunting or fishing restrictions, size of group, and other factors are most effectively understood in advance of a trip. Emphasis on major environmental sustainability techniques related to keeping the environment safe and pristine is not only important for the trip but also important for changing attitudes and lifestyles with respect to sustainability practices.

COMFORT

Experiencing nature can be challenging from a comfort standpoint. When a tourist is unprepared for heat or cold due to wearing the wrong clothes or shoes, the experience can become a disaster. Failing to apply proper sunscreen for outdoor events can become a liability after one day and affect the comfort for the remainder of the excursion. Tourists need to be better prepared for prolonged exposure to sun, rain, wind, temperature fluctuations, and other experiences that can be challenging and risky.

CHALLENGE

Finally, the challenge of the planned tour is also an important aspect of the nature tourism experience. Getting involved in the natural environment is not without risk. There are many medical conditions that can occur with an unprepared tourist—such as blisters, cuts, and bruises; heat related illnesses, rashes and reactions to food and drink, and many other conditions. Planners need to be prepared to treat these conditions and have a sound risk management plan in place. Further, aside from the risk, it is important to assist tourists with accepting risk and learning new adventures that will provide quality, memorable experiences. While safety is foremost, those leading tours must be able to handle the capsized canoe, a fall on a path, or the effects of overexposure in a way that provides a lesson and a memory.

Reflection—Returning

Tourists want memories of their experiences. A nature tourism experience not only provides memories, but it has the potential to cause many life changes as people learn about keeping the planet safe and sustainable. An advantage to sharing the messages inherent in protecting the environment is that people can also contribute to the overall sustainability and protection of resources once they return home. It is the remembrance of the experience that can be life changing, and that remembrance can cause individuals to want to return again and again to gain more skill and awareness about the delicate ecological balance present in the world's ecosystems. To this end, the drumbeat of sustainability needs to reverberate through a tourist experience so that individuals may make important adjustments in real life. These adjustments may be creating a home that both produces and consumes energy, or it could be that an individual may participate in community beautification projects. Either way, many individuals who experience the delicate relationship among ecosystems are often permanently moved to action by the experience.

SUSTAINABILITY MESSAGING

It is reasonable to expect, at the very least, that sustainability messaging be designed not only to prepare the individual for the nature experience, but also to provide ways to continue on a pathway long after the trip has been completed. At the very most, a strong curriculum, designed to educate and encourage important sustainability approaches, can contain everything from what nature tourism is to how to live in a way that is less wasteful of natural resources.

RETURN RATE

It is important to note that few people return to repeat a tour experience; however, many tour companies have been successful in producing relevant and repeatable experiences by varying the location and trip features around a theme. In nature tourism, the sustainability theme is an important current retainer in all programs. With the recurring theme, tourists may learn more and more about how each trip maintains a standard that protects the environment. Planners need to learn about all aspects of sustainability and be able to be excellent resources and examples for others to follow. A strong message throughout a trip will provide lasting memories and encourage repeat visitation.

VISITOR SATISFACTION

Efforts to evaluate the visitor upon completion of a trip should be made in any trip or excursion. It is especially important in a nature tourism experience to gauge what additional information is desired, how the trip may be adjusted to improve the visitor experience, and what the visitor has learned from the experience.

Education for Sustainability

Perhaps the most important aspect of providing for a nature tourism experience is training of staff and the way tourists are educated about many aspects of sustainability. In order to educate, tourism professionals should be well-trained in the understanding of what makes a tour sustainable, what makes lodging and events low impact on the environment, and what tourists need to know about the delicate ecological balance of flora, fauna, and human travel. This section provides an outline of key areas that should be covered when engaging in this form of tourism.

From the time that Rachel Carson wrote *Silent Spring* in 1962 and certain pesticides were banned due to deleterious effects on the environment, there has been increased awareness of the effect that human activities exert on the environment. From the Stockholm Declaration in 1972 developed at the United Nations Conference on the Human Environment in which there was a united stand on safeguarding natural resources and wildlife to contemporary concerns about global warming and other issues occurring in the environment, individual and collective efforts have been geared to addressing several issues. In tourism, the following areas are of significant importance in considering how to make something sustainable.

As an example for those who are planning to make a more sustainable area for nature tourism, the experience of a safari may be a good starting point. Longleat is a safari and adventure park located in Warminster, Watshire, UK. Originally opened in 1966, this nature and adventure atmosphere has been undergoing many changes due to expert planning and an effort at authenticity. In keeping with the natural habitats of the animals housed there, the heritage-status property includes a safari park, buildings and 900-acre grounds, and entertainment attractions. The plans have resulted in increased growth in attendance in 2015.

Components

"Reduce, recycle, reuse," is the hallmark of all efforts to save the planet. Known as the Rs of green, the concept was initiated through the Environmental Protection Agency and extended with standards developed by several "green" agencies.

Individuals are called upon to do what they can to lessen negative impacts on the environment. As for tourism the components below comprise those areas of most importance to the continuum of services provided by tourism professionals:

1   Traffic, congestion changes leading toward greater use of carpooling and public transportation.
2   Health and wellbeing with particular emphasis toward walkability, air quality, ample parks and recreation areas.
3   Resources improvement in regard to cleaner water, air, food, built, and natural environment.
4   Personal changes in uses of non-renewable resources through recycling, reuse, and other techniques to lower use.

The concept of sustainability means that efforts are made to see that there is no waste and that one may use and produce resources for improved living. In the tourism area, this means that all aspects of travel and visitation are able to follow many guidelines for making the environment last. The more that tourists know prior to visiting a pristine environment, the greater is the chance that proper practices will minimize impact on the environment.

Walking the Talk: Green Programs

Starting with marketing, it is important to eliminate deceptive marketing techniques that fail to provide the fully educated story about natural tourism. This means accurate information and follow through on acceptable practices for planning trips and tours, for selecting "green" hotels, for educating tourists, and for conducting tours and experiences with an idea toward "net zero" use of resources. In this section, it is suggested that all accommodations, transportation mechanisms, and actual experiences are "green". While this is not necessarily attainable, it is possible that over time, solutions will supplant current conditions and improve the environment.

Tourism planners may plan more buildings that have features that use resources more efficiently and effectively by following the standards noted in any one of three rating processes: Energy Star, LEED by the U. S. Building Council, and NAHB Green by the National Association of Home Builders. By implementing resource saving systems, hotels, restaurants, and other areas will contribute to reducing the carbon footprint (a measure of greenhouse gases) on the planet. For example, The Parisian in Macao opened 3,000 rooms with a LEED Silver certification. These three systems are briefly mentioned below:

1   Energy Star Home Energy Rating System allows for residences to be rated as above or below 100. A more energy efficient home is below 100, and a less energy efficient system is above 100.
2   The LEED certification certifies buildings according to silver, gold, and platinum ratings inclusive of innovations made to be more efficient with energy.
3   NAHB Green identifies ways to make homes more energy efficient.

With respect to buildings, the following construction and remodeling aspects have been known to save energy:

1   Well-oriented sites that take the most advantage of wind, sunlight, and climate.
2   Building foundations that consist of well-insulated materials such as insulated concrete forms.
3   Structural insulated panels that have a foam core, or other insulation such as denim, cellulose, and spray foam.
4   Siding made of fiber cement.
5   Windows and lighting using design and glazing.
6   Exterior doors made of medium density fiberboard.
7   Green roofing such as roof gardens, ones that regulate storm drainage, white colors, PV panels, and solar shingles.
8   Heating, Ventilations, and air-conditioning units that are sized right for the home, use forced air, solar, radiant, or geothermal.
9   Water uses to include grey water, lower flush devices, and energy efficient appliances.

Of course, those who manage tourist experiences should also be well versed in environmentally sustainable methods and be able to select appropriate "green" lodging, attractions, and amenities. This way individuals will come in contact with the standards used to certify facilities and areas as "green", and learn about things that can also be implemented in their own residences upon their return home. Tourist professionals may become aware of the efforts of hotels to gain Energy Star, LEED, or other ratings and then pattern their information according to the standards that are mentioned. In addition, any wilderness area or destination can be reviewed, and rules for visitation shared in promotional literature, while traveling to the destination, and during the experience itself. It is essential that information is accurate, and resources for gaining additional information should be provided.

Advocacy

It is also interesting to tourists to learn to become advocates of sustainability or aware of cultural needs of a community they visit. Early exposure to these principles may assist a tourist in identifying a cause and work for change to improve areas that are environmentally threatened. For example, warnings about endangered species have been very effective in garnering funding and programs to improve the viability of selected species such as the bald eagle, lions, tigers, whales, dolphins and other animals. So too have environmental areas been permanently protected due to the early warnings about using rainforests for the timber industry, or waterways that become polluted, and oceans that are "fished out".

The environmental message goes hand in hand with the education of visitors at every nature destination. By informing the public, and by directing individuals to additional information about a particular environmental need, it is possible to influence groups of informed individuals who can advocate for solving problems and changing habits. Being able to take a message back home is a powerful driver for change and improvements in and understanding of the environment.

One of the earliest efforts of a country to establish an ecotourism policy is Costa Rica. Responding to concerns about the devastation of razing rain forests for timber, policies were developed that changed the overall economic direction from "timber to tourism" and "better to build 1000 50-unit hotels than 50-1000 unit hotels. Since the mid-1950s, sustainable tourism has provided an economy that attracts tourists to the country's rich natural resources that include beaches, mountains, rain forests, waterways, and many other features. The story of how tourism fits in with the biodiversity of the region is best exemplified with this experience. While attending a 13-station zip line adventure close to Jaco Beach, those ascending a mountain to get to the highest line were told to stay in the middle of the elevated boardwalk and stairway to allow the ants to carry their food up to their anthill dwellings. In looking to the edge of the stairwell, the tourists were able to see hundreds of ants, carrying little squares of foliage ascending the stairs in a perfect line. It was further explained that the ants serve a purpose in consuming a large portion of the rainforest foliage per day, allowing the rainforest to not become overgrown.

Service

In light of the potential risks of nature tourism, professionals must be extremely alert to hazards that may cause injury. Initially, this could be a tourist who has simply not come prepared for lengthy walking, exposure to the weather, or the existence of insects and noxious plants. Tour professionals need to be prepared for addressing solutions to these issues before actually engaging in the tour. Extra equipment, extra skin treatments, water, sunglasses, hats, and other items will be very important for the trip to be successful for all tourists. It is important to note that even with a very precise orientation to the environmental experience, some tourists simply do not comply. This can provide a danger to other group members, and it also can challenge the success of the entire trip. In addition, handling the problems is important in order not to cast a pall on other tourists who may isolate this non-complying tourist.

Even the most thorough orientation to the out of doors can still cause problems, if the clients fail to listen or truly understand the difficulties that can ensue if advice is not followed. In one case, a beginning cross-country skiing class was being prepared for the course in an evening ground session before taking off a week later. The group of 16 was given a printed manual, and everything needed to prepare for the trip was included and reviewed in the 2½-hour session. Physical preparedness, diet including most appropriate foods to eat when skiing along a remote winter trail, safety considerations, clothing and equipment needs, and a review of skills was covered. One rule that was stressed was the no alcohol consumption on the trail. This was due to the possibility of dehydration, loss of judgment, and potential cold-related illness. One participant did not heed the instructions and brought a 6-pack of beer on the trail. She made a wrong turn and headed down a 4-mile trail and got lost. In the later part of the afternoon, rangers were called out to find her, as were her two instructors, and luckily she was retracing her steps. Had she not turned around, she could have been a casualty or a fatality due to the nightfall and snowstorm.

Resources

There are many resources available to tourist professionals that are helpful in a tour. For example, when a tour involves a trip to a national park, it is possible to locate a great deal of information in advance of the trip that will assist in learning regulatory constraints such as the handling of tour busses, the distance needed from animals, regulations concerning removal of litter and waste from the grounds, and many other matters. In addition, park personnel may be enlisted to guide tours and explain regulations and environmental approaches to the environment. They also become great contacts for those who wish to return and visit as individuals. The National Park Service, for example, follows standards regulations in all parks, and also rules that apply to a specific natural wonder. Getting to know general rules about the leader:group ratios and the general prohibitions for parks in general can prepare both the staff and the tourist group for a positive experience.

Tourist and tour guides may find important information about an area in detailed books that describe flora and fauna. For example, Jackson (2006) recommended "do not expect a cool walk on a hot sultry Indiana summer day. The trees block slight breezes, and if you are not protected by insect repellent, the mosquitoes, ticks, and flies can be a nuisance" (p. 185). This passage provides very important advice to the uninitiated and uninformed traveler. Tourist professionals can provide required reading prior to orientation events by listing readily available books from libraries or via order. An individual's preparation and education can also be encouraged.

Marketing

Since most marketing efforts are geared to wide range of tourists, the information received by all prospective tourists is an important way to educate the public. Sometimes, the environmental message in lost in a sea of advertising for accommodations, food, and amusements; therefore, few really get important information before they strike out on a trip, particularly one in the natural environment. Lack of information can be confusing to the prospective tourist and the tourist professional, and this confusion can result in mistakes made on trips that could easily be avoided.

Importance of Accuracy in Presenting the Natural World

Very specific rules and regulations are in place in many natural environments to protect air, water, and woods from pollution that may interfere with the delicate balance of the ecological system. For example, a simple rule of not feeding animals has been enforced for many years; however, in some remote parts of a park, tourists may not have been given that message. As a result, feeding of animals may destroy the natural habits of animals of prey and build an unhealthy relationship to humans that cannot be sustained.

One example of the sustainability message *not* getting to the tourist is a case of two tour buses that stopped for lunch at Wawona Campgrounds in Yosemite National Park. These, buses carried about 50 people and each stopped within about 15 minutes of each other at the parking lot and picnic grounds in the camp. The first bus unloaded and had lunches lacked into individual Styrofoam containers. The group proceeded to the picnic tables and ate their lunch. Within 5 minutes of their arrival a pack of coyotes also arrived. As the group finished their lunches, the Styrofoam boxes were stored just outside of the garbage cans since they did not fit into the bear-proofed trash containers. Some coyotes made a beeline for the trash container area while others approached tourists who were holding out leftover food for them to eat. The second tour bus arrived and these tourists left the bus with lunch bags. In this case, the tourists could easily place these bags in the bear-proof garbage cans when they were finished; however, the coyotes attracted some of these tourists who fed them. In either case, the tour companies sponsored these tours should have been responsible for giving their clients park rules that clearly state that no animals are to be fed. In addition, it should have been relayed to those who prepare lunches that Styrofoam containers were not to be used due to their size and problems with disposal.

The Delivery

The importance of specific guidance in message delivery cannot be stressed enough. Based on the curriculum provided earlier, the tourism professional should provide accurate information in all marketing outlets including the organizational website, collateral materials, and in any information provided to the tourist should reflect sound "green" philosophy from the clothing that is packed, through the wise use of resources during the experience, to the new habits adopted by the tourist upon return from the excursion. Every online and hard copy piece of paper should reflect adherence to the standards put forth by LEED and other organizations, by the World Ecotourism Society, and by the ratings used for accommodations and appropriate food sources. In every part of the experience, there should be an appropriate environmental message that is consistent with training and education of the tourism professional and tourist.

Safety and Security

Given the unknown nature of involvement in natural resources, tourism professionals must be aware of the dangers to individuals as well as the environment. In a compendium of actual cases of death in Grand Canyon National Park, Ghiglieri and Myers (2001) note that many of these deaths could have been avoided with a well-reasoned plan. These cases include falls, drowning, exposure, rock falls, bites from "venomous creatures" (p. 278) and other issues. The major theme that the reader came away with in these accounts is that the following caused the death or deaths:

1 Failing to anticipate the extreme heat or cold that is present on any given day.
2 Failing to accurately gauge the length of time it takes to hike rugged terrain.
3 Failing to adequately supply oneself with enough water and food.
4 Making faulty decisions counter to maps and pre-planning logic.
5 Failing to heed the advice of park staff.

The above issues have been repeated very commonly in many nature tourism programs. The tourist professional and the participant must be in sync and rules and regulations need to be researched and followed.

Regulatory Process: Origin of Typical Regulations for U. S. National Parks—An Example

The tourism professional may become educated to the laws and regulations that must be followed when venturing into a natural environment. While the law process differs by level of government and also by type of agency or business, the origin of regulations and the types of regulatory processes are similar. It takes research to learn a great deal about a specific area, and the ore knowledgeable the leader; the better the prospects are for the success of a trip.

The National Park Service I governed by Federal Laws and Executive Orders approved by the United States Congress. Sometimes these regulations require Presidential approval. Therefore, NPS may implement laws and enforce established policies. These policies apply to everyone and if one violates the law, the result can be a fine and/or imprisonment.

Regulations include a variety of rules that cover how visitors are to conduct themselves around pristine environments such as oceans, cultural resources, historic properties, archeological sites, hunting and fishing areas, and many other natural features. There are also general guidance regulations with regard to wilderness stewardship, accessibility of visitors, use of service animals for people with disabilities, sound preservation and noise management, trails, and wild/scenic rivers. The tables below show regulations governing the features that are prevalent in both Yosemite and Yellowstone National Parks.

Now that the importance of messaging and education has been reviewed, the delivery of the nature tourism experience should be conducted according to the unique characteristics of a particular destination. If tourism collateral materials are consistent and accurate about these destinations, then it should follow that the information secured for the tourist be also accurate and consistent with what is offered at the site of the experience. Table 9.1 and 9.2 show the types of regulatory information that should provide consistent messaging in promotion and business information. Again, carrying the message through to the tourist is important.

Table 9.1 Activities Prohibited in Yellowstone

1	Willfully remaining near or approaching wildlife including nesting birds, within any distance that disturbs or displaces the animal.
2	Traveling off boardwalks or designated trails in hydrothermal areas.
3	Throwing anything into thermal features.
4	Swimming in hot springs.
5	Removing or possessing natural or cultural resources (such as wildflowers, antlers, rocks, and arrowheads).
6	Travelling off-road by vehicle or bicycle.
7	Camping outside of designated areas.
8	Spotlighting wildlife (viewing with lights).
9	Imitating elk calls or using buglers. Imitating wolf howls.
10	Using electronic equipment capable of tracking wildlife.
11	Launching, landing, o operating unmanned aircraft (drones) on lands and waters.

Table 9.2 Activities Prohibited in Yosemite

1	Altering, damaging, or removing vegetation.
2	Vehicle use off established roads and parking areas.
3	Use of insecticides-herbicides and pesticides.
4	Loud noises. (60 decibels or higher between 100:00 p.m. and 6:00 a.m.
5	Nudity.
6	Use of meadow areas except on trails.
7	Smoking in buildings, on boardwalks, or in vegetated areas.
8	Harassment of wildlife or introduction of wildlife captured elsewhere.
9	Digging, scraping, chiseling, or defacing natural features.

Meeting Visitor Expectations

It is recommended that all nature tourists be exposed to a preliminary information meeting that depicts the unique and sensitive characteristics of a site. The following listing consists of potential rules that should be followed for a given site:

1 Description of site and features.
2 Topography and sensitivity of plants and trail construction.
3 Requests to enter and leave a site as it was, avoiding the picking up of rock or reef souvenirs, driftwood, pine cones, and other debris natural to the area.
4 Information regarding risky areas such as drop-offs in water, sliding rock or snow, slippery surfaces, and areas to avoid while walking or driving.
5 Presence of insects and animals that can be harmful with ways to avoid contact with either.
6 How to react if approached by an animal.
7 Avoidance of noxious elements in the environment such as plants, snakes, and other types of danger.
8 Tendencies for reactions to heat, cold, and other weather-related situations and how to handle them.

9 Avoidance of the use of alcohol, drugs, and other substances during the excursion.
10 Proper skin protection and clothing needed for comfort and safety.
11 The importance of having a buddy.
12 Following the lead of the tourism professionals who guide the experience.
13 Following local customs especially in interacting with residents.
14 Staying hydrated, properly fed for the exertion involved in the particular environment, and getting plenty of sleep.
15 How to handle accidents if you are a group member, and how to assist tourism professionals in a crisis situation.
16 In general, following rules and regulations that are present at the site.
17 Specifically, following the rules established by guides and tourism professionals.

Operating in a Natural Environment

As noted in the safety and security section, the natural environment is unpredictable. Having several plans for unforeseen circumstances will allow a trip to adapt to weather, impassable conditions, and other challenges that are presented.

The Outcome

Reflection.

When a tourist experience ends, there are many memories that sustain the experience for years on end. The organization that involves tourists in nature experiences should establish ways to connect after the trip is over. Simple things such as sharing e-mails and addresses, forming blog groups and providing newsletters either in hard copy or online, and keeping in touch with former participants are ways to encourage repeat business, but also to continue the conversation about environmental sustainability. For example, the Sierra Club has conducted trips and tours as a part of its message to individuals to respect and protect the environment. The club prints information about local trails, best ways to travel on the trails, and important environmental considerations when engaging in a trop or tour. Likewise, tour businesses can benefit from what has been organized by non-profit environmental organizations by respecting these messages and encouraging tourists to participate in local environmental organizations.

Advocacy

Individuals and groups who return from trips and tours in the many settings offering exposure to the natural environment may elect to get involved with one or more of the many outdoor-oriented groups that hike, bike, swim, and tour local natural areas. This involvement may extend the messages learned in a nature tourism experience and also increase the number of people who can commit to protecting important natural resources while changing their lifestyle to be less of a carbon footprint on the land.

The Tourism Professional as a Part of a Sustainability Team

Likewise, the tourism professional may also serve locally as a positive example of and resource for the promotion of sustainable practices in all tourism ventures that take place. Participating in local groups will also serve to increase the professional's credibility when conducting nature tours and when responding to questions about the natural environment.

Summary

This chapter involved discussion of the importance of coordinating the message about sustainable practices in the environment with education about environmental practices during the preparation for a nature tourism event. In addition, the importance of maintaining and being an advocate for sustainable tourism practices is stressed in anticipation of, during, and as a follow-up to experiencing the natural environment. The importance of the tourism professional demonstrating sound knowledge of these practices was emphasized as well as the role of the tourist in extending the knowledge of sustainable practice upon return from a satisfying exposure to the natural environment.

References

Ghiglieri, M. P. and Myers, T. M. (2001). *Over the edge: Death at the Grand Canyon.* Flagstaff, AZ: Puma Press.

Holtzman, B. (2012). *Wilderness survival skills.* New York: Chartwell Books.

Jackson, M. T. (2006). *The Nature Conservancy's guide to Indiana preserves.* Bloomington, IN: Quarry Books, Indiana Press.

Masberg, B. A. and Jamieson, L. M. (1999). The visibility of public park and recreation Facilities in tourism collateral materials: An exploratory study. *Journal of Vacation Marketing,* 5(2), 154–166.

Sellers, R. W. (1997). *Preserving nature in the national parks: A history.* New Haven: Yale University Press.

United States Department of Justice. (2016). *Information and technical assistance on the Americans with Disabilities Act.* (Retrieved from ada.gov homepage, 6/28/16).

United States Department of the Interior. (2016). *Rules and regulations.* (Retrieved from nps.gov/nature, 6/6/16).

10 A National Park in Turmoil

The Case Study on Vanoise National Park in the Alps

Isabelle Frochot

Introduction

This chapter reviews the history of national parks in France and discusses a pressing case relating to Vanoise National Park in French Northern Alps. The following analysis touches on the characteristics of charters, the stakeholders involved, the outcome of the recent charter renegotiation and the dilemma of the rejection in contrast to the fact that other national parks usually witness an approval rate of 75–100 per cent by the local districts involved. To what extent have local villages no longer accepted the regulations and is the local-level decision putting a break on national parks approval? Is a economic gain causing a threat to the existence of national parks and what kinds of solutions are able to reunite the stakeholders for approving a new national park charter?

France does not have a long history of national park development in comparison to the United States since its first national park was only created in 1963. However, the idea of preservation has existed in the French society for some time. Historically, the first natural areas protected were associated with feudalism. The objective was then for property owners to protect hunting grounds in order to manage their water, wood and game resources and the only real attempt to delimit an area to protect it came in 1861 with Napoleon III, in the forest of Fontainebleau (on the outskirts of Paris). Walking paths and cycling routes were constructed within the protected areas with the objective of leisurely consumption. During the 19th century, the first juridical and regulation bodies started stating how nature should be used and the first attempts at protecting species emerged. Towards the end of the 19th and early 20th century, biological woodland reserves appeared in France along with national hunting reserves with the aim to protect some areas. This resulted from a combined understanding that those spaces not only had biological but also aesthetic values (Richez, 1992). Behind the scenes, one institution, "Les Eaux et Forêts" (a body protecting water and forest resources) was particularly proactive at encouraging the protection of some sites. The Bird Protection League (LPO) and the National Society for Nature Preservation also became active in their own fields. The protection of flora species was a concern that appeared last in France as it was only in 1976 that the protected flora species were identified and a picking ban established on the most endangered ones. At the end of the Second World War, France was one of the few countries not to have any national formal structure and regulations regarding national parks. At that time, the rapid rise of alpine sports (skiing) was seen as a risk to fragile mountain environments and accelerated the need to officially identify protected areas.

The establishment of national parks in the United States has greatly influenced development of national parks in France and other parts of Europe as well. However, in France it took a centenary to establish the national park system compared to the United States. In France, it was on 27 November 1946 that a decree created the National Council towards Nature Preservation which established the statuses of the future national parks. Elaborated by the Ministry of Agriculture, the law instituting the national parks was adopted in 1960 and then, one after the other, seven parks were created. The Vanoise and Port-Cros National Parks were established in 1963, Occidentales Pyrénées in 1967, the Cévennes in 1970, the Ecrins in 1973, the Mercantour in 1979, the Guadeloupe (an island in the Caribbean) in 1989 and the Callanques park (near Marseille, metropolitan France) in 1992. In 2007, two new national parks were added: Réunion Island in the Indian Ocean and Guyana Amazonian National Park in South America. At present, the creation of a new national park is in progress in the Burgundy/ Champagne regions.

Some parks encountering pressing issues are examined in the next paragraph using the Vanoise case. With regard to marine interests, the parks have encountered a lot of objections. For instance, a new 2006 law had strengthened the possibility of creating a marine national park in Brittany. The project has been elaborated for several years but local opposition has been fierce as boat owners and local fishermen are worried that the marine park will constrain their activities. Picking shellfish is both a leisure and professional activity that has brought opposition to the notion of creating a park. Therefore, attempts at setting up a marine national park, given the intensity of holiday activities (the seaside is the prime destination in the summer in France) is proving to be complex.

In France, the national parks are under the administrative supervision of the Ministry of Ecology and Sustainable Development and under the Environment Law Articles L331 and R214. Every year, French national parks welcome 7 million visitors (Guide Gallimard, 1998; Merveilleux du Vignaux, 2003).

The Concept of National Parks in the French Context

A national park covers an area that has been qualified as being of an exceptional nature at a national and international level, due to a mixture of geological, biological diversity and landscapes of outstanding value. To some extent, the national parks have been considered as areas that are an entire part of France history and identity to the same extent that major heritage sites are part of France's legacy. However, the notion of nature cannot be conceptualised in isolation as it is necessarily intertwined with that of traditional human activities that have satisfied the need of local inhabitants within this fragile environment. These local activities essentially involve livestock and forestry occupations and the role of those activities in moulding the landscapes encountered is well acknowledged and has therefore been integrated in the management strategy of the park.

National parks are divided into several zones, each of which have different preservation objectives (Girand, 2003; Laslaz, 2004). The centre of the park represents an area that is the focus of preservation: human activities are usually forbidden apart from some forestry and agricultural activities that can be tolerated. These activities are accepted as long as they do not disrupt the flora and fauna of the park. Usually, when carefully managed, they contribute to the general upkeep of the park. However, park development is highly regulated concerning industrial and commercial activities, water usage, hunting and fishing. Public access is allowed in the centre area and various interpretation and guide services are provided. In this zone, all telephone and electric cables have to be concealed and motorised access is heavily regulated.

Within the centre area, a smaller area can be isolated, named the "integral reserve", where all activities and public access are forbidden in order to protect fragile fauna and flora ecosystems. This area gives scientists the opportunity to observe how species evolve when there is no human interference and of course an opportunity to guarantee the total protection of species. So far, two integral reserves have been created in the Écrins National Park and the Port-Cros National Park.

A third zone, the peripheral zone, is constituted by the land of the adjoining districts that have agreed to ratify the park charter. It allows some districts to be part of the park without having to face overly restrictive obligations. In this area, regulations are more flexible and much less limiting. However, the villages who have signed the charter need to develop planning and urbanism bylaws in accordance with the rules of the park, even though planning permission for new buildings remain in the hands of local mayors.

The Objectives of National Parks

The Original Objectives

National Parks missions include the preservation of natural, cultural and landscape heritage, the development of knowledge and the continuous monitoring of this heritage, the interpretation of this knowledge for a wider public and the encouragement of the public to respect the environment. The staff have various roles, from keeping counts of wildlife and flora species' evolution, to guiding and informing visitors as well as checking and regimenting public behaviour.

Any new park opening has to respect procedures set out in several steps. First, preliminary studies are conducted to evaluate the ecological profile of the park, followed by a consultation with local constituencies and then a public enquiry/survey is conducted among the local population. The Environment Ministry appoints the director of the park and the park administration is then undertaken by a public body whose administrative board is made up of state representatives, elected councillors, scientists, hunters, fishermen and park visitors' representatives. For instance, the parks involve the hunters in the decision to open or restrict some zones for hunting and careful planning of the hunting zones and seasons guarantees its role in the controlled growth of some game species. Some parks, like the Cévennes, even allow hunting of wild boars, stags and row dears in the central part of the park in order to limit their damaging impact on the local ecosystem. The preservation of species also involves more controversial actions such as the protection of bears in the Pyrenees which has led to an ongoing conflict with the hunters' community (the last female bear was accidentally killed by a hunter in 2006). The success of the preservation initiatives has been evidenced by the return of species no longer present or on the verge of extinction: ibexes, capercaillies, otters, Tengmalm owls, Lynx, wolves etc. A scientific committee advise the administrative council of the park and develops the relevant scientific programs for the park (preservations schemes, research programmes and scientific inventories etc.).

Another objective of the park is the preservation of landscapes. Indeed, officials are willing to undertake various actions to maintain or restore their landscapes. This can involve reducing human activities' visual impact such has concealing electric lines and/or landscaping and hiding car parks. Local traditional style is also preserved with regulations applied to the planning and materials used in the buildings' construction or restoration. If the implementation of preservation objectives would exceed the current budget of the districts, some subsidies may be provided to meet the excessive cost. Memory is also the object of preservation with some parks investing time in collecting memories from local inhabitants (legends and literature in the Cévennes for instance).

More importantly, one of the leading and common problems for mountain parks has been landscape closure. Due to a declining agricultural activity, the forest tends to overtake the landscape and in order to keep this landscape open, local agriculture has to be maintained. For instance, the parks have been encouraging the persistence of pastoral activities, often through subsidies. The aim is to sustain or restore animal grazing that will maintain the landscapes as they were when local farming activities were still heavily present (Finger-Stich and Ghimire, 1997).

The parks have engaged an important work in terms of interpretation. Providing interpretation services for visitors and informing them about the nature surrounding them is indeed an important mission. All the parks have organised paths with ample information being provided on signs and leaflets. The other objective of course is to explain the rules behind the functioning of the park and clarify its constraints to visitors. Newsletters, leaflets, maps, events, guided visits, local museums, education packs for schools, visitor centres are all part of the vast production of materials by the parks. Signage on site has to respect a national graphic chart that states the shape, size and colour (brown and yellow) of the signs displayed.

The New Statuses Established in 2006

The statuses of French national parks were renewed in 2006 as so far the national parks were the result of a national policy emanating from the government, although some local stakeholders felt that it was in some ways imposed top-down by national instances. The revision of the statuses aimed to give greater voice to local park stakeholders. With the new statuses, the French government keeps a very dominant power in the central zone where it controls most of the decision powers, and local authorities are given a consultative role only. However, the state has less control in the peripheral zone where districts can choose to belong or not to the zone and where regulations are less restrictive. The new law has increased the presence of local authorities and users in the administrative commission. The 2006 law also sets out to have more transparent decision processes and an increasing involvement of different users of the park.

The president is still elected by the Ecology minister but the local park administration body puts forward a choice of three candidates. Beyond the protection of natural resources, the 2006 law expands the parks' missions to landscapes and cultural heritage. What used to be called the central zone becomes the heart zone of the park (the "coeur du parc") and the peripheral zone is renamed the optimal membership zone ("aire optimale d'adhésion"). The park charter has two objectives: for the heart zone it identifies the objectives of protection of natural and cultural resources, including landscapes, and details how rules and laws are implemented. The second objective concerns the membership optimal zone by stating the general protection objectives and how sustainable development should be implemented and by which means.

The objections of the 2006 law have been of several kinds. On one side, nature lovers have been worried that the central zone could come under increasing pressure from local economic, forestry and agricultural interests which might gradually reduce the preservation of this area. On the other hand, local districts have been concerned that the regulations applied to the central zone might gradually expand to the peripheral zone, making their economic activities and users' interests more constricted. The administrative council of the park is assisted by groups of all the existing parks. This body has created a brand, "Esprit Parc National", that aims to federates all the actors within its vicinity.

The Case of Vanoise National Park

The History of Vanoise National Park

As stated previously, Vanoise National Park was among the first two national parks created in France in 1963. Before this date, the park was already a national hunting reserve (1936–1943) developed under the pressure of the Alpine Club and the Touring Club along with local hunters. This motivation came from the recognition that both the ibexes and chamois populations were slowly but increasingly reducing. At this stage, the reserve extended from Tignes to Val d'Isère (in the Tarentaise valley), including Bessans and Bonneval-sur-Arc (in the Maurienne valley). This zone was extended between 1943 and 1955 under the pressure of naturalists who considered that the original zone was too narrow to effectively protect the species concerned. From 1955 to 1959, the foundations of the future national park were gradually set with the development of a central zone aimed at protecting nature and educating the general public. A peripheral zone where local natural and cultural assets were valorised along with agriculture and tourism activities and various information, training and events around those elements were developed (Hermann, 2014).

This park covers a superficies of 52,839 hectares and it is located in the French region of Rhône-Alpes within the Savoie Department. The park has 14 kilometres of common frontier with the national Parc of Grand Paradis in Italy. The park has five nature reserves observing specific rules: Bailletaz (Val d"isère), Grande Sassière (Tignes), Hauts de Villaroger (Villaroger), Plan de Tueda (les Allues) and Tignes-Champagny (Tignes, Champagny).

The park covers altitudes ranging from 1,280 meters to 3,855 meters high and is spread over two valleys, that of the Tarentaise and the Maurienne. The central zone covers 535 kilometres squared, and its maximum zone is 1,465 kilometres squared, including 29 districts for a population of 37,700 inhabitants (Hermann, 2014). Its flora includes 1,200 different species (200 of whom are remarkable species and several of which are protected). The fauna includes 1,800 ibexes, 4,000 chamois and 120 species of nesting birds. Some of those species are protected and it is a major site for the protection of bearded vultures (reintroduced in 1986). In terms of tourism provision, the park has 600 kilometres of walking paths, 53 refuges and 10 gîtes (www.vanoise-parcnational.fr, 2016).

On another dimension, the Tarentaise valley, and to a lesser extent, the Maurienne valley, are the biggest skiing zones in France for a total of 30,3000 tourist beds. This ski industry is of a massive scale grouping: 520 ski lifts (449 in Tarentaise and 71 in Maurienne); three linked ski areas (Trois Vallées, Les Arcs, Espace Killy); 940 hectares of slopes with artificial snow for a total of 4,500 hectares of skiing slopes. Overall, and outside the nature reserve areas, the ski resorts represent 18 per cent of the park surface (27 per cent in Tarentaise and 5 per cent in Maurienne).

The Regulations and Administrative Bodies

The Vanoise park regulations stipulate that in the heart zone it is forbidden to pick flowers, fruits, minerals, fossils and insects. It is also forbidden to camp but light tents are allowed next to refuges in July and August. Dogs are forbidden, even on a lead. Noise should be avoided (shouting, bringing audio equipment to listen to music etc.) as well as making fires outside. Gliding sports such as hand gliding or gliders are forbidden if the glide takes place less than 1,000 meters above the ground. All types of bicycles are forbidden but a few mountain biking paths have been officially authorised by the National Park. Any motorised vehicles are only tolerated on roads, no off-roading is authorised. Visitors should not cause any arm, and hunting is forbidden. All visitors should take back with them their garbage, even if staying in a refuge.

The administrative committee of the park includes (Hermann, 2014):

- 7 representatives from the French government
- 18 representatives from local authorities (including 12 mayors)

- 16 personalities:
  - the president of the scientific committee
  - 8 individuals with local competencies and nominated by the Savoie prefect
  - 7 individuals with national competencies or representing national bodies
- 1 staff representative

The president administrates the committee and in particular the charter elaboration, monitoring and evaluation. The committee meets two to three times a year and delegates some of its activities to a bureau of 13 elected members.

The scientific committee members are proposed by the president, then advice is given by the administrative committee and validated by the prefect. This committee groups around 20 individuals and the scientific committee is consulted on questions related to the inventory and preservation of natural and cultural resources and on planning projects. It is also involved in the various studies and research projects with which the park is associated. The economic, social and cultural committee includes about 40 members and manages the contract policies and the implementation of the charter.

The management of the park itself is divided into four areas, each of which includes an area manager, a secretary and four to seven rangers (for a total of 50 employees for the park). Those agents are sworn officials who check visitors' respect of the rules, they undertake scientific intelligence, valorise the heritage, provide guidance to groups and visitors, restore the paths and take part in the local social and economic life.

The financial resources of the park come from the Environment ministry on top of subsidies received from the Regional and General Councils, along with some European funds and from other ministries on specific actions.

The Vanoise National Park Crisis since 2015

Initially the Vanoise park originated from a state decision but the 2006 law, which gave more power to local stakeholders, along with growing frustrations with the park restrictions, led to a major crisis in 2015. While the charter was up for renegotiation (it is renegotiated every 15 years), only two out of the 29 districts involved ratified it; so, in effect, the vast majority of the villages involved rejected it. The National Park still exists, the heart zone cannot be modified, but it is the peripheral zone that has changed, now only grouping two districts and not 29. In three years, the other 27 districts can choose to join again with Vanoise National Park. The situation is complex since some of those districts were only in the peripheral area and they will probably work much less in tune with the park in the future. However, other districts have not voted the charter but nonetheless have a part of their territory in the heart zone, so whether they want it or not, they will have to work with the park, to some extent.

The two districts which ratified it, Saint Martin de Belleville and Pesey-Nancroix, are both involved in intense skiing activity but this does not deter them from accepting the charter. So is the depth of the rejection more complex than just tourism-economic interests?

In all honesty, the ski business remains a limitation to the implementation of the park. To start, no other parks in France have received this amount of rejection, but no other parks have such strong economic activity associated with the park location. For years, the ski lobby (major hotel and ski lift companies) have put pressure on the government and other authorities to loosen park restrictions in order to develop more ski slopes and tourist accommodation. It is a fact that the Tarentaise and the Maurienne valleys have lost most of their industries over the years, and if local agriculture has survived, it is struggling economically. Moreover, the ways in which the tourism construction has taken place in ski resorts has led to a vast amount of accommodation leaving the commercial sector. Indeed, in order to finance the construction of ski resort accommodation from the 1960s onwards, the French government encouraged schemes whereby individuals would purchase accommodation. In exchange for an interesting private tax rebate over a 10-year period, they had to rent their accommodation most of the year. When the first 10-years period finished, most owners retrieved their flat from the rental market to benefit from it on their own. As a result, most ski resorts can now display a large number of tourists' flats but only a portion of them get out to the commercial market (this phenomenon is also known as the "closed shutters" or "cold beds"). So in order to keep attracting tourists and investment, and because real-estate prices remain very high within the resorts, there is strong pressure to build more accommodation. In itself, the logic of this building frenzy is questionable since statistics clearly show a slowing down of skiing demand in the French population, so the limits of the model have created various tensions.

Another objection to the park comes from local farmers, especially sheep farmers who have suffered from increasing wolf attacks over the last few years. The wolf is in fact protected and as a result the population has been increasing. The park does not authorise the hunting of wolves in the heart area and the Bern convention, in any case, protects wolves. Regularly, the wolves attack sheep at night but also increasingly by day. In the first nine months of 2015, 156 attacks have been recorded leading to the death of 600 sheep in the Vanoise park. Farmers can obtain governmental compensation for those losses but they claim that it insufficiently covers their losses. In September 2015, during a meeting with local farmers, the president of the park was confined for 15 hours in a town hall. The sheep farmers were unhappy due to the increase of wolf attacks on their livestock. By confining the president, their objective was to put pressure on authorities. Their main demand was the reduction of the wolf population, demanding that five wolves be killed in the Vanoise territory, as well as getting themselves authorised to react more rapidly in case of an attack. The local Savoie prefect soon reacted, promising a meeting with the farmers' representatives. The president was released and the farmers attended the meeting and as a result, the prefect promised to kill not five but six wolves. This is a particularly thorny situation. The French government authorises the killing of wolves every year in order to protect livestock (36 wolves to be killed in 2016). But, as we mentioned previously, the wolf is protected by several conventions and various environmental protection associations are currently contesting the government decision in front of tribunals.

More globally, it is the notion of national parks that creates in itself frictions, or, to be more precise, the ways in which some locals feel that they have been imposed on them by the government. In the early 1960s, sentiments were very strong against setting up such parks at first, and at this time land was taken over by the government to create the heart zone, removing it from the local districts' ownership, and several generations later this has created bitter feelings.

France remains a rural country with strong attachments to the local territory and local inhabitants and politicians still feel strongly that decisions should remain at a district level. A lot of local inhabitants tend to feel that, if the park is necessary and the heart zone is indeed a positive way to protect nature, they are more critical of the peripheral zones' implications. France is renowned for the heaviness of its administrative rules and burdens and the local districts feel that every time they set up a planning project, they have to face an increasing set of rules and regulations. In their eyes, the park adds more rules and regulations and also places expectations upon people to respect some local style that often implies an increased cost on building and restoration projects.

In retrospect, it is also true that Vanoise National Park has perhaps not developed close relationships through its lack of pedagogy with local politicians and populations. This lack of communication has certainly been detrimental to the park and even the rangers are not really trained with a vision of territorial development, which is greatly needed.

Whilst the 2006 law aimed to give more decision powers to local stakeholders, it has in fact perhaps created more problems than advantages in the Vanoise case since, for some of the local people, negative feelings about the park were already there and the new law allowed them to voice them even more officially. Vanoise National Park is aware of the various reasons that have led to the rejection of the charter by so many districts and it is currently looking back at the history of its charter, since its creation, to understand how the park has been perceived by the local populations. The park is currently launching a vast study to identify those various elements with the objective of undertaking better negotiations in the future and bringing back some of the districts that have recently rejected the charter.

Conclusion

The history of national parks in France is very recent compared to the United States or other European countries. Nonetheless, since the law setting up national parks was created in 1960, 10 parks have been set up in France and its associated territories. The park that has recently encountered the biggest opposition is that of the Vanoise in the Alps, where most of the districts involved have refused to ratify the new charter. The proximity of profit-making ski resorts certainly has a role to play, but rightly or not, local inhabitants in the peripheral area also feel that the rules of the park are too constraining and imposed from above.

Are the national Parks structures inadequate in a 21st century society? Most certainly not, but national parks have an essential role to play in the preservation of natural areas. The level of objections raised in the Vanoise is not representative of other French national parks that have accepted new charters with little opposition and most certainly, the economic pressures in the Vanoise area, not just the profit from ski resorts but also the weakening local economies, make local people feel that they have no other choice but to develop their economic resources from local tourism activities.

The necessity for a long-term vision is a key element but, unfortunately, it is sometimes found lacking amongst local actors or politicians. Further, resentment around the ways in which the park is felt as an imposed responsibility on locals also remains. The lack of communication with stakeholders is another limiting factor in this case.

When taking the specific case of parks located in mountain areas, a long-term vision is necessary and indeed, climate warming threats and modern living conditions mean that, if most of tourist demand is currently directed to the winter season, in the future, consuming mountains in the summer as one of the last-preserved natural areas could increase. As a result, the presence of the government as a directing body with a strong emphasis on environment preservation is a key factor. Even if participatory democracy remains a key element of 21st century decision-making processes, reality tends to show that environmental interests are best defended nationally.

References

Finger-Stich A. and Ghimire K. B. (1997). Travail, culture et nature, l'Harmattan, Paris.
Guide Gallimard (1998). Les Parcs Nationaux de France, Gallimard, Paris.
Giran, J.-P. (2003). Les Parcs Nationaux, une référence pour la France, une chance pour ses territoires, Rapport Parlementaire, Juin. Retrieved from www.ladocumentationfrancaise.fr/rapports-publics/034000496/index.shtml
Hermann M. (2014). Découvrir le parc national, Parc National de la Vanoise, Chambéry. Retrieved from www.vanoise-parcnational.fr/fr/parc-national-de-la-vanoise/letablissement-public
Garnier A. (2016). Outils juridiques pour la protection des espaces naturels (legislation guidelines). Retrieved from: http://ct78.espaces-naturels.fr/?arbo=les_fiches&sel=reste:fiche&val=6:17
Laslaz L. (2004). Vanoise, 40 ans d'histoire de Parc National : Bilan et perspectives, L'Harmattan, Paris
Merveilleux du Vignaux, P. (2003). L'aventure des Parcs nationaux, la création des Parcs nationaux français, fragments d'histoire, Édition de L'Atelier technique des espaces naturels, Montpellier.

Ministère de l'environnement, de l'énergie et de la mer (2013, Mars 26). Qu'est ce qu'un parc national? (Document). Retrieved from: www.developpement-durable.gouv.fr/ Qu-est-ce-qu-un-parc-national.html

Parcs Nationaux de France (2016). Official presentation of the body, aims and objectives. Retrieved from: www.parcsnationaux-fr.com/accueil/

Richez G. (1992). Parcs Nationaux et tourisme en Europe, L'Harmattan, Paris.

11   Listening to the Sounds of Silence

Forest-based Wellbeing Tourism in Finland

Raija Komppula, Henna Konu and
Noora Vikman

Nature experiences are seen to be a primary travel motive among foreign visitors to the Nordic region (Gössling & Hultman, 2006). For instance, in Finland, it has been estimated that one third of all foreign tourists take part in nature activities (Finnish Tourist Board, 2009). Today, the national tourism marketing organization promotes Finland as a tourist destination with three core values, which are "Silence, please", "Wild & Free" and "Cultural beat" (Visitfinland.com, 2015). This chapter focuses on the first two themes. "Wild & Free" refers to all-year-round nature-based activities, and "Silence, please" presents Finland as a counterpart to hectic urban life, a destination where the visitors can enjoy peace and quiet and have space to breathe (Visitfinland.com, 2015).

According to several studies (e.g. Lee et al., 2009; Li, 2010; Morita et al., 2007; Morita et al., 2011; Ohtsuka et al., 1998; Park et al., 2008; Tsunetsugu et al., 2010) it is widely believed that to come in contact with nature, especially with forest environments is somehow beneficial to human wellbeing and comfort. Forest-based nature tourism can hence be regarded as wellbeing tourism referring to culture, nature, peace and quiet in the countryside (Konu et al., 2010). Wellbeing tourism refers to emotional motivations, such as connection with community or nature, and hence, in several countries, it may be seen at least partly overlapping with rural tourism in terms of tourist motivations (Komppula & Konu, 2012; Pesonen & Komppula, 2010). According to Konu and Laukkanen (2010) motivation factors connected to health, physical activity and self-development were the most decisive that dictate the intention to take a wellbeing trip among potential Finnish wellbeing tourists.

In many descriptions of nature, the soundscape of the natural places is conceived as "silent" (Vikman, 2006). The general impression about nature is that it is a place where one can lounge and vegetate surrounded by relaxing and calming sounds, the silent or peaceful atmosphere being what people usually look for when they head to natural settings to spend time (Vikman, 2006).

The scenic beauty and sparse population in the Northern Karelia region in Eastern Finland offers many opportunities for visitors to experience silence in the nature. This chapter presents findings from two case studies that aim to develop products for two foreign wellbeing tourism segments, namely Japanese and Chinese, which are among the top ten foreign target markets of Finland as a tourist destination. Forest-based wellbeing tourism is defined as tourism taking place in or near a forest environment, including physical activities, relaxation and/or stress relief in the forest, utilization of natural resources of forests and learning activities related to how to use natural resources for wellbeing purposes (Konu, 2015b). These case studies are from the Northern Karelia region of Finland, where the University of Eastern Finland has, together with small local tourism businesses, developed nature-based tourism offering, which focuses on silence and forests.

Wellbeing Effects of Nature and Forests

Nature, especially forests have been proved to have beneficial effects on the physical and mental health and wellbeing of human beings (Park et al., 2009). Terms such as nature therapy (Lee et al., 2012) and forest therapy (Ohtsuka et al., 1998) have received lots of attention especially in Japan and recently also in Europe (e.g. Korpela et al., 2010). In Finland, benefits of green areas, nature and forest environment for wellbeing have been recognized (e.g. Korpela et al., 2014; Tyrväinen et al., 2014). Forest therapy, or "Shinrin-yoku" as it is called in Japan, refers to recreation and relaxation in forest environments, being a type of climatherapy or aromatherapy (Ohtsuka et al., 1998), in which walking in a forest and breathing in volatile substances called phytoncides, derived from trees, results in a hike in feelings of refreshment (Li, 2010), provides relaxation and reduces stress (Tsunetsugu et al., 2010).

According to the findings of Lee et al. (2009), experiencing forest landscapes may reduce stress, aid autonomic nervous system relaxation and enhance positive emotion, which suggests that the forest environments have a beneficial effect on mental health and Shinrin-yoku may be employed as a stress reduction method (Morita et al., 2007) as the scents of trees, the sounds of brooks and the feel of sunshine through forest leaves is believed to have a calming effect.

Such terms as tranquility, solitude, peace and silence are often connected to nature-based recreation, and are seen as a core component of this experience. They are also used as measures in the modified Recreation Experience Preference scale, which has been used as an instrument in the development of perspectives on recreation experience (e.g. Manfredo et al., 1996). The results of sound preference tests in different parts of Europe show that sounds of nature are mentioned most often when asking what the most pleasant sounds are for people (Järviluoma et al., 2009b; Vikman, 2009).

The pioneer of soundscape studies, R. M. Schafer (1977, in Järviluoma et al., 2009a), has defined noise as undesired, unmusical sound, loud sounds or meaningless sound as opposed to pleasant silence. In general, noise in the environment refers to something unpleasant and disturbing whereas silence is defined in terms of pleasantness. This reveals some ideals connected to the silent soundscape. It is acknowledged that there are many conventional settings, such as practicing religion, where silence is experienced, and reaching a silent state of mind often requires solitude and intimacy (Ampuja, 2014; Lappalainen, 1998; Sarlin, 2006). The variation between sounds and silences is also a key element when explaining the effects of sound to the human neurological system (e.g. Moran et al., 2013).

To practice "Silence" as a concept might come across as a bit complicated of an idea. However, "Silence" does not necessarily refer to a total lack of sounds; rather, spending time in the silent surroundings is an opportunity to relax, to listen and hear more clearly in a quiet, slow-paced environment. In the context of nature tourism, it means what many would describe as "quietness". According to several studies (Uimonen, 2006; Vikman, 2006 & 2009) people often equate the soundscapes in natural environments to silent soundscapes. For instance, people have described quiet natural environments by bringing forth diverse elements, such as sounds of the wind in the leaves of the plants, waves in the shore and sounds of birds and animals. It has been noted that people reach a similar state during collective listening walks when silently entering into natural environments (Vikman, 2010; Järviluoma et al., 2009b). Hence, it can be argued that a peaceful and slow "listening walk" in the forest in all its simplicity can be a strong positive experience.

The strong presumption on the background in development of wellbeing tourism is the search for silence or quietness, which is understood as an alternative to the everyday hectic tempo. While silence as an experience is expected to be pleasant and invigorating, it can be considered as a scene or a circumstance for wellbeing. The "good" soundscape has been defined by three qualities: balance, complexity and variety (Vikman, 2007). The qualities of alternative tourist spaces as pleasant environments can also be evaluated in the context of atmospheres which are "products" based on a multi-sensory, atmospheric and as such a holistic experience (Thibaud, 2011).

Case Silence

It was assumed in the development project *Silence and Listening as Resources of Tourism Expertise in North Karelia,* based on information from Chinese tourism experts as well as market research results of the national tourism organization of Finland, that the silent environment would be the main pull factor for the Chinese tourists to travel to Finland for an individual trip. The results of a study conducted among Chinese young people, born after 1990, show that 40 percent of this target group would like to travel to Nordic countries, with motivations referring to nature and peace and quiet (VisitFinland.com, 2015). Hence, two separate groups of Chinese young tourists were invited to visit North Karelia during 2014–2015 to test and experience a packaged "silence travel tour", which had been developed together with the entrepreneurs and researchers during the project. Both groups consisted of five Chinese, one man and four women in each group. They all were 28–31 years old and belonged to a Chinese consumer segment called "Tuhao" (New Rich, 土豪) (Hulme, 2014), which is one of the main target groups that are supposed to be the most interested in silence travel services. All participants in the test groups had a profession somehow connected to the tourism business, which enabled them to act in multiple roles, but first of all as an ordinary customer. During the trips, the participants were interviewed during and after each service module in order to increase understanding of the suitability of different service modules as part of a "silence travel tour". The Chinese assistant working in the project participated as a guide and interpreter, and answered the questions on their part.

Additionally, the project personnel were aware that for the test groups silence would be exotic and tempting, but at the same time also mysterious or even potentially frightening. During the trips, the perceptions and appreciation of silence changed when traveling to a quiet place and in different silent areas. The first important notion of the testing was that participants suggested that the daily programs should include more breaks and have a slower tempo. The first meeting with a silent place was experienced as encouraging, tempting to return to the place again. For many, it was the first step to experience how easily the ostensible "emptiness" gave space to rich perceptions and meanings and created a pleasant atmosphere and feeling of timelessness. One female participant suggested:

> Slow down the tour and add more free time, walking and maybe just lying on the lake shore, or in the forest to see the sky. Listening to the environment, this is something that makes me feel the silence inside and outside. Walking to a destination and focusing on the steps makes me feel hurried; it is not possible for me to calm down. But sitting in a natural environment would be the silence moment for me. During the sunny day, the sky and clouds here are very special.

Most of the customers appreciated and even wished to have more guidance on different types of "silent" activities helping them to reach a silent mood. One of the ladies commented:

> Further interpretation of its [activity] meaning by a professional guide would be needed, how the visitors could reflect on the inner self, how to recognize themselves in silence, find their spirituality. You should educate visitors on how to keep a calm mind in the busy city life, how to do self-decompression and regulation. Meditation and yoga can also carry out activities in nature.

The participants were asked about the suitability of different services in the "silence travel tour", which included during the winter trip, ice fishing, preparing salmon on a fire in a Finnish teepee, different saunas and ice swimming, cross country skiing, animal watching and a drum healing session. The summer trip included, for example, wild herb picking, slow forest walks with different themes (surviving in nature, hearing and other senses, quiet sitting moments in natural places, mushroom and berry picking, watching a sunset from a high place), a visit to a place which echoes and fishing in a small lake. One female visitor commented:

> Ice fishing is too exotic and exiting, but if tourists have a little bit longer time to do ice fishing, part of it could be silence travel product. But it is important to consider if a silence product needs to let the tourists to keep silent?

For Chinese it is not "natural" to keep silent. It would be worth considering, what is the bound between acoustic travel package and silence travel package? Is it possible to mix them together?

Most of the Chinese visitors were from big cities of China. Some of them had never seen blue sky and the idea of fresh air was exotic and new for them. For the researcher, sharing a tent one summer night with a young radio reporter from Hong Kong was a refreshing experience. She was extremely eager to wake up early and experience the sun rise, but a cloudy morning came as a disappointment. However, listening to the wind in a warm summer night made sleeping during the short night very exciting. The customers also gave suggestions on how to improve the program:

'Wild animal experiencing' may be a better product name than 'wild animal watching'. It is very hard to see wild animals. Tourists would be very disappointed when coming only for 'watching' them. But listening to wild animal is much more possible! Walking silently and slowly in the forest gives possibility to listen to different sounds of animals. When a sound appears, guide shows the picture of the animal to the tourists. It would supply the real experience of wild animal and forest. In case the tourists would not see wild animal during the tour they would still listen to them. If the animals do appear that would be a big surprise!

To sum up, the activities enforcing and preserving the silent atmosphere can be varied. The secret of applying silence as an attraction lies in creating stories, meditative working, designing the surroundings, giving space and time to enjoy the stories, sharing experiences, listening to one's bodily responses to existing elements such as temperature, humidity, in nature or in the sauna, smells of the flora and surprising sounds. The subtle tunes of the sound world create an intimate ambience.

Japanese Case

The second collaborative project was with nature tourism enterprises and the university. The aim was to develop service modules that could be included in a Forest wellbeing packaged tour for Japanese tourists. Desk research, focus group interviews and virtual testing phases (cf. Konu, 2015b) were first implemented, aiming to increase understanding of the needs and expectations of the target group. Based on the results of these phases, a one-week package tour was created together with the project personnel and the entrepreneurs. A Japanese tourist group of eight participants and two representatives of a tour operator were invited to participate on a test trip to experience a forest-based wellbeing tourism trip. An ethnographic study including participatory observation, questionnaires and interviews was conducted in order to increase understanding about the expectations and experiences of the participants (cf. Konu, 2015a).

After a long flight the itinerary at the destination included a visit to the spa followed by dinner. During the first day the guests went on a two-and-a half-hour walk in the Koli National Park. In the afternoon they visited a farm, which operates in a sustainable and organic manner. The next day was dedicated to preparation of local "superfood" based on ingredients from the natural environment. The third day was dedicated to nature-based activities such as hiking, canoeing, lunch by the camp fire and finally traditional sauna bathing. The fourth day contained educational activities such as visits to a botanic garden, forest research institute, arts and handicrafts quarters as well as a local winery.

Trip activities that were connected to nature and forests (e.g. hiking, kayaking and guided tours including "silent walks" and "nature as an energizer") were considered the highlight of the journey according to customer comments. One Japanese twenty-year-old woman commented as follows:

> The National Park was 'expansive' and open, and the trees did not grow as a thicket. Hence the atmosphere was really soothing and you could stay there at one's leisure. It made me feel healthier and even if the total schedule is rather tight we got to spend a long time there [in the forest]. The forest made me feel calm and energized.

Exercises focusing on "being in the moment", experiencing nature with time, silence and the fact that being in nature and the nature activities were not just simply considered as activities to be carried out (e.g. hike fast from one place to another), were seen as strengths of the nature activities. Experiencing nature by using all of their senses were recorded as very extraordinary and positive, and giving the participants a feeling of being empowered and taking part in therapeutic practices resulted in very powerful feelings for some test customers.

> I could feel with all my senses the life force of the nature and I felt so empowered.
>
> a woman, 60 years' old

> It was more like forest therapy than hiking in the forest.
>
> a man, 50 years' old

One service module included cooking with mushrooms and other ingredients that were harvested by the customers themselves from the forest. Here many of the test customers viewed the cooking *per se* as an experience. A 60-year-old woman talked a lot about cooking:

> Cooking in [the location] and making Karelian pies were the best. It is rare that you get to experience cooking in another country.

Other customers seemed to appreciate more the experience of tasting and gathering berries. A twenty-year-old woman said:

This was the most beautiful and mysterious place I have visited. I had the possibility to collect beautiful mushrooms and it was fun that you can find berries everywhere. In addition, I liked the most that I could lie down and relax anywhere [in the forest]. Also I don't have words to tell how interesting it was having a lunch in the forest. I was paddling for the first time on a lake ...

Customers also emphasized the service firm's (the guide's) role in facilitating their experiences. The guide gave guidelines and introduced possibilities related to how customers can interact and experience nature by using all of their senses. The customers valued good guidance, and this was mentioned several times when discussing forest activities:

The guide who guided us to the place where we had lunch was extremely good. Walking without talking is wonderful.

woman, 47 years' old

... In addition I had the possibility to get in touch with nature and refresh myself with the help and the guidance of the guide.

woman, 20 years' old

Two customers who were horticultural therapists wanted to visit plants and gardens of local people in addition to the botanical gardens that were included to the trip. One customer commented that instead of visiting the botanical garden they would have preferred seeing only the allotment area next to it:

I think that the visit to the botanic garden was unnecessary. I think that the private gardens close to church and the allotment area close to botanical garden were much more worth to see. Many Japanese housewives enjoy gardening. You should show Japanese the ways how people enjoy gardening here.

woman, 60 years' old

The researcher as well felt very relaxed during some exercises:

I really felt relaxing and calming down when I was lying on the rock with my eyes closed at the same time feeling the soft breeze and sun on my face. I heard just the wind. During this exercise I felt very relaxed and was surprised that I did not think anything else but that particular moment.

The Japanese customers highly valued the activities which took place in forest environment such as "a silent walk" and "feel nature as an energizer". The forests were seen to have a soothing and calming effect. Being in the moment, having time to experience the forest with all senses, and silence were the things that were appreciated the most. The guided activities also helped the Japanese customers to experience the forest environment with all senses which infused very strong positive emotions among the customers.

Conclusions

It has been stated that nature-based tourism is growing even faster than the tourism industry in general (Mehmetoglu, 2005). Travelling to remote and exotic places seems to have become almost a "life-necessity" for many people with reasonable income (Chen et al., 2016) and the demand for nature experiences is apparent globally (Cohen, 2008). Nordic people, at least the elderly, are used to free recreation in nature, and have quite easy access to the forests, lakes and mountains. Nordic countries are remote and cold even from the European perspective and taking shorter or longer walks in a more or less challenging terrain is a typical activity for older European tourists (Chen, Wang & Prebensen, 2016). Hence, nature-based tourism is often seen as tourism full of adventure and/or physical effort.

Nevertheless, as a nature-based tourism entrepreneur states in the article by Komppula (2006), "most of the products that sell well, are easy: cooking coffee and making sausages and pancakes by the fire" (p. 146). This is in accordance with the findings of this study, which indicate that very simple things, like experiencing nature with all senses, and especially feeling the sounds of silence can be a refreshing and rejuvenating experience for those who live their everyday lives in hectic environments. It is easy to recognize that the elements of the silent soundscape consists of natural sounds of the wind in the leaves of the plants, or just tree trunks and branches, in hay or waves on the shore. These elements belong to the quiet natural environment according to descriptions of the participants in all test groups, indicating that tourism revolving around silence could be an attraction in itself for Finland.

Tourism professionals should pay attention to the pace of the itinerary, and as noted in these case studies, give tourists an opportunity to take their time and enjoy the silence in nature without a tight schedule. This also supports the findings of Komppula and Konu (2012) who found that wellbeing tourists expect to relax, enjoy the opportunity to escape from daily routines and, on the other hand, have a physically activating break. However, in this study "physically activating" focuses more on experiencing nature with all senses instead of just carrying out physical exercises.

The cases show that the members of the test groups did appreciate the active role of the guides in enabling the nature experience by facilitating opportunities to see, hear, taste, smell and feel, and explaining the sources of the different experiences for the tourists. The case studies also showed that the tourists had diverse positive experiences in the forest environment and the forests had a soothing and calming effect helping them to gain a silent mood. This supports the findings of previous studies (Lee et al., 2009; Li, 2010; Morita et al., 2007; Morita et al., 2011; Ohtsuka et al., 1998; Park et al., 2008; Tsunetsugu et al., 2010) showing that being in touch with nature may increase customers' subjectively experienced wellbeing.

References

Ampuja, O. & Peltomaa, M. (Eds.). (2014). *Huutoja hiljaisuuteen. Ihminen ääniympäristössä.* Tampere: Gaudeamus.

Chen, J., Wang, W. & Prebensen, N. (2016). Travel companions and activity preferences of nature-based tourists. *Tourism Review,* 71(1), available at http://dx.doi.org/10.1108/TR-06-2015-0024.

Cohen, E. (2008). The changing faces of contemporary tourism. *Society,* 45(4), 330–333.

Finnish Tourist Board (2009). *Border Interview Survey: Foreign Visitors in Finland 2008.* Finnish Tourist Board MEK A: 164.

Gössling, S. & Hultman, J. (2006). An introduction to ecotourism in Scandinavia. In S. Gössling & J. Hultman (Eds.), *Ecotourism in Scandinavia: Lessons in Theory and Practice* (pp. 1–9). Ecotourism series 4. Wallingford: CABI.

Hulme, A. (2014). *The Changing Landscape of China's Consumerism.* Oxford: Chandos Publishing.

Järviluoma, H., Kytö, M., Truax, B., Uimonen, H. & Vikman, N. (Eds.) (2009a). *Acoustic Environments in Change.* Tampere: TAMK University of Applied Sciences. Tampereen ammattikorkeakoulun julkaisuja Sarja A, Tutkimuksia; 13. Kirjallisuuden ja kulttuurin tutkimuksia/Joensuun yliopisto, humanistinen tiedekunta; 14.

Järviluoma, H., Kytö, M., Uimonen, H. & Vikman, N. (2009b). Soundscapes in change: From 1975 to 2000. In H. Järviluoma, M. Kytö, B. Truax, H. Uimonen & N. Vikman. (Eds.), *Acoustic Environments in Change.* Tampere: TAMK University of Applied Sciences. Tampereen ammattikorkeakoulun julkaisuja Sarja A, Tutkimuksia; 13. Kirjallisuuden ja kulttuurin tutkimuksia/Joensuun yliopisto, humanistinen tiedekunta; 14.

Komppula, R. (2006). Developing the quality of a tourist experience product in the case of nature-based activity services. *Scandinavian Journal of Hospitality and Tourism,* 6(2), 136–149.

Komppula, R. & Konu, H. (2012). Do wellbeing tourists expect memorable experiences? In M. Kozak & N. Kozak (Eds.), *Proceedings Book of 6th World Conference for Graduate Research in Tourism, Hospitality and Leisure* (pp. 462–474). Anatolia, Ankara, Turkey.

Konu, H. (2015a). Developing a forest-based wellbeing tourism product together with customers: An ethnographic approach. *Tourism Management,* 49, 1–16.

Konu, H. (2015b). Developing forest-based wellbeing tourism products by using virtual product testing. *ANATOLIA,* 26(1), 99–102. DOI:10.1080/13032917.2014.921633.

Konu, H. & Laukkanen, T. (2010). Predictors of tourists' wellbeing holiday intentions in Finland. *Journal of Hospitality and Tourism Management,* 17, 144–149.

Konu, H., Tuohino, A. & Komppula, R. (2010). Lake Wellness: A practical example of a New Service Development (NSV) concept in tourism industry. *Journal of Vacation Marketing,* 16(2),125–139.

Korpela, K. M., Ylen, M., Tyrväinen, L. & Silvennoinen, H. (2010). Favorite green, waterside and urban environments, restorative experiences and perceived health in Finland. *Health Promotion International,* 25(2), 200–209.

Korpela, K., Borodulin, K., Neuvonen, M., Paronen, O. & Tyrväinen, L. (2014). Analyzing the mediators between nature-based outdoor recreation and emotional well-being. *Journal of Environmental Psychology,* 37, 1–7.

Lappalainen, T. (Ed.) (1998). *Hiljaisuuden etsijöitä. Ihmisiä elämän perimmäisten kysymysten äärellä.* Juva: WSOY.

Lee, J., Park, B.J., Tsunetsugu, Y., Kagawa, T. & Miyazaki, Y. (2009). Restorative effects of viewing real forest landscapes, based on a comparison with urban landscapes. *Scandinavian Journal of Forest Research*, 24, 227–324.

Lee, J., Li, Q., Tyrväinen, L., Tsunetsugu,Y., Park, B.-J., Kagawa, T. & Miyazaki, Y. (2012). Nature therapy and preventive medicine. In J. Maddock (Ed.), *Public Health: Social and Behavioral Health*, InTech, available at www.intechopen.com/books/ public-health-social-and-behavioral-health/nature-therapy-and-preventivemedicine.

Li, Q. (2010). Effect of forest bathing trips on human immune function. *Environmental Health and Preventive Medicine*, 15, 9–17.

Manfredo, M. J., Driver, B. L. & Tarrant, M. A. (1996). Measuring leisure motivation: A meta-analysis of the recreation experience preference scales. *Journal of Leisure Research*, 28(3), 188–213.

Mehmetoglu, M. (2005). A case study of nature-based tourists: Specialists versus generalists. *Journal of Vacation Marketing*, 11(4), 357–369.

Moran, J. M., Kelley, W. M. & Heatherton, T. F. (2013). What can the organization of the brain's default mode network tell us about self-knowledge? *Frontiers in Human Neuroscience*, 7, 391, available at http://doi.org/10.3389/fnhum.2013.00391.

Morita, E., Fukuda, S., Nagano, J., Hamajima, N., Yamamoto, H. & Iwai, Y. (2007). Psychological effects of forest environments on healthy adults: Shinrin-yoku (forest-air bathing, walking) as possible method of stress reduction. *Public Health*, 121, 54–63.

Morita, E., Naito, M., Hishada, A., Wakai, K., Mori, A., Asai, Y., Okada, R., Kawai, S. & Hamajiva, N. (2011). No association between the frequency of forest walking and blood pressure levels of the prevalence of hypertension in a cross-sectional study of Japanese population. *Environmental Health Preventive Medicine*, 16(5), 299–306.

Ohtsuka, Y., Yabunaka, N. & Takayama, S. (1998). Shinrin-yoku (forest-air bathing and walking) effectively decreases blood glucose levels in diabetic patients. *International Journal of Biometeorol*, 41, 125–127.

Park, B. J., Tsunestugu, Y., Morikawa T., Ishii, H., Furuhashi S. & Hirano, H. (2008). Physiological effects of Shinrin-yoku (taking in the atmosphere of the forest) in mixed forest in Shinano Town, Japan. *Scandinavian Journal of Forest Research*, 23, 278–283.

Park, B. J., Tsunestugu, Y., Morikawa T., Kasetani, T., Kagawa, T. & Miyazaki, Y. (2009). Physiological effects of forest recreation in a young conifer forest in Hinokage Town, Japan. *Silva Fennica*, 43(2), 291–301.

Pesonen, J. & Komppula, R. (2010). Rural wellbeing tourism: Motivations and expectations. *Journal of Hospitality and Tourism Management*, 17(1), 150–158.

Sarlin, T. (Ed.) (2006). *Hiljaisuutta etsimässä*. Helsinki: Kirjapaja.

Schafer, R. M. (Ed.) (1977). *Five Village Soundscapes*. Vancouver: A.R.C. Publication.

Thibaud, J.-P. (2011). *A Sonic Paradigm of Urban Ambiances*. *Journal of Sonic Studies*, 1(1), 1–14.

Tsunestugu, Y., Park, B. J. & Yoshifumi, M. (2010). Trends in research related to "Shinrin-yoku" (taking in the forest atmosphere of forest bathing) in Japan. *Environmental Health and Preventive Medicine*, 15, 27–37.

Tyrväinen, L., Ojala, A., Korpela, K., Lanki, T., Tsunetsugu, Y. & Kagawa, T. (2014). The influence of urban green environments on stress relief measures: A field experiment. *Journal of Environmental Psychology*, 38, 1–9.

Uimonen, H. (2006). Mieluisat ja meluisat – ääniympäristön veto ja vastenmielisyys. In H. Järviluoma, A. Koivumäki, M. Kytö & H. Uimonen (Eds.), *Sata suomalaista ääni-maisemaa* [One hundred Finnish Soundscapes] (pp. 55–67). SKS:n toimituksia 1100. Helsinki: SKS.

Vikman, N. (2006). Suomalaisuuden sydänääniä luonnon helmassa. [Heartbeats of Finnishness in the Nature]. In H. Järviluoma, A. Koivumäki, M. Kytö & H. Uimonen (Eds.), *Sata suomalaista äänimaisemaa* [One hundred Finnish Soundscapes] (pp. 12–22). SKS: n toimituksia 1100. Helsinki: SKS.

Vikman, N. (2007). Eletty ääniympäristö. Pohjoisitalialaisen Cembran kylän kuulokulmat muutoksessa [The Lived Acoustic Environments: Cembra's Changing Points of Ear] (Doctoral dissertation). Retrieved from Acta Universitatis Tamperensis, available at http://urn.fi/urn:isbn:978-951-44-7126-1.

Vikman, N. (2009). Silence depends on muscle power: An ethnographic pilgrimage into a cultural interruption. 2003/2009. In H. Järviluoma, M. Kytö, B. Truax, H. Uimonen & N. Vikman. (Eds.), *Acoustic Environments in Change* (pp. 72–89). Tampere: TAMK University of Applied Sciences. Tampereen ammattikorkeakoulun julkaisuja Sarja A, Tutkimuksia; 13. Kirjallisuuden ja kulttuurin tutkimuksia/Joensuun yliopisto, humanistinen tiedekunta; 14.

Vikman, N. (2010). Alussa oli askel - katsaus kuuntelukävelyyn ympäristökulttuurin tutkimuksen metodina [In the beginning there was step. An overview to listening walks as a method of environmental-cultural research]. In J. Pöysä, H. Järviluoma & S. Vakimo, (Eds.), *Vaeltavat metodit* [Wandering Methods] (pp. 190–214). Suomen kansatietouden tutkijain seura, Kultaneito VIII, Joensuu.

VisitFinland.com (2015). Kiinan nuoret unelmoivat matkasta Pohjoismaihin [Young Chinese dream about a trip to the Nordic Countries], available at www.visitfinland.fi/news/kiinan-nuoret-unelmoivat-matkasta-pohjoismaihin/ (accessed May 18, 2016).

12 Nature Tourism in Germany's Protected Areas

Marius Mayer and Manuel Woltering

Introduction: Germany as Tourism Destination

Although internationally more renowned for its export industries, Germany is also an important tourism destination accounting for 166.8 million arrivals and 436.2 million overnight stays in 2015 (Destatis, 2016a). Together with an estimated amount of 2.95 billion day-trips (Harrer & Scherr, 2013) the tourism sector contributes directly to 4.4 percent of the gross value added (9.7 percent including indirect effects) supporting in total about 2.9 million jobs (BMWi & BTW, 2012). Incoming tourism in Germany has grown strongly in the last two decades increasing the share of overnights stays from 11 percent (1995) to 18.3 percent in 2015 (Destatis, 2016a). Incoming tourism concentrates on larger cities and cultural highlights situated in rural areas, e.g. Neuschwanstein Castle or the Romantic Road. Only a few nature-based tourism destinations attract a significant share of foreign visitors like Eifel, Sauerland or Schwarzwald due to their location close to the German border, as well as some destinations in the Alps (Kagermeier, 2016).

It is only in the last two decades that Germany has more actively promoted itself as nature(-based) destination. In 2005, the umbrella brand "National Natural Landscapes" (Nationale Naturlandschaften) was created to market tourism in national parks, biosphere reserves and nature parks (EUROPARC Deutschland, 2016). The German National Tourist Board even declared 2016 the year of "fascinating nature holidays in Germany" (DZT, 2015). Nature tourism thus plays an important role for German tourism, especially for the domestic market: it avoids international trips which further increase the negative balance of travel payments, but also acts as a relatively sustainable form of tourism due to shorter distances and less air travel.

The following chapter gives a state-of-the-art overview of nature(-based) tourism in Germany and Germany's protected areas (PA). A description of nature tourism in Germany in general followed by a presentation of PA categories provides the background. We then give an insight into Germany's PA tourism, provide visitation numbers, inform about the motivations of park visitors and the economic impact of PA tourism. A final section discusses the insights and draws conclusions.

Nature(-based) Tourism in Germany

It is widely acknowledged that nature(-based) tourism suffers from ambivalent definitions impeding comparability and consistent measurement (Fredman & Tyrväinen, 2011). The terms nature tourism (NT) and nature-based tourism (NBT) are often used interchangeably and mixed-up easily:

- In a wider sense, NT/NBT generally refers to all tourism activities in natural settings, to "any type of tourism that relies mainly on attractions directly related to the natural environment" (Weaver, 2001, p. 350).
- In a stricter sense the setting of NT/NBT is limited to "relatively undisturbed phenomenon of nature" (Valentine, 1992, p. 108), "natural resources in a wild or undeveloped form" (Goodwin, 1996, p. 287) and requires the motivations of "study and observation" (Newsome et al., 2002, p. 13) respectively "experiencing" (Strasdas, 2006, p. 56) those areas.

Depending on the understanding, the scope of NT/NBT in Germany varies considerably. The broad perspective encompasses all tourism except for urban tourism, cultural tourism in smaller towns and rural areas as well as health/spa tourism. In terms of activities, also beach tourism at the coasts or ski tourism is included. Nevertheless, it is difficult to assess the quantitative dimension of this NBT perspective for the following reasons:

- As the geographical location does not determine the form of tourism, only very rough assumptions could be made whether the overnight stays in one municipality or even a whole county fulfill this NBT definition. For instance, in the mid-mountain ranges tourists could either visit health/spa resorts or pursue outdoor activities like walking or hiking. Thus, tourism statistics cannot help in assessing the market volumes.
- Day-trips and local outdoor recreation are not covered by any official statistics, although considerable shares of both are nature-based.
- Neither leisure activities nor travel motives are reliable discriminating factors for NBT, because of multi-optional guests driven by manifold motives and pursuing different activities in space and time. Thus, there are no NBT tourists as such.

These methodological problems notwithstanding, in the following we provide an overview of the existing data to show the importance of NBT in the wider sense.

Zeiner & Harrer (2012) determine for 2006 that rural areas in Germany account for about two thirds of overnight stays and about 40 percent of day-trips. However, rural tourism does not equal NBT thus it is helpful to use a survey from the mid-1990s, which identified that 80 percent of non-urban tourism in Germany takes place in or adjacent to PA (Paesler, 1996).

As representative surveys show, "nature" and "nature experience" play important roles for the travel decisions of Germans. In 2015, 28 percent of the holidays (longer than five days) of the German speaking population were "nature holidays"

(Natururlaub) if multiple responses were considered (domestic holidays at 36 percent in 2011) (FUR, 2016, p. 4; Porzelt, 2012, p. 172), and 7 percent if only the main travel motive is taken into account (FUR, 2014, p. 46 ff.). Holidays and nature experience are closely linked for many Germans: 53 percent name the travel motive "experience nature (beautiful landscapes, pure air, and clean water)" as very important, 43 percent healthy climate and 16 percent to get out of polluted air (FUR, 2013). According to another representative survey about the importance of offers in holiday destinations, 66 percent of the respondents stated that nature experience offers like guided hikes, animal observations etc. were important or even very important. Those offers were deemed more important than cultural offers (63 percent), wellness (56 percent) or childcare (44 percent) (Job et al., 2013, p. 99).

Concerning day-trips in Germany, Harrer & Scherr (2013) report that the third most important main reason for day-trips are specific activities like hiking, swimming, surfing or skiing with 12.4 percent or 302.8 million day-trips. Overall, 27.6 percent or 786.5 million day-trips are made in rural areas (defined here as municipalities with less than 20,000 inhabitants). This proves that NBT is an important market segment also for day-trips.

The second, narrower perspective on NT focuses on German protected areas (PA). Nowadays, most NT destinations in Germany are located inside or nearby PA. This encompasses the seaside resorts at the North and Baltic Sea and its islands (part of the three Wadden Sea national parks and two national parks on the shores of the Baltic Sea). Furthermore, destinations in the mid-mountain and alpine ranges also have high shares of PA. These facts suit the importance of unspoiled nature and less polluted environments as travel motives. However, the majority of these PA have been designated after tourism development had been in place for decades (Woltering, 2012). Thus, not all NT activities in these destinations can be assigned to PA.

Protected Areas in Germany: An Overview

The history of PA and thus NT in a stricter sense in Germany differs considerably from North America. Due to the long cultural history and the high population density, there are only very few areas with pristine nature in Germany (Figure 12.1).

Most areas are cultural landscapes strongly influenced by human activities (Jäger, 1994). The German conservation movement started in the 19th century as a reaction to the consequences of the fast industrialization of landscapes and environment. In contrast to the North American example of the national park idea protecting vast unspoiled wilderness, the focus remained on small-scale protection units. Today more than 8,600 nature conservation areas are evidence of this fact; more than 60 percent are smaller than 50 ha (BfN, 2016). It was only one decade after the Second World War that large-scale protected areas (defined here as covering >10,000 ha and being managed by an institution of its own) were finally introduced in Germany with the creation of the first nature park (Naturpark) in 1957. The first national park was not designated before 1970 in the Bavarian Forest (Figure 12.2).

Figure 12.1 Guided Tour through the Wadden Sea in Lower Saxony Wadden Sea National Park, by Marius Mayer, by Marius Mayer

Figure 12.2 Hiking Trail through Dead Wood Areas in Bavarian Forest National Park, by Marius Mayer, by Marius Mayer

Table 12.1 Protected area categories in Germany*

Category	Number	Terrestrial Area (ha)	Share of Terrestrial area (%)
Large Scale with Full-Time Administration			
National Parks	16	214,558	0.6
Biosphere Reserves	17 (15 UNESCO)	1,311,636	3.7
Nature Parks	103	9,946,967	27.8
Small Scale (predominantly) with no Full-Time Administration			
Nature Conservation Areas	8,676	1,378,140	3.9
Flora-Fauna-Habitat-Areas	4,606	3,323.321	9.3
Special Protected Areas for Birds	740	4,009,604	11.2
Landscape Protection Areas	8,531	10,150,656****	27.9
National Nature Monuments**	–	–	–
Natural Monuments***	–	–	–
Protected Landscape Components**	–	–	–

Source: Bundesamt für Naturschutz (BfN), 2016, slightly changed.

Notes

* Some categories overlap and it is therefore not possible to add them all in order to calculate the grand total.
** Usually very small-scale phenomena without nationwide inventory overviews.
*** New type with no representative until now.
**** 2011 values.

Over time, 10 different PA categories developed (Table 12.1), which often overlap, i.e. national parks can be biosphere reserves at the same time. As the large-scale PA play the most important role for NT/NBT due to their size, attractiveness, management and marketing resources, the remainder of this section is devoted to their presentation and nexus with tourism:

National Parks (NLP)

Compared to North America, the history of NLP in Germany is very short. 12 out of 16 NLP have only been designated since 1990. The legal mandate of NLP is to protect endemic species and ecological integrity on large-scale territories of mostly pristine character. As long as this mission is not compromised, NLP are open to scientific research, environmental education and to the experience of nature for the general public (BNatSchG, 2009, §24). Beyond this priority of protection, however, the designation of NLP more often than not also follows political rationales of attracting tourists to peripheral regions and promoting regional development (Mayer et al., 2010). Many German NLP are so-called "development NLP", which means that they still have to be developed towards natural ecosystem dynamics by giving up human use like forestry, fisheries, etc. (Figure 12.2). Only small shares are already "real" wilderness. Figure 12.3 shows that German NLP are located in peripheral regions with comparably low economic power, either squeezed to the country's borders or positioned in remote highlands. However,

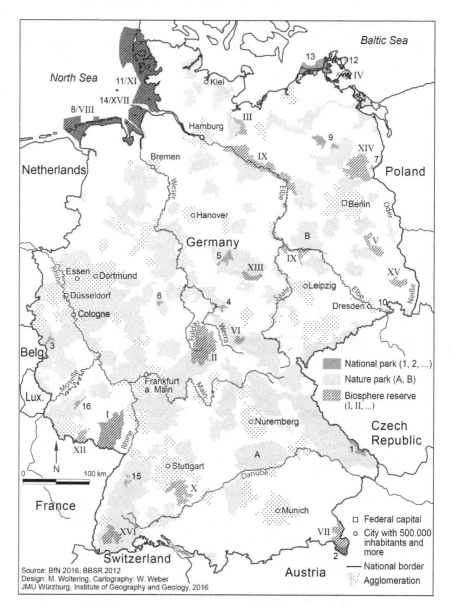

Figure 12.3 Large-scale Protected Areas in Germany

Source: own design.

this remoteness and structural weakness are a crucial precondition to have at least some natural landscapes preserved.

Nature Parks (NP)

In contrast to the NLP, NP and BR focus on cultural landscapes and their preservation. They are also permanently inhabited. According to BNatSchG (2009, §27) NP aim at two major goals: First, the conservation, development or restoration of cultural landscapes characterized by diverse uses. Second, NP are regarded as particularly suitable for recreational purposes because of their landscape assets and are areas in which sustainable tourism should be encouraged to foster sustainable regional development. In contrast to NLP, many NP are situated near agglomerations (Figure 12.3) and were intended to supply outdoor recreation possibilities. These NP are predominantly visited by day-trippers. A second large group covers nearly all low- and mid-mountain ranges in Germany and are characterized by overnight NBT in the broad sense (see also Job & Metzler, 2006). Compared to their ambitious tasks the financial and personal resources of most NP are weak, especially in contrast to NLP (Mayer, 2013, p. 465).

Biosphere Reserves (BR)

Since 1979 UNESCO biosphere reserves exist in Germany. BR are characterized by a broader approach of being model regions for sustainable development (Blab, 2006). Interestingly, their legal mandate does not mention recreation or tourism promotion at all, but stresses the "primary purpose of conserving, developing or restoring landscapes shaped by traditional, diverse forms of use", "ways of developing and testing forms of economic activity that are especially conserving of natural resources" as well as "purposes of research, of observation of nature and landscape and of education for sustainable development" (BNatSchG, 2009, §25). However, as Job et al. (2013, p. 15) show, NBT activities are widely used by BR managements to foster regional development and to promote regional agricultural or artisanal products.

Tourism in Germany's Large-scale Protected Areas

Representative Surveys

Representative population surveys provide a first approximation of the NBT potential of German PA. In 2010, 14 percent of the respondents stated that the national natural landscapes (NLP, BR, NP) play a very important and rather important (36 percent) role for their destination choice (Job et al., 2013, p. 99). In 2011/12, Job et al. (2013, p. 107 ff.) revealed rather weak spontaneous, i.e. unsupported knowledge of national natural landscape categories: 5.7 percent named NLP, 5.6 percent NP and 5.7 percent BR. Not surprisingly, the aided awareness of the PA categories is much higher: 97.7 percent know NLP, 89.5 percent NP, 51.8 percent BR but only 18 percent the umbrella brand "national natural landscapes". 54 percent of the respondents know at least one German NLP, 17.8 percent have visited one, while only 18.5 percent know a German BR and 9.2 percent have visited one. In total, nearly 31 percent of the German population regard NLP as potential holiday and 36 percent as potential day-trip destinations. The respective shares for BR are considerably lower with 8 percent and 13 percent.

Official Tourism Statistics

In order to estimate the quantitative dimension of NT in German NLP and BR official tourism statistics could be used (Destatis, 2016b). By applying a GIS query combining the PA and municipalities we identified the municipalities lying in PA, sharing some parts of their area with PA or directly bordering PA. We thus follow the definition of NLP-destinations by Hannemann and Job (2003).

In 2014, the 203 NLP-municipalities accounted for 7.88 million guests with 34.37 million overnight stays. This corresponds to nationwide shares of 4.9 percent respectively 8.1 percent. In the 690 BR-municipalities 10.76 million arrivals (6.7 percent) and 43.79 million overnight stays (10.3 percent) were counted.

However, these results have to be interpreted with caution due to the following restrictions:

- They do not include day-trippers and local outdoor recreationists.
- Not every person staying overnight is also a NT/NBT (the motivations and activities could be differing, e.g. visiting family/friends, business trips etc.) and/or does actually visit the PA itself.
- Non-commercial accommodations like holiday cottages, apartments and small inns with less than 10 beds are not covered by official tourism statistics. Especially in the rural PA destinations this excludes a considerable share of guests.
- Both values for NLP and BR should not be added up in any case because of the huge overlap of both PA categories. If one accounts for this fact and eliminates double values, then 15.1 million arrivals (9.4 percent) and 59.5 million overnight stays (14.0 percent) are counted in 804 German NLP and BR municipalities.

Economic impact of PA tourism in Germany

Due to negative attitudes towards PA by local populations (Ruschkowski & Mayer, 2011) there is a trend to highlight the economic effects of PA tourism. Economic impact studies face major difficulties: Firstly, Germany has a free access policy for PA resulting in a lack of visitor data (see above). Especially in BR and NP such figures are hard to obtain due to locals living inside the PA. Secondly, data on tourism expenditures are rare and those available are not representative for PA. Thus, costly field research including extensive visitor counting and surveying is required.

Funded by the German Federal Ministry of Environment, Job et al. (2003, 2005, 2009, 2013) established a standardized procedure for estimating the economic impact of tourism in large-scale PA and undertook various case studies in all types of PA. Table 12.2 gives an overview of the key findings. The results show that many large-scale PA in Germany are important tourism attractions which generate considerable regional economic impact.

The visitor days and structure as key parameters for economic impact studies are influenced by the location of PA with regard to the agglomerations: The distance between potential source regions and the PA is crucial. For example, Bavarian Forest NLP with its long distances to major cities is dominated by overnight visitors, whereas NLP Eifel south of the Rhein-Ruhr megalopolis is highly frequented by day-trippers (Woltering, 2012). In total, extrapolated for all German NLP there are about 50.9 million visitor days p.a. (as for 2012). The two Wadden Sea NLP dominate, constituting about 80 percent. The extrapolated results for all German BR total 65.3 million visitor days per year (Mayer & Job, 2014, p. 83; Job et al., 2013, p. 97). For the 103 NP there are not even rough estimates of the total visitation volume.

All German NLP generated a gross turnover of EUR 2.1 billion in 2012, showing huge variability and leading to an income equivalent of around 69,250 persons (Woltering, 2012, p. 235). All German BR create an extrapolated amount of EUR 2.94 billion gross turnover with income equivalents of approximately 86,200 persons (Job et al., 2013, p. 97). The high values of the two Wadden Sea NLP and Southeast Rügen BR can be explained by the fact that all three are coastal areas with a long tradition as destinations for beach/spa tourism and were designated as PA only recently. Therefore, it makes sense to assess the importance of the PA for visitors' travel motivation. Knowledge about the status as PA and its relevance for visitation is analyzed with the help of several successive questions (see Figure 12.4).

Depending on a region's history of tourism development the PA status represents the main visiting reason for a certain proportion of guests. These can be termed as visitors with a high PA affinity (VHPAA). Among the NLP the Bavarian Forest achieved the highest value with a share of 45.8 percent VHPAA, followed by the Lower Oder Valley with 31.6 percent while the Lower Saxony Wadden Sea reaches only 10.9 percent because of its beach/spa tourism tradition. For the BR these results are a little lower: Schaalsee with its relatively short tourism history shows the highest share of VHPAA (21.5 percent). The Rhön has a share of 13.7 percent whereas Southeast Rügen reaches only 4.9 percent. This means that only this small share of visitors would not come to the region if the BR did not exist.

Regarding this core group of VHPAA (which could also be interpreted as NT in the stricter sense because they are motivated by the PA status) the results of the economic impact analysis have to be adapted: Overall, for all NLP, the average share of VHPAA is 20.6 percent leading to 10.5 million visitor days and gross turnover of EUR 431 million p.a. The total income from tourism for the twelve NLP analyzed totals EUR 183.1 million for the VHPAA and EUR 1.196 billion respectively for all NLP visitors (Mayer & Job, 2014, p. 83). For the BR the

Table 12.2 Tourism Indicators for Selected German National Parks, Biosphere Reserves and Nature Parks (numbers and letters refer to Fig. 12.1)

Name	Area [ha]	Designation Year	Survey Year	Visitor Days [Million]	Share of Day Trippers [%]	Share of Foreign Visitors [%]	Share of Visitors with High PA Affinity [%]	Average Spending per Person and Day [€]	Gross Turnover all visitors [Million €]	Income Equivalent all visitors [Person]
National Park										
1 Bavarian Forest	24,217	1970	2007	0.76	33.0	3.8	45.8	36.57	27.8	904
2 Berchtesgaden	20,804	1978	2002	1.13	23.0	–	10.1	44.27	4.6*	206*
3 Eifel	10,770	2004	2007	0.45	76.0	11.7	27.3	19.31	8.7	251
4 Hainich	7,513	1997	2007	0.29	76.0	1.4	40.7	17.25	5.0	168
5 Harz	24,732	1990/1994	2012/13	1.75	49.8	4.9	24.4	42.57	74.3	2,312
6 Kellerwald-Edersee	5,738	2004	2007	0.20	59.0	5.8	25.8	19.48	3.9	111
7 Lower Oder Valley	10,323	1995	2008	0.21	92.0	–	32.1	9.45	1.9	61
8 Lower Saxony Wadden Sea	345,000**	1986	2007	20.65	15.0	1.5	10.9	50.37	1,040.2	34,525
9 Müritz	32,200	1990	2004	0.39	39.0	–	43.7	34.30	13.4	628
10 Saxon Switzerland	9,350	1990	2009	1.71	46.0	6.3	28.8	34.30	58.7	1,878
11 Schleswig-Holstein Wadden Sea	441,500***	1985	2012/13	18.80	18.5	1.8	17.1	57.19	1,065.6	30,401
Biosphere Reserves										
I Palatinate Forest	180,969	1992	2011/12	5.72	60.6	3.6	3.5	38.20	229.0	5,271
II Rhön	243,323	1991	2010/11	6.37	68.1	1.0	13.7	45.57	185.6	4,786
III Schaalsee	31,000	2000	2011/12	0.49	82.4	0.7	21.5	22.97	11.6	336
IV Southeast Rügen	22,800	1991	2011/12	5.29	6.7	2.8	4.9	71.43	379.3	14,281
V Spree Forest	47,509	1991	2011/12	1.94	48.7	1.0	8.7	62.16	90.0	2,971
VI Vessertal-Thuringian Forest	17,081	1979	2010/11	0.49	64.1	6.7	11.1	24.89	12.7	392

Name	Area [ha]	Designation Year	Survey Year	Visitor Days [Million]	Share of Day Trippers [%]	Share of Foreign Visitors [%]	Share of Visitors with High PA Affinity [%]	Average Spending per Person and Day [€]	Gross Turnover all visitors [Million €]	Income Equivalent all visitors [Person]
Nature Parks										
A Altmühltal	296,617	1969	2004	0.91	63.0	–	15.3	22.80	20.7	483
B Hoher Fläming	82,718	1997	2004	0.30	83.0	–	4.1	20.60	6.2	211

* Data available just for visitors with high national park affinity; ** About 93.0 % water surface; *** About 97.7 % water surface.

PA in Fig. 1 but without data in Tab.2: National parks: 12 Jasmund; 13 Vorpommersche Boddenlandschaft; 14 Hamburgisches Wattenmeer; 15 Schwarzwald; 16 Hunsrück-Hochwald. Biosphere Reserves: VII: Berchtesgadener Land; VIII: Lower Saxony Wadden Sea; IX: Flusslandschaft Elbe; X: Schleswig-Holsteinisches Wattenmeer und Halligen; XII: Bliesgau; XIII: Karstlandschaft Südharz; XIV: Schorfheide-Chorin; XV: Oberlausitzer Heide- und Teichlandschaft; XVI: Schwarzwald; XVII: Hamburgisches Wattenmeer.

Source: Job et al., 2003, 2005, 2009, 2013; Woltering, 2012; Mayer & Job, 2014.

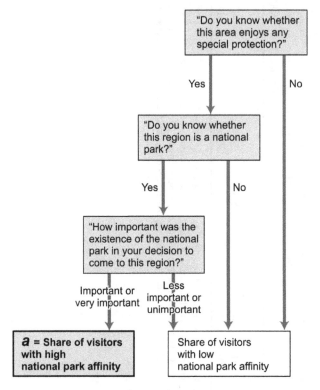

Figure 12.4   Decision Tree to Determine Visitors with High National Park Affinity
Source: Mayer et al. 2010: 75.

extrapolated results for all German BR reduce to 4.2 million visitor days motivated by the BR status p.a. generating gross turnover of about EUR 181.5 million and 5,261 income equivalents (Job et al., 2013, p. 97). Overall, the large gap of results for both PA categories indicates that there is still huge tourism potential, especially looking at those visitors attracted mostly by the PA. This holds also true for the two NP analysed where the share of VHPAA is very low (only 4.1 percent in Hoher Fläming).

Table 12.2 also reveals the marginal shares of foreign visitors to German large-scale PA. Only Eifel NLP registers more than 10 percent of incoming guests due to the proximity to Belgium and the Netherlands. The shares are even lower in the BR, potentially due to their limited prominence.

Conclusion

NT/NBT in Germany is more important than the common image as urban and cultural tourism destination suggests. However, it is not possible to determine the exact quantity of NT/NBT due to the varying understanding of NT/NBT, the lack of spatially explicit visitor, activity and travel motivation data and multi-optional tourists. Nevertheless, representative surveys prove the high importance of nature experiences for the travel decisions of Germans and the important role of PA as guarantors for these assets. These surveys also show that Germans are not especially familiar with the term BR and the PA umbrella brand of "national natural landscapes". These are not ideal preconditions for concise tourism marketing using these PA labels.

With 50.9 million visitor days in NLP and 65.3 million in BR the German large-scale PA are important although mostly domestic destinations. However, only relatively small shares of these visitors are actually motivated by the PA categories in the first place. This shows that NT in the strict sense are in Germany also consists of a rather limited core group of nature aficionados, while the majority of PA visitors might have visited the places anyway. Furthermore, the widely adopted NT definitions referring to "undisturbed, wild" nature only apply for the German NLP but not for the BR and NP focusing on cultural landscapes. Therefore, an understanding of NT better adapted to Central Europe might be useful, which includes also near-natural cultural landscapes and their traditional agricultural products (see Siegrist et al., 2015).

In general, the economic impact analyses of German PA tourism prove that PA play a very important role in NBT in the mostly peripheral rural PA regions in Germany, where they are often part of regional development strategies by stimulating tourism. Additionally, the considerable number of case studies in German PA using the same methodology serves as the base data necessary for a national socio-economic PA monitoring system but also for international comparisons (Woltering, 2012).

References

BfN (Bundesamt für Naturschutz) (2016). *Protected Areas*. URL: www.bfn.de/0308_gebietsschutz+M52087573ab0.html (03/21/2016).

Blab, J. (2006). Schutzgebiete in Deutschland – Entwicklung mit historischer Perspektive. *Natur und Landschaft*, 81(1), 8–11.

BNatSchG (Bundesnaturschutzgesetz, Gesetz über Naturschutz und Landschaftspflege) (2009). German Federal Law on Nature Conservation. Neufassung vom 29. Juli. Bundesgesetzblatt I: 2542. URL: www.bmub.bund.de/fileadmin/Daten_BMU/Download_PDF/Naturschutz/bnatschg_en_bf.pdf (03/31/2016).

Bundesministerium für Wirtschaft und Technologie (BMWi) & Bundesverband der Deutschen Tourismuswirtschaft (BTW) (2012). Wirtschaftsfaktor Tourismus Deutschland. Kurzfassung. Berlin. URL: www.bmwi.de/BMWi/Redaktion/PDF/Publikationen/wirtschaftsfaktor-tourismus-deutschland,property=pdf,bereich=bmwi2012,sprache=de,rwb=true.pdf (03/25/2016).

Destatis (Statistisches Bundesamt) (2016a). Ankünfte und Übernachtungen in Beherbergungsbetrieben: Deutschland, Monate, Wohnsitz der Gäste 1992-2015. URL: www-genesis.destatis.de/genesis/online Statistik 45412-0009 (03/20/2016).

— (2016b). Tourismus in Zahlen 2014. URL: www.destatis.de/DE/Publikationen/Thematisch/BinnenhandelGastgewerbeTourismus/Tourismus/TourismusinZahlen.html;jsessionid=ABF45DB2A2FDEE37E8303247448A1982.cae3 (03/20/2016).

Deutsche Zentrale für Tourismus e.V. (DZT) (2015). Themenkampagne 2016: "Faszination Natururlaub in Deutschland". URL: www.germany.travel/media/content/presse/de/pressemitteilungen_2015/06_PM_DZT_Natururlaub.pdf (03/25/2016).

EUROPARC Deutschland e.V. (2016). Nationale Naturlandschaften – unter einem Dach vereint. URL: www.nationale-naturlandschaften.de/ (03/25/2016).

Fredman, P., & Tyrväinen, L. (2011). Introduction. In P. Fredman & L. Tyrväinen (Eds.), *Frontiers in Nature-based Tourism: Lessons from Finland, Iceland, Norway and Sweden* (pp. 5–15). Abingdon: Routledge.

Forschungsgemeinschaft Urlaub und Reisen e.V. (FUR) (2013). Hauptsache "schönes Wetter"! Newsletter 10/2013. URL: www.fur.de/fileadmin/user_upload/Newsletter/Newsletter_Okt2013/RA-Newsletter10-2013_Urlaubsmotive.pdf (04/01/2016).

— (2014). Reiseanalyse 2014. Kurzfassung. Kiel.

— (2016). Erste ausgewählte Ergebnisse der 46. Reiseanalyse zur ITB 2016. URL: www.fur.de/fileadmin/user_upload/RA_2016/RA2016_Erste_Ergebnisse_DE.pdf (04/01/2016).

Goodwin, H. (1996). In Pursuit of Ecotourism. *Biodiversity and Conservation*, 5, 277–291.

Hannemann, T., & Job, H. (2003). Destination "Deutsche Nationalparke" als touristische Marke. *Tourism Review*, 58(2), 6–17.

Harrer, B., & Scherr, S. (2013). *Tagesreisen der Deutschen*. München: dwif.

Jäger, H. (1994). *Einführung in die Umweltgeschichte*. Darmstadt: WBG.

Job, H., & Metzler, D. (2006). Naturparke + Tourismus = Regionalentwicklung? *Natur und Landschaft*, 81(7), 355–361.

Job, H., Metzler, D., & Vogt, L. (2003). *Inwertsetzung alpiner Nationalparke. Eine regionalwirtschaftliche Analyse des Tourismus im Alpenpark Berchtesgaden*. Kallmünz/Regensburg: Lassleben.

Job, H., Woltering, M., & Harrer, B. (2009). *Regionalökonomische Effekte des Tourismus in deutschen Nationalparken*. Bonn-Bad Godesberg: Landwirtschaftsverlag.

Job, H., Kraus, F., Merlin, C., & Woltering, M. (2013). *Wirtschaftliche Effekte des Tourismus in Biosphärenreservaten Deutschlands*. Bonn-Bad Godesberg: Landwirtschaftsverlag.

Job, H., Harrer, B., Metzler, D., & Hajizadeh-Alamdary, D. (2005). *Ökonomische Effekte von Großschutzgebieten. Untersuchung der Bedeutung von Großschutzgebieten für den Tourismus und die wirtschaftliche Entwicklung der Region*. Bonn-Bad Godesberg: BfN.

Kagermeier, A. (2016). *Tourismusgeographie*. Konstanz: UVK.

Mayer, M. (2013). *Kosten und Nutzen des Nationalparks Bayerischer Wald. Eine ökonomische Bewertung unter Berücksichtigung von Forstwirtschaft und Tourismus*. München: Oekom.

Mayer, M., & Job, H. (2014). The Economics of Protected Areas – A European Perspective. *Zeitschrift für Wirtschaftsgeographie*, 58(2–3), 73–97.

Mayer, M., Müller, M., Woltering, M., Arnegger, J., & Job, H. (2010). The Economic Impact of Tourism in Six German National Parks. *Landscape and Urban Planning*, 97(2), 73–82.

Newsome, D., Moore, S. A., & Dowling, R. K. (2002). *Natural Area Tourism: Ecology, Impacts and Management*. Clevedon: Channel View.

Paesler, R. (1996). Regionalwirtschaftliche Auswirkungen der Ausweisung von Großschutzgebieten aus der Sicht des Tourismus. In P. Bartelheimer, E. Gundermann, E., M. Moog & M. Suda (Eds.), *Großschutzgebiete. Ökonomische und politische Aspekte* (pp. 57–71). München: LMU München.

Porzelt, M. (2012). Naturtourismus in Schutzgebieten am Beispiel der deutschen Naturparke. In H. Rein & A. Schuler (Eds.), *Tourismus im ländlichen Raum* (pp. 171–189). Wiesbaden: Gabler.

Ruschkowski, E. V., & Mayer, M. (2011). From Conflict to Partnership? Interactions between Protected Areas, Local Communities and Operators of Tourism Enterprises in Two German National Park Regions. *Journal of Tourism and Leisure Studies*, 17(2), 147–181.

Siegrist, D., Gessner, S., & Ketterer Bonnelame, L. (2015). *Naturnaher Tourismus. Qualitätsstandards für sanftes Reisen in den Alpen.* Bern: Haupt.

Strasdas, W. (2006). The Global Market for Nature-based Tourism. In H. Job & J. Li (Eds.), *Natural Heritage, Ecotourism and Sustainable Development* (pp. 55–64). Kallmünz/ Regensburg: Lassleben.

Valentine, P. S. (1992). Review: Nature-based Tourism. In B. Weiler & C. M. Hall (Eds.), *Special Interest Tourism* (pp. 105–127). London: Belhaven Press.

Weaver, D. B. (2001). Ecotourism as Mass Tourism? Contradiction or Reality? *Cornell Hotel and Restaurant Administration Quarterly*, April, 104–112.

Woltering, M. (2012). *Tourismus und Regionalentwicklung in deutschen Nationalparken.* Würzburg: Geographische Gesellschaft Würzburg.

Zeiner, M., & Harrer, B. (2012). Wirtschaftliche Bedeutung des Tourismus im ländlichen Raum. In H. Rein & A. Schuler (Eds.), *Tourismus im ländlichen Raum* (pp. 11–26). Wiesbaden: Gabler.

13 Governing Nature Tourism in Eastern and Southern Africa

René van der Duim, Jakomijn van Wijk and Machiel Lamers

Introduction

Conservation in sub-Saharan Africa has undergone significant changes. In recent decades, against the background of shifting global discourses on conservation and international development, conservation organisations, international development organisations, tourism businesses, state agencies and local communities in Africa have increasingly attempted to synthesize their diverging objectives to find new solutions for the protection of nature and wildlife outside state protected areas, often by developing nature tourism to generate livelihood opportunities. Whereas communities have long been excluded from such conservation work, they have become actively involved in conservation especially since the 1970s and 1980s (see also Hulme & Murphree, 2001; Suich, Child & Spencely, 2009). Moreover, conservation is increasingly underpinned by market logic. This chapter provides an overview of this transition in the governance of nature tourism by first describing the main logics in the conservation discourse over time. We next discuss four institutional arrangements for nature tourism in Africa – conservancies in Namibia, private game reserves (PGR) in South Africa, tourism conservation enterprises (TCE) in Kenya and Transfrontier Conservation Areas (TFCAs) – to illustrate how communal and private landowners have come to play a pivotal role in conservation on the one hand and how conservation increasingly is undergirded by neoliberal principles on the other (see also Van der Duim, Lamers & Van Wijk, 2015). After comparing these arrangements and highlighting the main internal and external challenges associated with these governance arrangements, we finalize with a conclusion.

Shifting Conservation Logics

Especially in colonial Africa, strictly protected game reserves became the backbone of conservation through the first half of the twentieth century (Adams, 2004). While these reserves became "a resort for gentleman hunters, whether traveller or colonial servant to experience hunt and kill 'wild' nature" (Adams & Hulme, 2001: 154), traditional subsistence hunting by pastoralists became illegal and was framed as "poaching" (Akama, 1996). Concerns about declining wildlife numbers led to the establishment of national parks in Africa from the 1940s onwards (Adams, 2004). The *conservation logic* thus promoted the protection of wildlife in designated areas like nature reserves and national parks from which local communities were excluded, ignoring their traditional rights and needs. This approach to conservation, that seeks to preserve wildlife and their habitat through forceful exclusion of local people who have traditionally relied on the environment in question for their livelihoods, is also known as "fortress conservation" (Brockington, Duffy & Igoe, 2008).

In situ protection of wildlife became contested in the 1970s. As Adams & Hulme (2001) argue, the social impact of protected areas began to be widely acknowledged in the 1970s and the idea that parks should be socially and economically inclusive slowly began to become part of mainstream conservation thinking. Wildlife still roamed outside national parks, causing human–wildlife conflicts, and the decrease of wildlife numbers made clear that community land was necessary to ensure healthy wildlife populations. Based on the idea that conservation and development could be simultaneous achieved, a community-based conservation and *development logic* became included in the conservation discourse (Hulme & Murphree, 2001; Suich et al., 2009; Van der Duim et al, 2015). At least on paper, communities became 'partners' rather than 'poachers' and people and parks became reconnected again, albeit this link was only indirectly established. Community involvement in conservation, aiming at 'sustainable use' and 'incentive-based conservation', was strengthened by means of Integrated Conservation and Development Projects (ICDPs) and Community-based Natural Resource Management (CBNRM) (Adams & Hutton, 2008). As part of these projects communities neighbouring national parks were 'pacified' through community projects like the building of water pumps, health clinics and schools and park revenue sharing programs. In many countries also tourism became an important tool for rural people to gain an economic interest. For instance, the community lodge Il Ngwesi was founded in Kenya in 1996 so as to increase the socio-economic benefits accruing from wildlife to park-neighbouring communities (e.g. Manyara & Jones, 2007; Zeppel, 2006).

However, many of these projects were very much dependent on external donor funding and involved communities lacked the entrepreneurial savvy to turn these enterprises into commercially viable businesses (Hulme & Murphree, 2001; Van der Duim, 2011). This set the stage for private sector involvement in conservation outside national parks and nature reserves. Contracts were established between communities and private parties that allowed the latter to run ecolodges on community land in exchange for sharing a percentage of the tourist dollars. As such, communities assumed the role of wildlife asset owners with wildlife paying its way through tourism. The conservation discourse was thus expanded with the *market logic*. Table 13.1 summarizes the three logics in the conservation discourse.

Table 13.1 Logics in the Conservation Discourse (adapted from Van Wijk, 2015)

	Conservation Logic	*Development Logic*	*Market Logic*
Value of wildlife	Intrinsic value	Economic value	Economic value
Role communities	Excluded	Beneficiary, partner & participant	Wildlife asset manager
Logic of community involvement	n.a.	Empowerment	Incentivize landowners for conservation
Dominant organizational form	National Parks and Nature Reserves on public land	Community lodges and other community based projects adjacent to national parks on communal land	Ecolodges managed by private party and owned by community on communal land
Key proponents	Wildlife Authorities Conservation NGOs	Development NGOs	Conservation NGOs Impact investors
Main benefit streams from tourism	Park entrance fees (flowing to government)	Tourism revenue sharing programs (percentage of park entry fees is shared with local villagers neighbouring parks)	Payment for services
		Payment for services (e.g. cultural tours) or products (e.g. handicraft shops)	Annual concession fee paid by private tourism operator to communal land owners
		Direct and indirect employment	Direct and indirect employment

Contemporary Institutional Arrangements in Africa

This section illustrates the inclusion of market logic and its related neoliberal principles in conservation by highlighting four institutional arrangements that have emerged in the 1990s (see Table 13.2) in eastern and southern Africa, namely conservancies in Namibia, tourism conservation enterprises (TCE) in Kenya, private game reserves (PGR) in South Africa and Transfrontier Conservation Areas (TFCAs). Their importance is well illustrated by the sometimes impressive growth in numbers. The total of conservancies increased from 1 in 1995 to 82 in 2015 (NACSO, 2015), the number of private game reserves from 10 in the 1960s to 11,600 in 2012 (van Hoven, 2015) and the total of AWF tourism conservation enterprises from 1 in 1991 to more than 60 in 2013 (AWF, 2014).

Conservancies

While the emergence of the conservancy regime in Namibia was a collective process, the government, supported by NGOs, has played a pivotal role in developing

Table 13.2 Overview of the Key Events in the Emergence of the Institutional Arrangements under Study (adapted from Van Wijk et al., 2015b: 242)

Institutional Arrangement	Birth of Arrangement	Main Driving Force/Project
Conservancies in Namibia	• 1992: first draft of conservancy policies developed • 1993: start of LIFE programme • 1995: first joint venture between Torra Conservancy and Wilderness Safaris • 1996: Nature Conservation Amendment Act • 1998: first four communal conservancies registered	• Coalition of government officials, NGO personnel and the new Minister of Wildlife, Conservation and Tourism • USAID's Living in a Finite Environment (LIFE) Programme
Tourism Conservation Enterprises in Kenya	• 1996: Il Ngwesi (community enterprise) • 2000: Koija Starbeds lodge • 2007: The Sanctuary at Ol Lentille • 2007: Satao Elerai lodge	• USAID's COBRA project (1992–1998) • USAID's CORE (1999–2005) • Funding by Embassy of the Kingdom of the Netherlands in Nairobi (2007–2014)
Private Game Reserves in South-Africa	• 1987: formal recognition of wildlife ranching as agricultural activity by Department of Agricultural Development	• Practice was ahead of policy, driven by economics (e.g. land with wildlife sold at higher prices than land without wildlife; some landowners already harvested wildlife to commercially produce biltong) • Changing discourse that promoted game ranching (in scientific and non-scientific magazines)
Transfrontier Conservation Areas	• 1997: foundation of Peace Parks Foundation • 2000: first TFCA opened (Kgalagadi) • 2007: MoU for the Selous-Niassa TFCA	• USD 260,000 grant by Anton Rupert, the President of the Southern African Nature Foundation • Peace Parks Foundation • German government, UNDP/GEF and other donors

and promoting conservancies. It introduced national legislation in 1996 that granted communal area residents' rights over wildlife and tourism on their land if a conservancy had been instated. A conservancy is an organizational form aimed at effectively managing common property resources like game within the area's geographical boundaries. For instance, a representative committee needs to be launched and methods for distributing benefit flows among community members should be well established (Jones, Diggle & Thouless, 2015). Conservancies are incentivized to protect the biodiversity and game on their land by accruing benefits from it. Many conservancies do so by contracting private sector parties to develop ecolodges on their land. This transition towards market-based conservation in Namibia was strongly supported by the US Agency for International Development (USAID), which became a central player in nature conservation in Africa in the 1980s (Corson, 2010). USAID's 1993 LIFE project supported the Namibian government in its efforts to develop the conservancy approach and still runs under the name LIFE Pus. At the end of 2014, 82 conservancies were registered covering almost 20 per cent of Namibia with over 180,000 residents (NACSO, 2015).

Tourism Conservation Enterprises (TCEs)

The institutional arrangement of tourism conservation enterprises (TCEs) emerged through a process of trial-and-error by the African Wildlife Foundation (AWF) to achieve its conservation mission. Again USAID played a pivotal role in the emergence of this arrangement through its COBRA and CORE projects of which AWF was a subcontractor (Van Wijk et al., 2015a). TCEs are partnerships between a community and private sector party brokered by AWF to generate direct benefit flows from wildlife to communities. Communities typically allow a private sector party to build a lodge and other tourism facilities on their land and manage it for a given period of time. The private sector incentivizes the community to protect the wildlife on their land for tourism by paying different kinds of fees like bed-night fees and conservation fees (Lamers et al., 2014; 2015). AWF has launched over 60 enterprises of which 65 per cent are tourism related and 35 per cent are related to agriculture and livestock management (AWF, 2014). These enterprises have collectively secured a significant amount of land for conservation. For instance, according to AWF, 73,000 hectares have been allocated to conservation through the launch of six TCEs (Pellis et al, 2014). Whereas CBNRM in Namibia is firmly rooted in national legislation, TCEs in Kenya lack such regulatory embedding. NGOs other than AWF have also welcomed the enterprise model to promote conservation on community land (Pellis et al., 2014). With the Kenyan government having neglected these developments for almost two decades, this has resulted in a large variety of community-related and wildlife-focused enterprises in Kenya. This divergence has only recently prompted the Kenyan government to look for ways to create a level playing field in the conservation enterprise sector (Pellis, Lamers & Van der Duim, 2015a).

Private Game Reserves (PGRs)

The institutional arrangement of private game reserves (PGRs) also emerged from the grass-roots level. South-African ranchers started to welcome wildlife on their land and began to commercially exploit the animals by producing biltong. This was an illegal practice at that time because wildlife ownership was not yet determined by where the wildlife was found (Van Hoven, 2015). The South-African government responded reactively to the developments by legalizing private ownership of wildlife in 1987. PGRs are governed by governmental regulations as well as professional standards established by trade associations. The PGR industry has grown significantly over time. There are 11,600 today which cover 18 per cent of the land surface. Collectively, this has led to a 40-fold increase in wildlife numbers in this era (Van Hoven, 2015).

Transfrontier Conservation Areas (TFCAs)

With the increasing pressure from, for example poaching, the loss of biodiversity, and the lack of funding to properly manage protected areas, in the late 1990s the need to augment protected areas beyond national parks and across countries was increasingly recognized. In 1997 the Peace Parks Foundation was founded and promoted the development of transfrontier conservation areas (TFCAs). TFCAs involve various states as well as non-state actors and are governed by international treaties. According to Hanks & Myburgh (2015), at present there are ten TFCAs in Africa with a signed Treaty of Memorandum of Understanding. Apart from conservation, an additional objective of TFCAs is the provision of ecosystem goods and services to Africa's rapidly growing human population. According to Hanks & Myburgh (2015) TFCAs certainly have the potential to open up a number of development opportunities, especially related to nature-based or wildlife-based tourism, including safari hunting. Although South Africa, Botswana and Namibia already have a reasonably well-developed tourist infrastructure, particularly Angola, Mozambique, Zambia and Zimbabwe, there is still a lot of room for the development of nature tourism.

Internal Challenges

With the exception of PGRs, where the ranch owner is the main decision-maker, the other arrangements are multi-actor arrangements. The involvement of parties with different interests, value frames and resources poses internal challenges of getting these parties to agree on conservation and development objectives, establish legitimate governance structures and achieve the set objectives (Van Wijk, Lamers & van der Duim, 2015b).

First, challenges emerge when negotiating and agreeing on conservation and development objectives. In order to streamline such negotiations, AWF has developed a tool book for establishing TCEs (AWF, 2011). While outlining procedures and designing formats were intended to advance uniform arrangements, in practice the enterprise model has been applied quite differently by different arrangements of actors across Kenya (Lamers et al., 2015). Similarly, in the case of Namibian conservancies, major differences exist in how communities and private sector parties collaborate. Jones et al. (2015) distinguish different joint venture models, varying from the conservancy owning and managing the lodge to the conservancy owning the lodge, but leaving the management to a private sector party. Such divergence indicates that institutional arrangements in conservation are tailor-made, and their establishment is thus time-consuming and costly. For instance, community mobilization may take at least one to two years, while providing and developing capacity for community institutes with management knowledge and skills in tourism, business and conservation may take many more years. Since private investors are not willing to finance such community mobilization and empowerment, donor funding is critical in the birth of such arrangements. Also in the establishment of TFCAs, general steps and milestones have been identified. Yet getting different parties on the same page is no easy feat. As Hanks and Myburgh (2015: 166) argue: "The establishment of TFCAs is a complex and time-consuming process, requiring intensive and extensive advocacy and facilitation work in all participating countries, with each having a sense of ownership of the whole process." Divergence among TFCAs also exists, as Noe (2015) points out. She argues that countries that are part of a TFCA differ in their tourism infrastructure, which creates significant differences in the revenues generated from tourism among these countries.

Second, once agreements on the objectives, the financial arrangements and the decision-making structures have been reached, the execution of these arrangements poses another set of challenges. With respect to TCEs, Lamers et al. (2014; 2015) show how communities and private sector parties may be in discord because of different expectations (see also Ahebwa et al., 2012; Nthiga, 2014). For example, despite agreements made to not graze with cattle or hunt in the conservation areas, some members of the community (or of other communities) might not be abiding by those rules. In these cases, some members of the community still perform the role of poacher, while the role of the entrepreneur is not always understood and valued by the community. This often leads to distrust between the entrepreneur and community, local political tensions and conflicts (Lamers et al., 2014; 2015). Similar challenges are also found among Namibian conservancies. For instance, drawing on a case study of the Tsiseb Conservancy, Lapeyre (2015) shows how issues of accountability, elite capture, weak community governance mechanisms and confusion about user rights amongst others hamper the efficacy of the conservancy. Pellis, Duineveld and Wagner (2015b) similarly show how conflicts have played a central role in the development of the Anabeb conservancy. On a transnational scale, TFCAs are formalized in MoUs that are signed by the governments involved, which are then codified in international treaties (Hanks and Myburgh, 2015). However, Noe (2015) points out that such agreements are often ambiguous when it comes to who has the authority and legitimacy to govern the cross-border space.

Third, the distribution of benefit flows from these conservation agreements poses major challenges (see Van der Duim et al., 2015). While in the case of PGRs, tourist dollars go to individual landowners, income generated through tourism in conservancies and TCEs is predominantly shared at the group level. This collective distribution of benefit flows is in some cases challenged by community members who would rather see benefit-sharing at the individual level or by those who ensure that they benefit disproportionally through corrupt behaviour (see also Ahebwa & van der Duim, 2013). The number of beneficiaries also differs greatly per arrangement. In Kenya, at the Koija Starbeds lodge (a TCE), tourism benefits have to be shared among 5,500 people, whilst at the Satao Elerai lodge there are only 638 beneficiaries (Lamers et al., 2015). Moreover, benefit-sharing comes with major governance challenges. The heterogeneity of the actors involved in, for example, conservancies or TCEs and the shifting power balances between these actors lie at the root of these challenges (see, for example, Ahebwa et al. 2012; Lamers et al. 2014; Van der Duim 2011). Besides governance challenges, community members may spend the income generated from tourism in such a way that it counters the conservation objectives. For instance, community members may buy more livestock, which may negatively affect the tourism product when the conservancy is overrun with goats and cows rather than wildlife. In the case of TCEs this clearly triggers tensions between tourism entrepreneurs and communities (see Lamers et. al., 2014). This requires continued facilitation from reliable trustworthy third parties like NGOs to safeguard the realization of conservation objectives, accountability and transparency, and maintain the permanency of the institutional arrangement. Especially related to TFCAs, critics like Noe (2015) even paint a much darker picture of the socio-economic benefits brought about by TFCAs. Her case study illustrates unfulfilled expectations, reflecting that conservation distributes both fortune and misfortune (see also Brockington et al., 2008).

External Challenges

Besides internal challenges a number of developments also pose external challenges to the governance of these arrangements, namely global market fluctuations, challenges related to climate change, developments in both non-consumptive and consumptive forms of tourism, governance and the growth of private sector capital for conservation (Van Wijk et al., 2015b).

First, in order to be financially sustainable, all of the institutional arrangements draw heavily on tourism. For instance, since 2005 the Namibian Tsiseb conservancy's operational costs for nature conservation have been fully covered through tourism (Lapeyre, 2015), and tourism is expected to be the core driver for economic development in TFCAs (Noe, 2015). However, tourism is a volatile market. For instance, Kenya has faced deadly terrorist attacks over the last two years which have led to a 25 per cent fall in visitor numbers, denting the country's tourism industry. Kenya lost a quarter of its visitors in the first five months of 2015 – 284,000 down from 381,000 in 2014 (Morris, 2015). The financial dependency of the discussed institutional arrangement for conservation and livelihood on tourism income makes them highly vulnerable with regard to global tourism market fluctuations.

Second and similarly, climate change may cause significant changes in tourism patterns. Gössling, Peeters & Scott (2008) argue that mitigation policies addressing the aviation industry's emissions eventually will alter the costs and mobility of traveling, which will have major repercussions for long-haul holiday destinations. At the same time climate variability and change is also likely to harm and alter the ecosystem services on which tourism depends (e.g. biodiversity, water, scenic landscape) and consequently might discourage tourism. However, some of the climate change mitigation policies, including REDD+, are gradually influencing existing institutional arrangements for natural resource use; in some countries carbon-related income is developing into a land-use option for landowners already involved in nature tourism (see for example AWF, 2012).

Third, research shows that over the past decades, support for trophy hunting as an incentive for conservation has significantly changed. Sport hunting plays a key role in South Africa and Namibia in particular. According to Van Hoven (2015), devolving the ownership of wildlife to private landowners and the related growth of sports hunting has positively contributed to wildlife populations. Recently Naidoo et al. (2016) evaluated financial and in-kind benefit streams from tourism and hunting in 77 conservancies in Namibia from 1998 to 2013. Based on data collected annually for all conservancies to characterize whether benefits were derived from hunting or tourism, they concluded that across all conservancies total benefits from hunting and tourism increased at roughly the same rate although conservancies typically started generating benefits from hunting within three years of formation as opposed to after six years for tourism. However, their research also indicated that a simulated ban on trophy hunting significantly reduced the number of conservancies that could cover their operating costs.

Whereas in South Africa, Namibia but also Tanzania sport hunting is propagated, in the birthplace of African trophy hunting, Kenya (Lindsey, Roulet & Romañach, 2007), sport hunting was banned in 1997. While in Uganda trophy hunting was reintroduced in 2001 (Ochieng, Ahebwa & Visseren-Hamakers, 2015), in Botswana, where hunting was central to Botswana's CBNRM work, it was outlawed in 2014. These shifting dynamics illustrate the lack of consent about hunting as a tool for conservation. The latent threat of radical policy change creates doubts about the balance between consumptive and/or non-consumptive forms of tourism and uncertainty for communities, investors and entrepreneurs involved in tourism–conservation–development arrangements.

Fourth and related, changes at one policy level may set in motion changes at other policy levels and vice versa. Coherently embedding institutional arrangements as discussed in this chapter in multiple institutional arenas increases their stability, as well as their resilience to external forces. But it may also create new and salient governance challenges (Lamers et al., 2014). Such governance complexities are also likely to increase and intensify in the future, if community members become more entrepreneurial.

Fifth, traditionally, government and donor funding and philanthropy have been the main sources of finance for conservation. To address the deficit in funding for conservation, private sector capital increasingly is considered crucial.

Gutman and Davidson (2007) estimate that global investment in conservation is only 30 per cent of the total required investment to achieve the objectives of the Convention on Biodiversity Conservation. According to Gutman and Davidson (2007), the increase in innovative, often international, market-based and experimental financing mechanisms will gradually build on or replace existing financing mechanisms run by governments and NGOs. Especially scholars like Brockington et al. (2008) distrust the premise of placing monetary values on biodiversity, ecosystems and their goods and services, and suggest that the increasing 'neo-liberalization' of conservation is leading to the re-regulation of nature through increasing forms of commoditization. This shift in problem-based financing towards opportunity-based financing therefore is likely to foster changes not only in the way institutional arrangements for tourism, conservation and development are financed, but also where such institutional arrangements will be developed.

In Conclusion

This chapter showed how the logics in the conservation discourse over time have expanded from a conservation to a development and market logic, allowing communal and individual landowners to play a pivotal role in conservation by assuming the roles of entrepreneur and wildlife asset manager. We illustrated this market-based approach to conservation by discussing and comparing four institutional arrangements that have emerged in eastern and southern Africa in the 1990s. In each of these arrangements nature tourism has been the main mechanisms for accruing benefits from wildlife to support conservation and community livelihoods. Although most of these arrangements emerged in the 1990s, their origins are to be found in the experimentation with different conservation approaches in the 1970s and 1980s. We furthermore discussed several internal and external challenges that hamper these arrangements to achieve their objectives. Political economists and political ecologists suggest that these challenges mainly emanate from the neoliberal frame of reference in which these arrangements are strongly embedded (Brockington et al., 2008; Corson, 2010). Clearly, as Adams & Hulme (2001) argue, one of the consequences of the growing importance of neoliberal approaches to conservation is the growing involvement of the private sector in the tenure and management of protected areas, raising complex issues of rights, ownership, governance and legitimacy. While the commodification and financialization of conservation are undoubtedly the root of many of the governance problems associated with these arrangements, it is unlikely that the market logic will become subordinate in the conservation discourse in the near future. It is thus important to grapple with governance complexities associated with the market-based approach to conservation. This is all the more salient with communities increasingly taking on the role of risk-taker as grant funding is being replaced with debt funding. Cross-case analysis, monitoring and learning could lead to a better oversight of differences between and within institutional arrangements, and, based on that, development of governance systems which are able to address the many internal and external challenges these arrangements are facing.

References

Adams, W. M. (2004). *Against extinction: The story of conservation*. London: Earthscan.

Adams, W. M. & Hulme, D. (2001). Conservation & community, changing narratives, policies & practices in African conservation. In D. Hulme & M. Murphree (Eds.), *African wildlife & livelihoods. The promise and performance of community conservation* (pp. 9–23). Oxford/Portsmouth: James Currey Publishers/Heinemann.

Adams, W. M. & Hutton, J. (2007). People, parks and poverty: Political ecology and biodiversity conservation. *Conservation and Society*, 5(2): 147–183.

Ahebwa, W. M. & van der Duim, V. R. (2013). Conservation, livelihoods and tourism: A case study of the Buhoma-Mukono Community-based Tourism Project in Uganda. *Journal of Park and Recreation Administration*, 31(3): 96–114.

Ahebwa, W., van der Duim, V. R. & Sandbrook, C. (2012). Private–community partnerships: Investigating a new approach to conservation and development in Uganda. *Conservation and Society*, 10(4): 305–317.

Akama, J. S. (1996). Western environmental values and nature-based tourism in Kenya. *Tourism Management*, 17(8): 567–574.

AWF (2011). *Conservation enterprise: A decision support toolkit*. Nairobi, Kenya/ Washington, DC: African Wildlife Foundation.

AWF (2012). *Mbirikani carbon, community and biodiversity project: Reducing emissions from deforestation and forest degradation and protecting a critical landscape for Kenya's wildlife and communities*. Nairobi/Washington, DC: African Wildlife Foundation.

AWF (2014). Recording of live webinar on African Wildlife Capital with AWF's CEO, Patrick Bergin. Retrieved May 6, 2014, from www.youtube.com/watch?v=pzEbzsZQZ00

Brockington, D., Duffy, R. & Igoe, J. (2008). *Nature unbound: Conservation, capitalism and the future of protected areas*. London: Earthscan.

Corson, C. (2010). Shifting environmental governance in a neo-liberal world: USAID for conservation. *Antipode*, 42(3): 576–602.

Gössling, S., Peeters, P. & Scott, D. (2008). Consequences of climate policy for international tourist arrivals in developing countries. *Third World Quarterly*, 29(5): 873–901.

Gutman, P. & Davidson, S. (2007). *A review of innovative international financial mechanisms for biodiversity conservation with a special focus on the international financing of developing countries' protected areas*. Washington, DC: WWF–MPO.

Hanks, J. & Myburgh, W. (2015). The evolution and progression of transfrontier conservation areas in the Southern African development community. In V. R. van der Duim, M. Lamers & J. van Wijk, (Eds.), *Institutional arrangements for conservation, development and tourism in eastern and southern Africa* (pp. 157–179). Dordrecht: Springer.

Hulme, D. & Murphree, M. (2001). *African wildlife and livelihoods: The promise and performance of community conservation*. Oxford: James Currey Ltd.

Jones, B. T. B., Diggle, R. W. & Thouless, Chr. (2015). From exploitation to ownership: Wildlife-based tourism and communal area conservation in Namibia. In V. R. van der Duim, M. Lamers & J. van Wijk (Eds.), *Institutional arrangements for conservation, development and tourism in eastern and southern Africa* (pp. 17–37). Dordrecht: Springer

Lamers, M., Nthiga, R., Van der Duim, V. R. & Van Wijk, J. (2014). Tourism–conservation enterprises as a land-use strategy. *Tourism Geographies*, 16. DOI:10.1080/14616688. 2013.806583

Lamers, M., Van der Duim, V. R., Nthiga, R., Van Wijk, J. & Waterreus, S. (2015). Implementing tourism-conservation enterprises: A comparison of three lodges in Kenya.

In V.R. van der Duim, M. Lamers & J. van Wijk (Eds.), *Institutional arrangements for conservation, development and tourism in eastern and southern Africa* (pp. 219–238). Dordrecht: Springer.

Lapeyre, R. (2015). The Tsiseb Conservancy: How communities, the state and the market struggle for its success. In V. R. van der Duim, M. Lamers & J. van Wijk (Eds.), Institutional *arrangements for conservation, development and tourism in eastern and southern* Africa (pp. 39–58). Dordrecht: Springer.

Lindsey, P. A, Roulet, P. A. & Romañach, S. S. (2007). Economic and conservation significance of the trophy hunting industry in sub-Saharan Africa, *Biological Conservation*, 134(4): 455–469.

Manyara, G. & Jones, E. (2007). Community-based tourism enterprises development in Kenya: An exploration of their potential as avenues of poverty reduction, *Journal of Sustainable Tourism*, 15: 628–644.

Morris, H. (2015). Kenya visitor numbers fall 25 per cent as terrorism hits tourism. *The Telegraph*. At: www.telegraph.co.uk/travel/destinations/africa/kenya/articles/Kenya-visitor-numbers-fall-25-per-cent-as-terrorism-hits-tourism. Accessed 27 February, 2016.

NACSO (2015). *Community conservation in Namibia: A status summary of communal conservancies, community forests and other CBNRM initiatives. Summary 2014/2015.* Windhoek: Namibian Association of Community Based Natural Resource Management (CBNRM) Support Organisations (NACSO).

Naidoo, R., Weaver, Chr., Diggle, R. W., Matongo, G., Stuart-Hill, G. & Thouless, Chr. (2016). Complementary benefits of tourism and hunting to communal conservancies in Namibia. *Conservation Biology*, 30(3): 628–638.

Nthiga, R. W. (2014). Governance of Tourism Conservation Partnerships: Lessons from Kenya. PhD thesis. Wageningen: Wageningen University.

Noe, C. (2015). The Selous-Niassa transfrontier conservation area and tourism: Evolution, benefits and challenges. In V. R. van der Duim, M. Lamers & J. van Wijk (Eds.), *Institutional arrangements for conservation, development and tourism in eastern and southern Africa* (pp. 181–201). Dordrecht: Springer.

Ochieng, O., Ahebwa, W. M. & Visseren-Hamakers, I. (2015). Hunting for conservation? The re-introduction of sport hunting in Uganda examined. In V. R. van der Duim, M. Lamers & J. van Wijk (Eds.), *Institutional arrangements for conservation, development and tourism in eastern and southern Africa*. Dordrecht: Springer.

Pellis, A., Anyango-van Zwieten, N., Waterreus, S., Lamers, M. & Van der Duim, V. R. (2014). *Tourism captured by the poor: Evaluation of aid investments in the tourism sector of Kenya's ASALs*. Wageningen: Wageningen University.

Pellis, A., Lamers, M. & Van der Duim, V. R. (2015a). Conservation tourism and landscape governance in Kenya: The interdependency of three conservation NGOs. *Journal of Ecotourism*. DOI:10.1080/14724049.2015.1083028

Pellis, A., Duineveld, M. & Wagner, L. (2015b). Conflicts forever: The path dependencies of tourism conflicts; the case of Anabeb Conservancy, Namibia. In G. T. Jóhannesson, C. Ren & V. R. van der Duim (Eds.), *Tourism encounters and controversies: Ontological politics of tourism development*. Farnham: Ashgate.

Suich, H., Child, B. & Spencely, A. (2009). *Evolution and innovation in wildlife conservation: Parks and game ranches to transfrontier conservation areas*. London: Earthscan.

Van der Duim, V. R. (2011). New institutional arrangements for tourism, conservation and development in Sub-Saharan Africa. In V. R. Van der Duim, D. Meyer, J. Saarinen & K. Zellmer (Eds.), *New alliances for tourism, conservation and development in eastern and southern Africa* (pp. 83–106). Delft: Eburon Academic Publishers.

Van der Duim, V. R., Meyer, D., Saarinen. J. & Zellmer, K. (Eds.) (2011). *New alliances for tourism, conservation and development in Eastern and Southern Africa.* Delft: Eburon Academic Publishers.

Van der Duim, V. R., Lamers, M. & Van Wijk, J. (Eds.) (2015). *Institutional arrangements for conservation, development and tourism in eastern and southern Africa.* Dordrecht: Springer.

Van Hoven, W. (2015). Private game reserves in southern Africa. In V. R. van der Duim, M. Lamers & J. van Wijk (Eds.), *Institutional arrangements for conservation, development and tourism in eastern and southern Africa* (pp. 101–118). Dordrecht: Springer.

Van Wijk, J. (2015). "Wildlife is a boon, not a barrier": How a conservation organization mobilized around seemingly opposite logics to create a hybrid organizational form. Paper presented at the 2015 Annual Meeting of the Academy of Management, Vancouver, Canada.

Van Wijk, J., van der Duim, V. R., Lamers, M. & Sumba, D. (2015a). The emergence of institutional innovations in tourism: The evolution of the African Wildlife Foundation's tourism conservation enterprises. *Journal of Sustainable Tourism*, 23(1): 104–125. DOI:10.1080/09669582.2014.927878

Van Wijk, J., Lamers, M. & van der Duim, V. R. (2015b). A dynamic perspective on institutional arrangements for tourism, conservation and development in eastern and southern Africa. In V. R. van der Duim, M. Lamers & J. van Wijk (Eds.), *Institutional arrangements for conservation, development and tourism in eastern and southern Africa* (pp. 239–259). Dordrecht: Springer.

Zeppel, H. D. (2006). *Indigenous ecotourism: Sustainable development and management.* Oxfordshire: CABI.

14 Emerging Trends in Wildlife and Tiger Tourism in India

Krithi K. Karanth, Shivangi Jain and Dincy Mariyam

Introduction

Wildlife tourism has emerged as an important sector of tourism globally. It is estimated to comprise 10 percent of global GDP (Balmford et al., 2009; Weaver, 1999). The multitudes of economic benefits provided by offering tourism opportunities in and around wildlife or nature reserves are recognized (Balmford et al., 2009; Kiss, 2004). However, the negative impacts on reserves, wildlife and local communities are also widely debated (Gaughan et al., 2008; West & Carrier, 2004). Specific criticisms have included the negative ecological impacts on habitats and behavioral impacts on animals that result from heavy vehicular traffic, disturbance caused by people and trash generated (Charnley, 2005; Farrell & Marion, 2001; Gössling et al., 2002; Krüger, 2005), as well as over reliance on flagship species and the neglect of others (Lindsey et al., 2007; Rastogi et al., 2015). Additional concerns include tradeoffs between income generated by private enterprises and jobs provided by them, versus leakage of revenue, the dilution of cultures and affordability-accessibility to the reserves for people who live around these reserves (Archabald & Naughton-Treves, 2001; Banerjee, 2012; Bookbinder et al., 1998; Bruyere et al., 2009; He et al., 2008; Rastogi et al., 2015; Sandbrook, 2010; Stone & Wall, 2004). Lastly, depending on revenue generated from wildlife or nature, focused tourism initiative may be insufficient to sustain conservation and management efforts in reserves (Banerjee, 2012; Buckley et al., 2012; Karanth & DeFries, 2011; Naidoo & Adamowicz, 2005; Wells, 1993). Globally, as wildlife and nature-based tourism continues to grow, emerging economies such as India contribute millions of new visitors with disposable incomes and growing interest in wild places (Balmford et al., 2009; Karanth & DeFries, 2011), making it imperative that we understand these trends and enact policies to sustain growth and mitigate negative impacts.

With a growth rate averaging 7.8 percent in the last decade (2005–2015, ranging from 5.1 percent in 2012–2013 to 10.3 percent in 2009–2011), and a sizable middle class (267 million people), India has emerged as a major market for domestic and international tourism (Beinhocker et al., 2007; Das, 2009; Gandhi & Orr, 2007; Shukla, 2010). The estimated growth rate of total number of visits (including multiple visits by a person) from 1991–2014 was 13.75 percent across all States and Union Territories

(Ministry of Tourism Government of India, 2014). Current estimates for foreign exchange earned through tourism averages $13.7 billion, ranging from $5.73 billion in 2005 to $20.24 billion in 2014 (Ministry of Tourism Government of India, 2005–2014). In 2014, domestic travel spending was 81.4 percent ($80.48 billion) of direct Travel and Tourism GDP compared to 18.6 percent ($18.39 billion) foreign travel spending (WTTC, 2015). By 2025, these are expected to grow to $171.94 billion for domestic and $35.70 billion for international spending, respectively (WTTC, 2015).

Complemented by rich biodiversity and natural heritage, and specifically housing the largest global populations of wild tigers and elephants—the demand for wildlife tourism only grows in India (Karanth et al., 2012; Karanth & DeFries, 2011; Karanth & Karanth, 2012). Wildlife and nature-centered tourism comprises a niche sector within the larger tourism sector. Despite this rapid interest and growth in wildlife tourism post 2000, there is still a lack of basic information on trends in visitors, gate fees and revenues generated from wildlife or nature-based tourism in reserves across India. Thus, providing the motivation to examine these factors, so that current tourism management efforts in reserves can be improved and sustained (ticketing, routes, caps on vehicles and visitor numbers) as the demands and pressures increase.

This study focused on understanding wildlife tourism in 528 terrestrial and peninsular marine (excluding island reserves) wildlife reserves in India. These reserves cover < 4.88 percent of total land area in India (ENVIS, 2016). Passed in 1972, the Indian Wildlife Protection Act contained provisions for establishing a list of protected species and habitats. This decade saw an emergence of formal wildlife reserves registered as National Parks and Sanctuaries in India, expanding from 127 in 1970, to more than 600 terrestrial and marine reserves today (ENVIS, 2016). Corbett National Park and Tiger Reserve (Uttarakhand) was the oldest reserve established in 1936 under British governance, and Cauvery North Wildlife Sanctuary (Tamil Nadu) is the newest reserve established in 2014 (ENVIS, 2016).

This expansion of India's reserve system was complemented in 1973 with the launch of the Project Tiger scheme with the objective of preserving a viable population of tigers and tiger habitat as a national heritage. This scheme recognized reserves with significant tiger populations and designated them as tiger reserves, thereby according them more importance and higher levels of funding, and enhanced protection (Rangarajan, 2001). Originally establishing 11 tiger reserves across India in the 1970s, this scheme has now grown to include 49 tiger reserves that cover 1.2 percent (39,669 kilometers squared) (ENVIS, 2016) of India's geographical area.

This study focused on examining wildlife tourism in terrestrial and peninsular marine National Parks and Wildlife Sanctuaries, and excluded the 106 island marine reserves. Specifically, this included examining trends in visitor numbers and gate fees in 176 wildlife reserves including 36 tiger reserves, and comparisons between tiger reserves and non-tiger reserves. Due to widespread public interest in tigers, it was expected that there would be a greater increase in tourist numbers and gate fees for tiger reserves compared to non-tiger reserves (Karanth et al., 2012; Karanth & Karanth, 2012). The overall aim was to assess emerging trends in wildlife tourism and specifically, tiger-driven tourism in India over the past decade.

Methods

This study focused on understanding tourism trends in 524 National Parks and Wildlife Sanctuaries, excluding 66 conservation and 26 community reserves which had no systematic data available. According to chapter IV of the Wildlife Protection Act 1972, a National Park constitutes

> an area that is notified by the state government, whether within a sanctuary or not, by reason of its ecological, faunal, floral, geomorphological, or zoological association or importance, needed to for the purpose of protecting and propagating or developing wildlife therein or its environment.
>
> (Wildlife Protection Act, 1972)

Whereas, a Wildlife Sanctuary covers "any area, other than the ones comprised with any reserve forest or the territorial waters, which is of adequate ecological, faunal, floral, geomorphological, natural or zoological significance, for the purpose of protecting, propagating or developing wildlife or its environment" (Wildlife Protection Act, 1972). There were five reserves where tourism was not allowed by the government due to ecological and political reasons. The reserves covered 4.76 percent of India's total geographical extent. The reserves varied in size from 0.02 kilometers squared to 7,506 kilometers squared, with an average size 257 kilometers squared (ENVIS, 2016).

Information on (1) visitor numbers from 2005–2015 for 176 of 524 PAs (34 percent), (2) gate fees from 103 of 176 PAs (59 percent) for year 2014–2015 and (3) visitation and gate fees for 36 tiger reserves was collected. The accessibility of each reserve to India's top 44 urban centers, defined as cities with populations > 100,000 people with an airport or major railway station was mapped (Karanth & DeFries, 2011). Data collection was dependent on ease of access to government records, which varied across states. Data were collected by writing to and filing right to information act requests with all state forest and wildlife departments across India (Right to Information, 2005).

Results and Discussion

The study compiled information on 50 National Parks and 126 Wildlife Sanctuaries across India. These comprise 34 percent of all National Parks and Wildlife Sanctuaries, and 75 percent of tiger reserves in India. There were five reserves where no tourism was allowed, and these were excluded from the analysis.

Visitors

In 2014–2015, 4,623,134 tourists visited 118 wildlife reserves in India. This includes 3,233,665 people visiting National Parks, and 1,851,280 visiting Wildlife Sanctuaries. Among tiger reserves the total visitors were 1,466,728. Visitors to tiger reserves comprised 32 percent of all visitors to wildlife reserves in India. Records showed that for 24 reserves (N = 94) in 2005-2006 and 15 reserves (N = 118) in 2014–2015, the total visitor count was 0. In 2005–2006, among National Parks (N = 31), there were no visitors to Rajiv Gandhi (Andhra Pradesh) and Murlen (Mizoram). In 2014–2015, the lowest number of 16 visitors was reported in Mouling (Arunachal Pradesh) (N = 37). For Wildlife Sanctuaries in 2005–2006, 23 sanctuaries (N = 69) had 0 visitors and in 2014–2015, 15 sanctuaries (N = 90) had 0 visitors. For details, please see Table 14.1.

From 2005 to 2015, the average numbers of visitors increased from 17,997 (N = 95) to 39,179 (N = 118), a 117 percent increase. In 2005–2006, National Parks visitors averaged 29,841 and in Wildlife Sanctuaries it was 13,407. By 2014–2015, the average number of visitors for National Parks had increased to 87,396 and in Wildlife Sanctuaries it grew to 20,569. The increase in visitors was 192 percent in National Parks compared to 53 percent for Wildlife Sanctuaries. Among tiger reserves, the average increased from 32,061 to 61,113 people in this decade, a 90 percent increase. See Table 14.1 for details.

The annual growth rates were estimated in 69 wildlife reserves, and 17 tiger reserves that had continuous data available from 2005–2015. These rates vary from –37.1 to 37.2 in all reserves versus –24.3 to 16.6 in tiger reserves (Figure 14.1). Year-to-year increments in each reserve over 10 years were calculated using the formula {(ln (Visitor number in year 2014–15) – ln (Visitor number in year 2005-06))*100}/ (Number of years). These increments ranged from –0.16 percent to 1.09 percent for National Parks, -0.24 percent to 4.06 percent for Wildlife Sanctuaries and 0 percent to 0.45 percent for tiger reserves (Karanth & DeFries, 2011).

Tourist numbers between tiger and non-tiger reserves were compared. In 2013–2014, as predicted, it was found that the number of tourists visiting tiger reserves was higher than non-tiger reserves (t-test, $p < 0.05$). However, due to high standard deviations and low sample sizes, the results must be interpreted with caution.

In 2005–2006, the highest number of visitors (N = 95) was 171,409 people going to Ranganathittu bird sanctuary (Karnataka), and by 2014–2015 (N = 114), 1,055,691 people visited Rajiv Gandhi (Rameswaram, Andhra Pradesh). Among National Parks (N = 31), in 2005–2006 Corbett (Uttarakhand) had 130,043 people visiting, and by 2014–2015 (N=37), the highest number of people, 1,055,691 visited Rajiv Gandhi (Rameswaram, Andhra Pradesh). Among Wildlife Sanctuaries (N = 69), in 2005–2006, 171,409 people visited Ranganathittu (Karnataka) and by 2014–2015 this number increased to 315,968 people in Ranganathittu. Among tiger reserves, Dampa (Mizoram) reported 71 visitors in 2005–2006 (N = 19) and eight in 2014–2015 (N = 24). For highest visitors, in 2005–2006, Corbett

Table 14.1 Visitors and Gate Fees in Indian Wildlife Reserves

Year	2005–2006			2014–2015				
Category	Total tourists	Indians	Average tourists (N)	Total tourists	Indians	Average tourists (N)	Average Gate Fees Indians USD (Rs)	Average Gate Fees International USD (Rs)
All Reserves	1,713,575	90%	17,136 (100)	4,623,1355	96%	37,587 (123)	1 (67)*	6.5 (432)
National Parks	925,072	85%	28,909 (32)	3,233,665	95%	85,097 (38)	1.5 (100)	8 (533)
Wildlife Sanctuaries	928,940	97%	12,725 (73)	1,851,280	98%	19,694 (94)	1 (67)	6 (400)
Tiger Reserves	609,164	83%	30,458 (20)	1,466, 728	89%	58,669 (25)	1 (67)	9 (599)

Notes

2005-2006: There were no visitors to 2 National Parks and 22 Wildlife Sanctuaries

2014-2015: There were no visitors to 15 Wildlife Sanctuaries

*We have converted Indian rupees to US dollars at the base year 2016 exchange rate of 66.58 rupees to the dollar. We have rounded up the values to the nearest whole number.

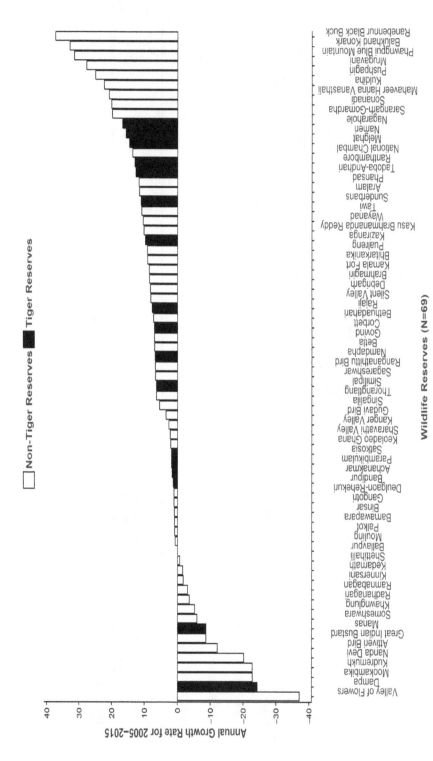

Figure 14.1 Annual Tourist Growth Rate from 2005 to 2015 across 69 Wildlife Reserves in India including 17 Tiger Reserves

(Uttarakhand) hosted 130,043 people and by 2014–2015, Ranthambore had 374,134 visitors. Additional details are in Table 14.1.

Across all wildlife reserves, domestic visitors increased from 90 percent to 96 percent from 2005 to 2015. In National Parks, domestic visitors increased from 85 percent to 95 percent in this decade (Table 14.1). In Wildlife Sanctuaries, domestic visitors also increased from 97 percent to 98 percent in 2014–2015. Among tiger reserves, domestic tourism increased from 83 percent to 89 percent (see Table 14.1).

From 2005 to 2015, visitors increased in 126 reserves and decreased in 30 reserves (including 7 tiger reserves). Across all reserves (N = 120), the highest positive growth of 34,050 percent was reported by Burchapur Wildlife Sanctuary in 2005–2015. Among National Parks, the highest positive growth, 1,582 percent was reported from Phawngpui Blue Mountain (Mizoram). Additionally, negative growth was reported by eight National Parks, with the Valley of Flowers (–96.5 percent) reporting the highest negative growth (Uttarakhand). Among Wildlife Sanctuaries Burchapur had the highest positive growth and 22 Wildlife Sanctuaries had negative growth during this period. Among tiger reserves (N = 35), Nameri (Assam) reported the highest positive growth rate of 306 percent, and Satpura (Madhya Pradesh) had the highest negative growth (–90.6 percent) from 2005–2015.

To examine accessibility of these reserves, the distance to the nearest urban center relative to the type and size of reserves was mapped. Across all reserves, the average distance was 212 kilometers (Ranging from 1.5 kilometers for Keoladeo Ghana National Park to 819 kilometers for Ngengpui Wildlife Sanctuary). For tiger reserves, the accessibility was a distance of 214.33 kilometers (ranging from 35 kilometers in Rajaji National Park to 585 kilometers in Namdapha National Park).

Gate Fees

Gate fee information (the fee charged for people visiting a reserve, excluding camera fees or vehicle fees) was collected from reserves for 2014–2015. Gate fees varied for Indians and international visitors. Fees ranged from Rs 0 in Chakrasila WLS (Assam) to Rs 240 ($4) in Phwangpui Blue Mountain (Mizoram) for Indians. Fees for international visitors ranged from Rs 0 in three reserves (Rajiv Gandhi and Lankamalleswara in Andhra Pradesh and Chakrasila, Assam) to Rs 1000 ($15) in many Karnataka and Odisha reserves. Across all reserves, the average estimated gate fees for domestic visitors was Rs 71 ($1, N = 96), and for international visitors was Rs 415 ($6, N = 89). The average estimated gate fees were higher for domestic visitors, Rs 98 ($1.5) in National Parks compared to Wildlife Sanctuaries, Rs 55 (< $1). It was also higher for international visitors, Rs 522 ($8) in National Parks compared to Wildlife Sanctuaries, Rs 413 ($6). Details are in Figure 14.2.

Among Tiger Reserves, fees ranged from Rs 20 ($0.30) in Satkosia (Odisha) to Rs 200 ($3) in Corbett (Uttarakhand) and all tiger reserves in Karnataka for domestic visitors. For international visitors, fees ranged from Rs 60 ($0.90) in

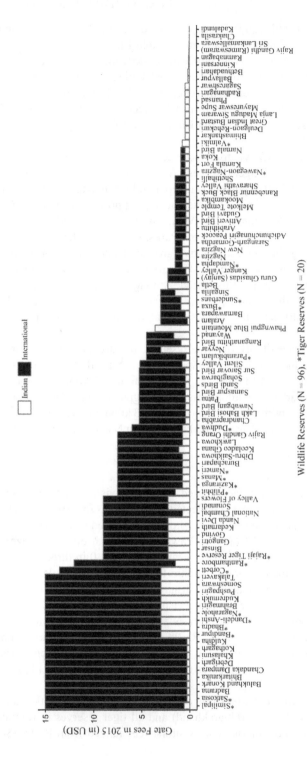

Figure 14.2 Gate fees in 2014–2015 across 96 Wildlife Reserves in India Including 20 Tiger Reserves

Nawegaon-Nagzira (Maharashtra) to Rs 1000 ($15) in Satkosia and Simlipal (Odisha), and all five tiger reserves in Karnataka. Average gate fees for domestic visitors in Tiger Reserves was Rs 94 ($1) and for international visitors Rs 608 ($9). Additional details are in Table 14.1.

Gate fees were compared for tiger and non-tiger reserves for the year 2015. As predicted, tiger reserves have higher gate fees for domestic visitors (N = 96, t-test, p < 0.1) and international visitors (N = 75, t-test, p < 0.05) compared to non-tiger reserves. However, these results must be interpreted with caution due to the high standard deviations and low sample sizes.

This paper finds that the growth of wildlife tourism in India mirrors growth of wildlife and/or nature-based tourism in other countries, and this has been linked to higher disposable incomes allowing more people to visit wild places and view nature (Balmford et al., 2009). Tourist visitation to all wildlife reserves, and tiger reserves specifically was found to have risen by 6 percent in the last decade in India. The number of domestic and international visitors has also increased, but domestic tourism is dominant. Domestic tourism comprises > 95 percent of wildlife tourism in India. This presents huge opportunities to engage the Indian public to care for, support and take pride in the nation's wildlife. However, this also brings significant challenges with regard to managing the onslaught of visitors, vehicular traffic and growth of tourism infrastructure (hotels and homestays) in each of these reserves (Farrell & Marion, 2001).

Previous assessments (Karanth & DeFries, 2011; Karanth & Karanth, 2012; TTF, 2005) have highlighted these challenges particularly in the context of managing the associated land-use change that accompanies growth in tourism around Indian reserves that are much smaller and less connected compared to their African and American counterparts. It has also been found that gate fees vary across reserves, and higher prices in some reserves might lead to reserves becoming inaccessible to local people (Charnley, 2005). Lack of accessibility and revenue-sharing opportunities and leakage of revenue may promote resentment against tourism by local people who live around these reserves but see very little direct benefit (Archabald & Naughton-Treves, 2001; Banerjee, 2012; Bookbinder et al., 1998; He et al., 2008; Rastogi et al., 2015; Sandbrook, 2010; Stone & Wall, 2004).

Gate fees in India were much lower compared to gate fees for reserves in Africa or the Americas. For example, in the United States Yellowstone and Grand Canyon National Parks charge $15/person (National Park Service, U.S. Department of Interior, 2016; Weaver, 2015). Among African reserves Maasai Mara (Kenya) charges $80/person for non-residents (Mara Conservancy, 2011), and Serengeti (Tanzania) charges $60/person for non-residents (Tanzania National Parks, 2013). Similarly in South America, reserves like the Galapagos National Park charge up to $100/person for non-residents (Lozano, 2013). Although gate fees were higher for international visitors, they can potentially generate more funds for conservation and/or subsidize the costs of visiting a reserve for Indians. Therefore, differential price mechanisms within the Indian context are perhaps worth exploring further, as has been done in Costa Rica (Chase et al., 2008).

At present, general tourism is estimated to directly contribute 2.2 percent of overall GDP, and in totality contribute 6.7 percent of GDP in India (WTTC, 2015). Wildlife tourism comprises an unknown fraction of this. This study is one attempt to unravel the contribution of wildlife tourism to the broader tourism sector in India, but the effort remains incomplete as many reserves still do not keep organized records of visitors, gate fees and associated revenues generated from wildlife–nature-based tourism. State and national governments need to establish and improve record keeping at every reserve so that accurate data on visitors and fees are collected and long term trends in visitors can be analyzed. Additionally, going beyond fees, economic analyses that tease out the direct and indirect contributions of the wildlife tourism sector to India's GDP will need to be implemented.

It is clear that tiger-focused tourism is a major force within wildlife tourism in and outside India, comprising 32 percent of all visitors and generating higher gate fees and revenues (Table 14.1). This assessment of tourism in a selection of Indian wildlife reserves finds that tourism growth is not universal; there are many wildlife reserves that are visited by few people and/or have experienced negative growth rates. This makes it challenging to sustain conservation efforts in these places in the absence of sufficient funds, as well as of broader public support and interest in these reserves. Buckley et al. (2012) have demonstrated that conservation efforts directed at threatened mammal species has become reliant on revenue from tourism to a previously unsuspected degree. They, along with others, highlight that although this provides new opportunities for conservation funding, heavy dependence on such an uncertain source of funding is a new, large and growing threat to other endangered species (Kruger, 2005).

Revenue sharing to generate conservation funds generated by tiger reserves varies by state; in some cases they are directed to a larger corpus of funds, while in others they remain with the reserve that generated this revenue. Such variability makes it imperative that we establish uniform policies and consistent revenue-sharing mechanisms directed at how tourism income generated from one reserve is spent regionally or nationally to benefit multiple reserves and species (He et al., 2008; Kiss, 2004; Lindsey et al., 2007), so that the fate of other reserves and wildlife species does not become tied to one species, as with Sariska in 2005 where tourism revenues and visitors dramatically declined when tigers went extinct locally (Karanth & DeFries, 2011; TTF, 2005).

Acknowledgements

The authors thank the forest and wildlife departments from Andhra Pradesh, Arunachal Pradesh, Assam, Bihar, Chhattisgarh, Jharkhand, Karnataka, Kerala, Madhya Pradesh, Maharashtra, Mizoram, Odisha, Rajasthan, Tamil Nadu, Telangana, Uttar Pradesh, Uttarakhand and West Bengal. They acknowledge institutional support from the Wildlife Conservation Society (New York and India) and the Centre for Wildlife Studies (India). They thank Shriyam Gupta and Anubhav V for assistance provided.

References

Archabald, K., & Naughton-Treves, L. (2001). Tourism revenue-sharing around national parks in Western Uganda: Early efforts to identify and reward local communities. *Environmental Conservation*, 28(2). doi:10.1017/s0376892901000145

Balmford, A., Beresford, J., Green, J., Naidoo, R., Walpole, M., & Manica, A. (2009). A global perspective on trends in nature-based tourism. *PLoS Biology*, 7(6), e1000144. doi:10.1371/journal.pbio.1000144

Banerjee, A. (2012). Is wildlife tourism benefiting Indian protected areas? A survey. *Current Issues in Tourism*, 15(3), 211–227. doi:10.1080/13683500.2011.599367

Beinhocker, E. D., Farrell, D., & Zainulbhai, A. S. (2007). Tracking the growth of India's middle class. *McKinsey Quarterly*, 3(3), 51–61.

Bookbinder, M. P., Dinerstein, E., Rijal, A., Cauley, H., & Rajouria, A. (1998). Ecotourism's support of biodiversity conservation. *Conservation Biology*, 12(6), 1399–1404. doi:10.1111/j.1523-1739.1998.97229.x

Bruyere, B. L., Beh, A. W., & Lelengula, G. (2008). Differences in perceptions of communication, tourism benefits, and management issues in a protected area of rural Kenya. *Environmental Management*, 43(1), 49–59. doi:10.1007/s00267-008-9190-7

Buckley, R. C., Castley, J. G., Pegas, F. D., Mossaz, A. C., & Steven, R. (2012). A population accounting approach to assess tourism contributions to conservation of IUCN-redlisted mammal species. *PLoS ONE*, 7(9), e44134. doi:10.1371/journal.pone.0044134

Charnley, S. (2005). From nature tourism to ecotourism? The case of the Ngorongoro Conservation Area, Tanzania. *Human Organization*, 64(1), 75–88. doi:10.17730/humo. 64.1.u8fer0aap3ceg4a1

Chase, L. C., Lee, D. R., Schulze, W. D., & Anderson, D. J. (1998). Ecotourism demand and differential pricing of national park access in Costa Rica. *Land Economics*, 74(4), 466–482. doi:10.2307/3146879

Das, D. K. (2009). Globalisation and an emerging global middle class. *Economic Affairs*, 29(3), 89–92. doi:10.1111/j.1468-0270.2009.01927.x

ENVIS Centre on Wildlife & Protected Areas. (2016). *Protected Areas of India*. Retrieved April 17, 2016, from: www.wiienvis.nic.in/Database/Protected_Area_854.aspx

Farrell, T. A., & Marion, J. L. (2001). Identifying and assessing ecotourism visitor impacts at eight protected areas in Costa Rica and Belize. *Environmental Conservation*, 28(3), 215–225. doi:10.1017/s0376892901000224

Gandhi, S. S., & Orr, R. J. (2007). Large scale urban development in India: Past and present. (Working Paper No. 35). Retrieved from Stanford University website: https://gpc. stanford.edu/sites/default/files/wp035_0.pdf

Gaughan, A. E., Binford, M. W., & Southworth, J. (2009). Tourism, forest conversion, and land transformations in the Angkor basin, Cambodia. *Applied Geography*, 29(2), 212–223. doi:10.1016/j.apgeog.2008.09.007

Gössling, S., Hansson, C. B., Hörstmeier, O., & Saggel, S. (2002). Ecological footprint analysis as a tool to assess tourism sustainability. *Ecological Economics*, 43(2–3), 199–211. doi:10.1016/s0921-8009(02)00211-2

Government of India. (1972). *Chapter IV: Wildlife Protection Act*. New Delhi, India.

Government of India. (2005). *Right to Information Act*. New Delhi, India.

He, G., Chen, X., Liu, W., Bearer, S., Zhou, S., Cheng, L. Y., ... Liu, J. (2008). Distribution of economic benefits from ecotourism: A case study of Wolong Nature Reserve for giant pandas in China. *Environmental Management*, 42(6), 1017–1025. doi:10.1007/ s00267-008-9214-3

Karanth, K. K., & DeFries, R. (2011). Nature-based tourism in Indian protected areas: New challenges for park management. *Conservation Letters*, 4(2), 137–149. doi:10.1111/j.1755-263x.2010.00154.x

Karanth, K. K., DeFries, R., Srivathsa, A., & Sankaraman, V. (2012). Wildlife tourists in India's emerging economy: Potential for a conservation constituency? *Oryx*, 46(3), 382–390. doi:10.1017/s003060531100086x

Karanth, K. U., & Karanth, K. K. (2012). A tiger in the drawing room: can luxury tourism benefit wildlife? *Economic and Political Weekly*, 47(38), 38–43.

Kiss, A. (2004). Is community-based ecotourism a good use of biodiversity conservation funds? *Trends in Ecology & Evolution*, 19(5), 232–237. doi:10.1016/j.tree.2004.03.010

Krüger, O. (2005). The role of ecotourism in conservation: Panacea or Pandora's box? *Biodiversity and Conservation*, 14(3), 579–600. doi:10.1007/s10531-004-3917-4

Lindsey, P. A., Alexander, R., Mills, M.G.L., Romañach, S., & Woodroffe, R. (2007). Wildlife viewing preferences of visitors to protected areas in South Africa: Implications for the role of ecotourism in conservation. *Journal of Ecotourism*, 6(1), 19–33. doi:10.2167/joe133.0

Lozano, G. (2013, February 28). *Entry Tax to Protected Areas*. Retrieved April 19, 2016, from: www.galapagospark.org/nophprg.php?page=programas_turismo_tributo

Mara Conservancy. (2011). *Conservation Fees*. Retrieved April 19, 2016, from: http://maratriangle.org/visit/conservation-fees/

Market Research Division Ministry of Tourism Government of India. (2005). *India Tourism Statistics 2005*. New Delhi, India.

Market Research Division Ministry of Tourism Government of India. (2006). *India Tourism Statistics 2006*. New Delhi, India.

Market Research Division Ministry of Tourism Government of India. (2007). *India Tourism Statistics 2007*. New Delhi, India.

Market Research Division Ministry of Tourism Government of India. (2008). *India Tourism Statistics 2008*. New Delhi, India.

Market Research Division Ministry of Tourism Government of India. (2009). *India Tourism Statistics 2009*. New Delhi, India.

Market Research Division Ministry of Tourism Government of India. (2010). *India Tourism Statistics 2010*. New Delhi, India.

Market Research Division Ministry of Tourism Government of India. (2011). *India Tourism Statistics 2011*. New Delhi, India.

Market Research Division Ministry of Tourism Government of India. (2012). *India Tourism Statistics 2012*. New Delhi, India.

Market Research Division Ministry of Tourism Government of India. (2013). *India Tourism Statistics at a Glance 2013*. New Delhi, India.

Market Research Division Ministry of Tourism Government of India. (2014). *India Tourism Statistics at a Glance 2014*. New Delhi, India.

Naidoo, R., & Adamowicz, W. L. (2005). Biodiversity and nature-based tourism at forest reserves in Uganda. *Environment and Development Economics*, 10(2), 159–178. doi:10.1017/s1355770x0400186x

National Park Service, U.S. Department of Interior. (2016). *Fees & Passes*. Retrieved April 19, 2016 from: www.nps.gov/grca/planyourvisit/fees.htm

Rangarajan, M. (2001). *India's Wildlife History: An Introduction*. Delhi, India: Permanent Black.

Rastogi, A., Hickey, G. M., Anand, A., Badola, R., & Hussain, S. A. (2015). Wildlife-tourism, local communities and tiger conservation: A village-level study in Corbett Tiger Reserve, India. *Forest Policy and Economics*, 61, 11–19. doi:10.1016/j.forpol. 2015.04.007

Sandbrook, C. G. (2010). Local economic impact of different forms of nature-based tourism. *Conservation Letters*, 3(1), 21–28. doi:10.1111/j.1755-263x.2009.00085.x

Shukla, R. (2010). *How India Earns, Spends and Saves: Unmasking the Real India.* New Delhi, India: SAGE Publications India.

Stone, M., & Wall, G. (2004). Ecotourism and community development: Case studies from Hainan, China. *Environmental Management*, 33(1), 12–24. doi:10.1007/s00267-003-3029-z

Tanzania National Parks. (2013). *Tariffs from 1st July 2013 to 30th June 2015.* Retrieved April 19, 2016 from: www.tatotz.org/downloads/2013/FINAL%20TANAPA%20 TARIFFS%20FOR%202013-2015.pdf

TTF, Tiger Task Force. (2005). *Joining the Dots: The Report of the Tiger Task Force.* Project Tiger Directorate, Union Ministry of Environment, Government of India, New Delhi.

Weaver, D. B. (1999). Magnitude of ecotourism in Costa Rica and Kenya. *Annals of Tourism Research*, 26(4), 792–816. doi:10.1016/s0160-7383(99)00044-4

Weaver, Traci. (2015, May 11). *Yellowstone National Park Announces New Entrance Fees Starting June 1.* Retrieved April 19, 2016 from: www.nps.gov/yell/learn/news/15028.htm

Wells, M. P. (1993). Neglect of biological riches: The economics of nature tourism in Nepal. *Biodiversity and Conservation*, 2(4), 445–464. doi:10.1007/bf00114046

West, P., & Carrier, J. (2004). Ecotourism and authenticity. *Current Anthropology*, 45(4), 483–498. doi:10.1086/422082

WTTC, World Travel and Tourism Council. (2015). *Travel and Tourism Economic Impact 2015 India.* London, United Kingdom. Retrieved April 19th, 2016, from: www. wttc.org/-/media/files/reports/economic%20impact%20research/regional%202015/ world2015.pdf

15 Chinese Approach to Sustainability

Challenges and Suggestions

Rui Song

Introduction

Endowed with large land territory, endemic flora and fauna, rich biodiversity, and diverse ecological systems, China has witnessed a booming development of nature tourism in the last three decades. Nature-based tourism (NBT), or nature tourism in short as it is known in the western world, is described as all forms of tourism that, " … use natural resources in a wild or undeveloped form—including species, habitat, landscape, scenery, salt and fresh-water features"; it is "travel for the purpose of enjoying undeveloped natural areas or wildlife" (Goodwin, 1996). However, as discussed in the following, Chinese perceive "wild" and "developed/undeveloped" in a culturally different tradition compared with westerners. Nature tourism, or nature-based tourism, a term seldom used in China both academically and practically, would be described as any travel to the natural environment, i.e. less humanly constructed areas in the Chinese context. This chapter focuses on tourism related to the natural resource sites which have diversified titles similar to "national park".

Tourism and Natural Resource Administration in China

Travel and tourism in China was not developed until 1978 when the prolonged economic reform and opening to the outside world began. Deng Xiaoping's visit to Huangshan Mountain in 1979 has been regarded as the milestone and starting point of modern tourism in China. He called for "Brand Huangshan out" and pointed out that tourism should be fully promoted and developed as an engine for local development (Xiao, 2006). Since then, tourism has been developed into a sizable industry, playing an increasingly important role in the country's social and economic development through "learning by doing".

With fast economic growth and social development in the last three decades, tourism has been triggered gradually. In 1995, the tourism sector started to develop as a pillar of the tertiary industry. In 1998, the State Council designated tourism as one of the three new growth points of the economy, in addition to the automobile and real estate sector. One year after the global financial crisis in 2008, tourism was regarded as the strategic pillar industry of national economy and modern service industry which aimed to improve people's living standard. In this context, tourism has witnessed boom both in demand and supply. On the demand side, billions of Chinese have been liberated ideologically, economically, and socially to enjoy travel and recreation with more disposable income, more leisure time, more vehicle ownership, and a stronger desire to travel. On the supply side, governments, state-owned enterprises, and private companies have invested abundantly in infrastructure improvement and tourism facilities. Consequently, China's tourism has witnessed striking growth and according to China National Tourism Administration (CNTA), Chinese domestic tourist arrivals increased 17 times since the statistics system was established in the mid-1980s. Domestic tourist expenditures increased 40 times in the last two decades and among the world's top source markets, China, with a double-digit growth in expenditure every year since 2004, continues to lead global outbound travel. In 2015, Chinese domestic tourist arrivals reached 4 billion RMB and created revenue of 3600 billion RMB.

The undergoing historically unprecedented boom of tourism has not only changed people's lifestyles, economic structure, and regional development pattern, but also increased pressure on natural resources.

Nature Tourism Resource Administration System

In general, the natural resources in China are administrated in a scattered way by dozens of different government departments, from forest, land, mountain, mining, river, and marine. Within this context, nature tourism resource administration has the following characteristics.

First, legislatively, nature tourism resource is administrated by different departments of ministries in the central government or quasi government agencies. Due to length limitations, this paper focuses on the important natural resource sites. Since 1956 when the first national nature reserve was established in Guangdong Province, a complicated natural reserves system has been established which covers nine categories and 8,900 sites in total, out of which 2,992 sites are at national level. The nine categories include National Nature Reserve, National Key Scenic Resorts, National Forest Park, National Water Reserve Park, National Wetland Park, National Geo-park, National Mining Park, and National Marine Park (see Table 15.1). On the one hand, this system enables all kinds of important natural resources under protection legislatively. This is crucial for China which has been undergoing fast economic development. On the other hand, this makes the management of any single site, as well as communication, coordination, and cooperation among different government departments very difficult. Obviously, each of these classifications is administered by a different department within a ministry, or even across different ministries. And many sites may have more than one title[1] and thus receive directives from multiple administrative agencies. Each administrative system has its own priorities and objectives, making any integrated and long-term strategic focus difficult, if possible.

Second, practically, the nature tourism resource is managed by the local government authorizes at vertical level. Compared to the central government

Table 15.1 National Natural Protection Systems in China

Category	Authority	Starting Year	Numbers
National Nature Reserve	State Forestry Administration, Ministry of Environmental Protection, Ministry of Agriculture, and State Oceanic Administration of P.R.C	1956	428
National Key Scenic Resorts	Ministry of Housing and Urban-rural Development of P.R.C	1985	225
National Forest Park	State Forestry Administration	1982	826
National Water Reserve Park	Ministry of Water Resources	2001	658
National Wetland Park	State Forestry Administration	2008	706 in total, 654 pilots and 52 certificated
National Geo-park,	Ministry of Land Resources	2000	218
National Mining Park	Ministry of Land Resources	2005	72
National Marine Park	State Oceanic Administration of P.R.C	2011	30

(responsible for overall approval and some of the funding) and provincial government (responsible for funding of operations and construction), local government at municipal and county level (responsible for provision of land and local resources, and community relations) are always the "real" managers of the nature tourism resource. There are always conflicts among governments of different levels and across agencies, in particular in terms of management rights. For example, Taishan Mountain, Changbaishan Mountain, Huangguoshu Waterfall, Zhangjiajie, Wuyishan Mountain, along with others, once suffered or have suffered conflicts among government authorities at provincial, municipal, and county levels, as well as across forests, housing, and urban–rural development, among environmental protection government agencies. Considering that almost all nature tourism resource sites involve the local community at different scales, the situation is more complicated. For example, the sustainability of Huangshan Mountain involves different entities and stakeholders. The relationship among them is quite complicated. Xu, Zhu, and Bao (2016), through a systematic analysis of the path towards sustainable development of Huangshan Mountain, describe the phenomenon of Chinese government-dominated mass tourism that a nature-based development model has evoked, into a dual structure with modern efficient management patterns at the core site and municipal scales, and a backward unsustainable situation at the community scale.

Third, the nature tourism resource sites are under complicated systems in terms of business operations. Although lack of funds is a common issue for protected areas worldwide, it is somewhat more serious in China. The nature tourism resource sites have been categorized as "self-funding organizations" in China (Li, 2004), meaning that they are expected to generate revenue to support operations, and to contribute to local economic development, major infrastructure development, poverty relief, and local employment. While the sites can apply to the central government for the funding of special projects such as roads, the central government does not provide funding for operating expenses. Provincial governments normally provide most of the financial support for infrastructure and facilities during the initial stages of development. They may also cover the initial operational expenses. However, the ongoing expenses should be covered by the administrations of the site who are therefore always involved in the operation of tour businesses, such as hotels, restaurants, souvenir shops, etc. Meanwhile, for the daily operation, administrations of the site or local authorities always explore a variety of other options for funding, including leased concessions and Build-Operate-Transfer (BOT) contracts. Peng (2003) summarized nine different models of governance and operation in nature tourism. Whatever the models, this arrangement often results in the sacrifice of ecological conservation and local community involvement (Wang, Innes, Wu, Krzyzanowski, Yin, Dai, & Liu, 2012).

Efforts towards and challenges of Sustainability

Efforts towards Sustainability

Globally, sustainability is defined and pursued in three dimensions simultaneously, i.e. economic, environmental, and social. However, in China, the unbalance between economic growth and environmental protection has been more severe and drawn more attention. After a duration of fast economic growth pushed by the mentality of "pollute first, control later", China began to make its transformation from economic growth to sustainable development in the early 1990s. Following the Earth Rio Summit in Brazil in 1991, protection of the environment was adopted as a fundamental state policy in 1993 (Sofield & Li, 2011). In 1994, it was expanded to encompass the principles of "ecologically sustainable development". Comprehensive sets of environmental laws and regulations have been enacted and environmental needs and priorities have been included in every state's Five-Year Plan for economic development since 1995. China began to grapple more seriously with issues of sustainability in all areas, i.e. energy, transport, manufacturing, mining, urban development, etc. (Sofield & Li, 2011). To promote more balanced patterns of development, the China Communist Party Central Political bureau commenced a new ideological campaign in 2005 to shift the focus of the official agenda from "economic growth" to "sustainable development". The concept of "Ecological Civilization" was introduced in 2007. The State Environmental Protection Administration (SEPA) was upgraded to the Ministry of Environmental Protection (MEP), directly under the State Council in 2008. Systems for integrated management, pollution prevention, control and supervision, and law enforcement have been gradually improved. To date, the National People's Congress (NPC) has created 10 environmental laws and 30 resource protection laws. Local people"s congresses and governments have developed more than 700 local environmental rules and regulations, and the departments of the State Council have issued hundreds of environmental regulations, including 69 regulations formulated by the MEP.

In this context, tourism has been one of the first proponents of a policy more attuned to western/international standards that incorporates sustainability in its planning, development, and operation. Since the mid-1990s, governments and academia have been trying to incorporate ecologically sustainable development (ESD) in tourism.

In nature tourism, the idea of serious conservation was introduced along with zoning, environment-friendly construction, resource-saving, conservation regulations, and protection methods in planning, regulations, and operations. Measures such as promoting environmental protection, dismantling inappropriate buildings, delineating core protected areas, and developing GIS monitoring systems have been undertaken. China promulgated new regulations, including the Regulation for Chinese National Key Scenic Resorts, the Resolution of Chinese Forest Park Development, and the Tourism Law of the P.R.C. for sustainable tourism development in natural areas. Although the economic element has still been the main pursuit (Xu Ding & Parker, 2008; Xu & Sofield, 2013), most nature-based destinations have made strong efforts to achieve the dual aim of environmental sustainability and economic growth. Xu Ding and Parker (2008) noted that Chinese tourism researchers and the tourism industry "are often criticized as lacking concern for sustainability" (but) "the multiple goals of tourism for development were perceived right from the start of tourism planning". For example, many nature tourism sites implemented the policy of "day tour in the park and overnight stay out of the park" to eliminated the negative impact on environment caused by tourist accommodations. Eco-toilet and eco-trails and eco-vehicles were utilized to minimize the environmental impacts. Many nature tourism sites such as Jiuzhaigou Valley have paid high attention to the ecological research and protection. Different kinds of environment monitoring stations and international collaboration labs have been established. Meanwhile, community involvement has been gradually emphasized, partly due to the introduction of western concepts by planning experts in favor of the western concept of community involvement for destination sustainability, and partly due to the conflicts between local community and managers and/or operators. For example, Jiuzhaigou Valley is described as one of the best practices in community involvement where the local community has been involved in the administration, policymaking, and benefits distribution at the very beginning. The leaders and employees of the administration are locals. The Community Committee was established to communicate with the administration. Locals have the privilege of working in the state-owned enterprise and joint venture companies and are encouraged to operate their own business on the site. Allied catering companies were established and the local community has the preferential right to get 77 percent profit, although their share in the company is only 49 percent. Meanwhile, the local community that lives inside the reserve gets 7 yuan RBM from every entrance ticket. However, tension between the community inside and outside the reserve has been gradually worsened because accommodation in the reserve had been forbidden since 2000 in order to protect the environment, in particular the water. The villagers outside the reserve have got more income from room rental, restaurant, and accommodation. The economic gap between the community inside and outside the reserve has increased and the administration is trying to compensate the community inside the reserve by constructing a new building outside the reserve.

Generally speaking, as Xu et al. (2016) point out, unlike most developed countries, China has its particular context and is testing a process of sustainable tourism development implemented through top-down institutional arrangements, using strict control systems to pursue both natural resource conservation and economic growth. The Chinese government-dominated mass tourism nature-based development model has brought a dual structure with modern efficient management patterns at the core site and municipal scales, and a backward unsustainable situation at the community scale. And more importantly, this model risks running into a potential path-dependency trap, which creates barriers to integrated sustainable development (Xu et al., 2016).

Challenges of Sustainability of Nature Tourism

Demand Side

China's nature tourism witnessed dramatic growth since the late 1980s when the government began to develop domestic tourism. Different than other developing countries, such as those in Africa, where the nature attractions are mainly utilized to attract western tourists, most of China's nature tourism received above 90 percent domestic tourists. And Chinese tourists have specific characteristics in terms of travel time, preference, behavior, and environmental awareness compared with westerners.

First, Chinese tourists' visits have been over-concentrated on public holidays. The potential of Chinese travel demand had been triggered in particular in 1998 when the Chinese government implemented an economic incentive policy called Golden Week Policy Two. Although it is a legislative right for any employee who has worked for any kind of institutions for at least one year to enjoy their annual paid leave, for many Chinese, especially who work for private companies, it is just a right on paper. A national survey I finished in 2013 shows that almost 40 percent of 2,552 respondents reportedly don't have annual paid leave. And only 30 percent of the respondents can arrange vacation time with paid leave by themselves. In this context, most Chinese need to use public holidays which have been scheduled by the central government annually, in particular the golden weeks, to travel with their family or friends. The Golden Week policy has substantially increased the need for outdoor recreation and nature tourism. It has also unintentionally made a mess of China's biggest landmarks and cities, with thousands and thousands of people and recently cars swarming the tourist attractions, especially the famous scenic sites. There is a popular ironic description of the travel experience in China which says that in the scenic spots, during the long holidays, the adults can only see the heads of others while children can only see the bottoms of adults (Godbey & Song, 2014). It is not surprising that the crowding caused chaos in many destinations. Mt. Huashan in Shaanxi Province, Jiuzhaigou Valley in Sichuan Province, among other natural attractions, once reported that tourists were stranded due to overcrowding during peak days. Although carrying capacity has ecological, psychological, physical, social, and economic dimensions, the base line for Chinese is safety, in other words, to ensure there is no accident or personal harm.

Second, the Chinese perception of and behavior related to nature and carrying capacity is different from westerners. There is a deep social and cultural content to virtually all nature tourism in China that distinguishes it from the west. For Chinese tourists, nature conservation does not mean the separation of human from nature but being within nature harmoniously (Xu, Chu, Sofield, & Li, 2014). Experiencing nature does not mean experiencing hardship in nature but means realizing the ideal life in nature. Chinese tourists in natural areas want easy access, and comfort, rather than physical exercise, and friendly companionship rather than the "pure" wilderness. Therefore, roads, concrete paths, stairways, hotels, and restaurants, even cable cars and elevators are regarded as necessary to facilitate ease of access for tourists. The peaks of many famous mountains are normally categorized as part of their core areas; however, for Chinese, climbing the peaks is amongst the most attractive activities and a cultural tradition dating back several thousand years. Consequently, violation of the conservation regulation is obvious and common. Conflicts arise when tourists are not allowed into mountain peak core areas, as is the case with many of China's new nature reserves that follow a modified western pattern of zoning. Such conflicts also occur between the institutions and their on-site management teams who want tourist income, and their superiors, whose responsibility is mainly to demonstrate their conservation efforts (Xu et al., 2014). Although the government tries to regulate nature tourism, most nature reserve managers are faced with the conflicts in trying to meet government regulation and Chinese tourist demands, a "middle way" or harmony way can usually be found. Meanwhile, with a huge population and high density of population, it is expected and widely accepted for most Chinese to live with the concept of "crowded" (Godbey & Song, 2014). Chinese visitors will tolerate many more people in a confined space without feeling uncomfortable than many westerners. Growing up in a collective culture, most Chinese like to visit the places which are famous and most frequently visited, such as the Five Famous Mountains, Jiuzhaigou Valley, and the West Lake. When Chinese visit these must-sees, it seems reasonable to be tolerant of the crowding.

Supply Side

On the supply side, there are lots of challenges to sustainability in nature tourism destinations.

First, the economic-orientation and Fordism production mode has been implemented in the tourism industry (Xu et al., 2016). Economic growth and GDP-dominated outlooks have been followed for more than three decades. And for tourism which has been positioned as an important industry and income earner, economic benefits have been given more importance, in particular in the undeveloped regions. Regional economic development is still an important responsibility for the local government authorities who are responsible for environmental protection at the same time. Without many income resources, tourism is regarded as the main, if not only economic engine in the nature tourism destinations which are always located in less-developed regions. Tourism income, coming from entrance tickets and infrastructure services, is the resource of taxation and community's living. More importance is attached to economic benefits rather than tourist experience or ecological impacts. The impulse of development is always stronger than the motivation for protection, in particular with the absence of punishment of violations. Hence, large-scale construction of man-made landscapes and tourism facilities has resulted in damage to natural landscapes and environmental degradation.

Second, there is gap between the policies and practices in terms of sustainability. Xu & Sofield (2013) examined sustainability components in China's tourism policies, including 56 tourism development policies by the State Councils and 31 provinces since the 1980s. They found that while sustainability was an important component in some of these policies, the meaning of sustainability in the tourism sector was confusing and pro-business tourism development still played a dominant role. Although sustainability is often stated as the purpose of development, and tourism development strategies are regarded as more environmentally oriented than other industries, little guidance is provided to make sure that sustainability principles are followed.

Third, the current nature tourism resource administration system seems to work un-efficiently and un-effectively to achieve the goals of sustainability. There is no unequivocally different function in terms of tourism and recreation utilization of these natural resources. Laws are lacking to clarify the goals, principles, management structure, financial systems, and protection for the abundant natural resource sites. Although each administration agency has its own regulations, planning, and policies, in the current complexity of the system, it is difficult for managers to follow all of the regulations. Meanwhile, the complexity of the administration system also leads to a "tragedy of the commons"—any individual administration department would not undertake the due responsibility of sustainable development. Generally speaking, the complicated and overlapped administration system makes integrated and holistic sustainable development very difficult, if possible. Problems with the overall system have sparked debate in China about how best to reorganize its administration and management. The debate focuses on two key aspects: organizational arrangements and financial structures.

Fourth, the implementation of the regulations is quite loose. Although the modern western-constructed conservation institutions have been established gradually, the violation of regulations is quite common and obvious. Sightseeing trails and commercial tourist facilities have been built in the core area of many natural reserves. Although there are regulations on carrying capacity, i.e. Regulations on Scenic Spots Planning (GB50298-1999) and General Specification for Tourism Planning (GB/T18971-2003) which are mandatory and require the tourist attractions to identify the limitation of tourist flows, as well as China's Tourism Law in 2013 which empowers the regulation on carrying capacity as a legal effect, only very few natural tourist sites have limited the numbers of tourist arrivals and their staying time. Since there is no operative mechanism and measure which compel the sites to implement the carrying capacity regulation, the related administrative and legislative regulations are just on paper.

Fifth, local community involvement is insufficient as community involvement and participation is crucial to sustainability. The ways of participation may vary in different countries, but generally include joining in the process of self-governance, responding to authoritative decisions that impact on one's life, and working cooperatively with others on issues of mutual concern (Til, 1984). As Tosun and Jenkins (1996) noted, in some developing countries, democratic institutions and regulations were only shared by some state and business elites. In China, of those reserves developing tourism, the survey in 1997 showed that only 10.7 percent benefit more than half of the local people, and about 22.7 percent never bring economic benefits to local communities. The current administration and management system has not encouraged the communities' participation during the process from planning to management, operation, economic benefits, and environmental protection. And developers and managers are always unwillingness to let the local community be involved in the planning process. Meanwhile, local residents' apathy and unawareness about participation is also an obstacle to implementing sustainability from a community perspective. Without well-constructed community organization, the participation of the community in the development process is based on individual capacity. This individual participation mode makes community cohesion ineffective. Although the introduction by the planning experts of the western concept of community involvement for destination sustainability became more and more common, the facts showed that the implementation is not easy.

Suggestions: Chinese Approach to Sustainability

Sustainable development which incorporates ecological, social, and economic aspects has been confirmed as the goal and framework of development in China. Aiming at achieving the "development that meets the needs of the present without compromising the ability of future generations to meet their own needs", Chinese government appeals to society to take efforts with this slogan of ecological civilization, harmonious society, and beautiful China. Tourism has been regarded as a pilot during this effort. However, due to reasons discussed above, there are plenty of challenges for the sustainability of tourism, as well as natural tourism.

From both sides of demand and supply, the following suggestions might be offered:

First, the Chinese cultural context should be considered when we are striving for sustainability. The different implementation of western concepts of sustainability via a Chinese approach is the general anthropocentrism and anthropomorphism inherent in the Chinese value system that is derived from Confucian philosophy and Daoism (Li, 2004). The index of sustainability in China should be constructed with the consideration of Chinese culture and social context. Meanwhile, not only the policymakers, managers, environmental protectors, but also the tourists and the public should be educated towards more sustainable consumption, production and administration modes.

Second, the "enlightened mass tourism" should be regarded as a philosophy of tourism development in general and nature tourism specifically. Noticing the contradictions and gap between the capitalist-based mass tourism thesis and the ethics-based alternative tourism antithesis, Weaver (2014) created a term of "enlightened mass tourism" as a constructive synthesis. He pointed out that sustainable tourism was contextualized as an evolving synthesis arising from the need to amalgamate the gap between mass tourism and alternative tourism because of internal contradictions that limit their contribution to development. Opportunities for expanding the ethical bridgehead in mass tourism created by adherence to corporate social responsibility policies derive from the integration of alternative tourism products within mass tourism destinations and itineraries, accompanying possibilities for transformational tourist learning, and the reassertion of indigenous rights. This idea should be clarified as the philosophy of tourism development in China.

Third, some efforts should be made to de-centralize Chinese vacation time. By enforcing the annual paid leave across the country with effective legal measure, or empowering the local government the right to schedule public holidays, the pressure from over-concentrating tourist flows would be alleviated to some extent.

Forth, the classification and administration system of natural resource sites should be reformed. The author suggests re-classifying the natural resource sites according to two independent dimensions, i.e. level of visitation and maintaining biodiversity. This classification reflects interconnectedness between tourism activities and natural assets in protected area settings. Implementation of this model requires the availability of comprehensive data about both protected area ecologies and tourist recreational activities. Based on this classification, a more effective administration and management, like the national parks system in U.S.A. should be established and cover those with high biodiversity. And the franchise system is suggested for those with high biodiversity and high visitation. Central government financial support is suggested for those with high biodiversity and low visitation. The new administration and management system will have an institutional structure capable of coordinating decision-making by inter-governmental agencies across national, provincial, and local scales, as well as by government departments, enterprises, and local community.

Fifth, reforms should be implemented to increase the collective participation of natural resource-dependent communities in the development and management of nature tourism. There are four prerequisites for community participation and involvement: namely, legal rights and opportunities to participate; access to information; provision of enough resources for people or groups to get involved; and genuinely public, that is, broad instead of selective, involvement from the concerned communities. Hence, it is necessary to empower the destination community at four levels, i.e. economic, psychological, social, and political (Scheyvens, 1999). The future of community involvement clearly hinges on the economic, political, psychological, and social empowerment of the local community through the communication of ideas, skills, and education among those peoples.

Sixth, the scientific survey and study should be carried out at national level as it is necessary to develop an improved inventory of natural resources such as species counts, vegetation surveys, and the analysis of soil and water quality, the quantification of visitor impacts including visitor counting, surveys of visitor satisfaction and experience, as well as measures of local conflict or benefit, and to conduct comprehensive and interdisciplinary management evaluations through a broader range of professionals.

Note

1 For example, Jiuzhaigou Valley is a national natural reserve, national key scenic resort, natural forest park, and World Natural Heritage. Zhangjiajie has the titles of national key scenic resort, natural forest park, natural geo-park, and World Natural Heritage.

References

Buckley, R. (2012). Sustainable tourism: Research and reality. *Annals of Tourism Research*, 39, 528–546.

Du Cros, H., Bauer, T., Lo, C., & Song, R. (2005). Cultural heritage assets in China as sustainable tourism products: Case studies of the Hutongs and the Huanghua section of the Great Wall. *Journal of Sustainable Tourism*, 13, 171–194.

Godbey, G. & Song, R. (2014). *Finding Leisure in China*. State College, PA: Venture Publishing.

Goodwin, H. (1996). In pursuit of ecotourism. *Biodiversity and Conservation*, 5(3), 277–291.

Li, W. (2004). Environmental management indicators for ecotourism in China's nature reserves: A case study in Tianmushan Nature Reserve. *Tourism Management*, 25, 559–564.

Murphy, P. E. (1985). *Tourism: A Community Approach*. London: Routledge.

Nianyong, H. & Zhuge, R. (2001). Ecotourism in China's nature reserves: opportunities and challenges. *Journal of Sustainable Tourism*, 9, 228–242.

Peng, D. (2003). *Governance of Tourist Attractions in China, Beijing*. China Tourism Publication (in Chinese).

Scheyvens, R. (1999). Ecotourism and the empowerment of local communities. *Tourism Management*, 20, 245–249.

Silva, J. A. & Khatiwada, L. K. (2014). Transforming conservation into cash? Nature tourism in Southern Africa. *Africa Today*, 61(1), 17–45.

Sofield, T. & Li, S. (1998). Tourism development and cultural policies in China. *Annals of Tourism Research*, 25(2), 362–392.

Sofield, T. & Li, S. (2011). Tourism governance and sustainable national development in China: A macro-level synthesis. *Journal of Sustainable Tourism*, 19(4–5), 501–534.

Su, D., Wall, G., & Eagles, P. F. J. (2007). Emerging governance approaches for tourism in the protected areas of china. *Environment Management*, 39, 749–759.

Til, V. J. (1984). Citizen participation in the future. *Policy Studies Review*, 3(2), 311–322.

Tosun, C. & Jenkins, C. L. (1996). Regional planning approaches to tourism development: The case in Turkey. *Tourism Management*, 17, 519–531.

Wang, G., Innes, J., Wu, S., Krzyzanowski, J., Yin, Y., Dai, S., & Liu, S. (2012). National park development in China: Conservation or commercialization? *AMBIO*, 41(3), 247–261.

Weaver, D. B. (2012). Organic, incremental and induced paths to sustainable mass tourism convergence. *Tourism Management*, 33(5), 1030–1037.

Weaver, D. B. (2014). Asymmetrical dialectics of sustainable tourism: Toward enlightened mass tourism. *Journal of Travel Research*, 53(2), 131–140.

Whitelaw, P. A., King, B. E., & Tolkach, D. (2014). Protected areas, conservation and tourism: Financing the sustainable dream. *Journal of Sustainable Tourism*, 22(4), 584–603.

Xiao, H. (2006). The discourse of power: Deng Xiaoping and tourism development in China. *Tourism Management*, 27(5), 803–814.

Xu, H. & Sofield, T. (2013). Sustainability in Chinese development tourism policies. *Current Issues in Tourism*, 19(3), 1337–1355. DOI:10.1080/13683500.2013.849665

Xu, H., Ding, P., & Packer, J. (2008). Tourism research in China: Understanding the unique cultural contexts and complexities. *Current Issues in Tourism*, 11(6), 473–491.

Xu, H., Zhu, D., & Bao, J. (2016). Sustainability and nature-based mass tourism: Lessons from China's approach to the Huangshan Scenic Park. *Journal of Sustainable Tourism*, 24(2), 182–202.

Xu, H., Cui, Q., Sofield, T., & Li, F. M. S. (2014). Attaining harmony: Understanding the relationship between ecotourism and protected areas in China. *Journal of Sustainable Tourism*, 22(8), 1131–1150.

16 Tourism in Preserved Nature Areas in Taiwan

Yu-Liang Tseng, Noriko Sato, Shih-Shuo Yeh and Tzung-Cheng Huan

Development of Nature Tourism in Taiwan

Study Background and Objective

The island of Taiwan (formerly known as "Formosa") was mainly inhabited by Taiwanese aborigines until the Dutch and Spanish settlement during the Age of Discovery in the 17th century, when Han Chinese began immigrating to the island. In 1624, the Dutch East India Company established a stronghold called Fort Zeelandia at Anping, Tainan. Subsequently in 1626, the Spanish Empire landed on and occupied northern Taiwan, at the ports of Keelung and Tamsui, as a base to extend their trading. This colonial period lasted 16 years until 1642, when the last Spanish fortress fell to Dutch forces. In 1662, the Dutch were expelled by the Qing dynasty which annexed Taiwan (Kelly & Brown, 2010; Wikipedia, 2016f). Eventually Taiwan was ceded to the Great Japanese Empire in 1895 because of Japan's success in the First Sino-Japanese War; however, Taiwan was taken over by the Chinese because of Japan's failure in World War II in 1945, and separated from mainland China in 1949 due to the Chinese Civil War (Kelly & Brown, 2010; Wikipedia, 2016f).

The history of nature tourism in Taiwan may be best described by two development stages. The first stage relates to the development of nature tourism during the Japanese occupation of Taiwan, from 1895 to 1945, that marked the end of the Second World War. The second stage is currently unfolding under the rule of the Republic of China since 1945 (Kelly & Brown, 2010). During the stage of Japanese occupation, nature tourism revolved around identifying locations for setting up wilderness areas to be used for recreational purposes. After 1945, nature tourism further evolved around national parks. Today, nature tourism in Taiwan has proliferated from national parks to National Scenic Areas, National Forest Recreation Areas, and so on (Kelly & Brown, 2010; Wikipedia, 2016g).

Taiwan was part of the Great Japanese Empire from 1895 to 1945 and in 1931 the Great Japanese Empire released the "Japan National Park Law". The Japanese followed American's model of the national park and requested the then Emperor of Japan to establish similar national parks in the Great Japanese Empire, including Taiwan. In 1933 the Taiwan National Park Investigation Committee was constituted for surveying and identifying scenic areas with rich biodiversity. This initiative formed the foundation for setting up national parks, and helped draft the Taiwan National Park Protocol based on the Japan National Park Law (Gissibl *et al.*, 2012; Tang, 2014; Wikipedia, 2016g). According to its findings, the committee further proposed to establish the following three national parks as the beginning of national park development: (1) Daiton National Park including what is now Yangmingshan, (2) Tsugitaka Taroko National Park which is now Taroko National Park and Shei-Pa National Park, and (3) Niitaka Arisan National Park which is now Yushan and Alishan national parks. In 1937 the Governor-General of Taiwan announced the official demarcation of the above three national parks. However, the process of consolidating the national parks in Taiwan was terminated because of the Pacific War (Gissibl *et al.*, 2012; Tang, 2014; Wikipedia, 2016g).

Post 1945, Taiwan was returned back to China and the national park movement was revived from 1961 onward. Subsequently, the Taiwan National Park Law passed in 1972 to protect the nature and wildlife with a mandate for conservation, education, recreation and research. Since 1982 nine national parks have been developed including (1) Kenting, (2) Yushan, (3) Yangmingshan, (4) Taroko, (5) Shei-pa, Kinmen (or Quemoy), (6) Donsha Atoll, (7) Taijiang, (8) South Penghu and (9) Shoushan falling under the jurisdiction of the Taiwan Ministry of the Interior (Gissibl *et al.*, 2012; Tang, 2014).

The island of Taiwan located on the western edge of the Pacific Ocean is about 35,883 square kilometres (13,855 square miles) in size, smaller than Switzerland and larger than Belgium. It lies approximately 180 kilometres (110 miles) off the southeastern coast of mainland China situated across the Strait of Taiwan. To the north is the East China Sea and to the east is the Philippine Sea. It has Bashi Channel of the Luzon Strait to the south and the South China Sea to the southwest. Smaller islands of the archipelago include the Penghu islands in the Taiwan Strait, 50 kilometers (31 miles) west of the main island, with an area of 127 square kilometers (49 square miles). The tiny islet of Xiaoliuqiu is off the southwest coast, and Orchid Island and Green Island are to the southeast, separated from the northernmost islands of the Philippines by the Bashi Channel. The islands of Kinmen and Matsu near the coast of Fujian across the Taiwan Strait have a total area of 180 square kilometers (69 square miles). To the east are inhospitable rugged mountains comprising of five ranges from the northern to the southern tip, while the inhabited plains lie in the west. Taiwan has been abundantly endowed with high mountains consisting of over 200 peaks over 3,000 meters high (Kelly & Brown, 2010; Wikipedia, 2016a, 2016f).

Thirteen national scenic areas falling under the control of the Tourism Bureau of Taiwan have been introduced for leisure and tourism purpose. The Northeast Coast National Scenic Area was set up in 1984, followed by Guanyinshan, Sun Moon Lake, Tri-Mountain, Alishan, Siraya, Southwest Coast, Maolin, Dapeng Bay, East Rift Valley, East Coast, Penghu, and Matsu National Scenic Areas. Furthermore, out of 22 national forest recreation areas in Taiwan, 18 are supervised by the Forestry Bureau, two by the Veterans Affairs Council and the other two by the National Taiwan University and National Chung Cheng University (Tourism Bureau, 2008; Wikipedia, 2016a).

Between 2002 and 2008, nature tourism thrived owing to a series of promotion campaigns such as the Plan for Doubling of Tourist Arrivals under the aegis of the Executive Yuan. Nature tourism has been booming in national parks, national scenic areas, and national forest recreation areas, and continues to be utilized for attracting international tourists (Tourism Bureau, 2008).

Today nine national parks (with a national nature park), 13 national scenic areas, and 22 national forest recreation areas are the main suppliers of nature tourism for locals and international visitors (Wikipedia, 2016a). To explore the nature-based tourism in Taiwan, this article focuses on nature tourism as it occurs in national parks and national scenic areas situated in high altitude, including Yushan National Park, Taroko National Park, and Alishan National Scenic Area. It also touches on small islands such as Kinmen National Park, Penghu National Scenic Area, Orchid Island, and Green Island which have recently emerged as popular nature attractions.

Unique Nature Tourism in Taiwan

Yushan National Park is home to Yushan, the highest peak of Taiwan and also the highest peak in Northeast Asia. The park was originally established as the Daiton National Park by the Governor-General of Taiwan on 12 December, 1937 when Taiwan was a part of the Empire of Japan (Wikipedia, 2016g). The park with a total of 103,121 hectares contains over thirty peaks, more than 3,000 meters with two-thirds of its area being above 2,000 meters. The elevation difference among recreation areas in the park could be up to 3,600 meters, characterized by peaks, canyons, cliffs, and valleys. Due its remoteness to the city and a cap on visitation, Yushan National Park is not the most visited national park; however, it still managed to attract 1,044,994 visitors in 2015 (Tourism Bureau, 2016).

Taroko National Park was named after the Taroko Gorge, the landmark gorge of the park. The park was originally established as the Tsugitaka-Taroko National Park by the Governor-General of Taiwan on 12 December, 1937 when Taiwan was a part of the Empire of Japan. In the year of 1945, the Chinese government subsequently ceased the development of the park and it was not until 28 November, 1986 when the park was reopened in some sense. The park plays a significant role in the ongoing environmental protection movement that attempts to protect natural scenery, historic relics and wildlife, and to facilitate scientific research and promote environmental education (Gissibl *et al.*, 2012; Tang, 2014; Wikipedia, 2016g). It was documented that the park hosted 6,605,985 visitors in 2015 (Tourism Bureau, 2016).

Alishan National Scenic Area, one of Taiwan's most-visited destinations, has been inhibited by the Taiwanese aborigines since time immemorial and Chinese migrants started making it their home only in the 19th century. Following the cession of Taiwan to Japan at the end of the First Sino-Japanese War, Japanese expeditions to the area found large quantities of cypress which led to the development of the logging industry in the area and the export of local cypress and Taiwania wood (Gissibl *et al.*, 2012; Tang, 2014; Wikipedia, 2016g). A series of narrow-gauge railways were built in the area during this time to facilitate the transportation of lumber from the mountains to the plains below, and brought a batch of visitors to the area and several new villages also began to sprout up along the railway lines. Development of this region took off only after the completion the Alishan Forest Railway in 1912 by Japanese which now entices a large number of tourists seeking the nostalgic. With the exhaustion of forest resources in the 1970s, domestic and international tourism overtook logging to become the primary economic activity in the area. The tourism industry continued to expand with the completion of the Alisan highway in the 1980s, displacing the railroad as the primary mode of transportation to the mountain. Today tourism represents the area's main engine of economic development (Gissibl *et al.*, 2012; Tang, 2014; Wikipedia, 2016g). The region was declared as a national scenic area in 2001 and facilitated 3,047,701 visitors in 2015 (Tourism Bureau, 2016).

Kinmen National Park is one of the most famous island national parks for nature tourism and is located just off the southeastern coast of mainland China. Situated about two kilometres (1.2 miles) east of the Chinese city of Xiamen, due to its strategic location, over the decades Kinmen has witnessed the significant change of geo-political climate from a historical battlefront to a present-day trading point between China and Taiwan. Quemoy is the name for the island in English and in many European languages. Because of its military significance, it limited the development on the island as an international tourist attraction. Nevertheless, in 2003 Kinmen opened itself up to tourists from Fujian in Mainland China which aided in the development of tourist infrastructure. Consequently, it became a popular weekend tourist destination owing to its quiet villages, vintage architecture, and serene beaches (Kelly & Brown, 2010; Wikipedia, 2016c). Meanwhile, those transiting via ferry between Quemoy and Xiamen also make a brief stop on the island (Kelly & Brown, 2010; Wikipedia, 2016c). Large parts of Kinmen form the Kinmen National Park, which includes old military fortifications and structures, historical dwellings, and natural scenery. In 2014, a period of the highest increase in passenger transit, 1.5 million passengers travelled by ferry between the two ports and 2,029,898 visitors (Tourism Bureau, 2016) came to the Kinmen National Park in 2015. It is important to note that starting January 2015, Chinese mainland tourists shall no longer require an Exit-and-Entry Permit in advance for visiting Kinmen, Penghu, and Matsu Islands. The new legislation is expected to further bolster tourism development in the area (Wikipedia, 2016c).

Penghu National Scenic Area covers most, but not all of the islands and islets that form Penghu County. These islands encompass a total of 320 kilometers of shoreline (Wikipedia, 2016e). Penghu National Scenic Area is divided into three recreation areas: North Sea recreation area, Magong recreation area, and South Sea recreation area. First, the North Sea Recreation Area is suitable for popular kinds of water sports and activities and represented by two famous spots. Xianjiao islet, situated south of Jibei islet, got its name owing to the vast amounts of submerged reefs (Xianjiao means dangerous reefs) and houses rich marine resources and beautiful sand beach. Its shallow coral ground is the best place for snorkeling and water activities. Tiejhan islet, a hill terrain attracting a variety of seabirds during the summer to dwell and breed, makes it a unique spot for bird-watching. Equally, Magong Island Recreation Area including Magong City and other townships was an important commercial and trade center across the Taiwan Strait, which gradually evolved into an important administration area for Penghu today. Xiyu Township is situated west of the Magong Island. The island is filled with well-known tourist sites, including the natural bay of Zhuwan, and the Dachi sand beach on the southwest side, which is the most famous beach in the national scenic area and the county. Baisha Township is a famous spot for bird-watching. Lastly, the northeast coast of Huxi Township is geologically complicated, and a long period of erosion has led to a multi-variant geological environment. Third, the south sea recreation area is known for its abundant geological features. For example, the entire Tongpan islet is surrounded by basalt columns of clear lines that form walls, the most enriched in Penghu, and has long been known as the Yellowstone Park of Penghu. Wang'an Island houses a harbor with a seabed composed of a mixture of sand beach and mud. In the early days, in addition to a coastal fishery and intertidal zone fishing, local residents used to round up catches with a drag net. Cimei islet is the fifth-largest island in Penghu, and situated at the south end of the archipelago (Wikipedia, 2016e) and its natural terrain is well preserved. In total, Penghu National Scenic Area attracted 1,323,993 visitors in 2015 (Tourism Bureau, 2016).

Green Island is a small volcanic island in the Pacific Ocean about 33 kilo-metres (21 miles) off the eastern coast of Taiwan. The island is administered as Lüdao Township, a rural township of Taitung County and one of the county's two offshore areas (the other being Orchid Island). Green Island is part of East Cost National Scenic Area and it is primarily noted for its prisons and penal colonies. The island was originally inhabited by the aboriginal Amis people. A short distance offshore from Taitung, Green Island is surrounded by beautiful coral reefs that make it a snorkeler's paradise. On the island itself, most of the scenic spots are linked by the 16.3 kilometer round the island concrete highway (Wikipedia, 2016b). Green Island attracted 363,045 visitors in 2015 (Tourism Bureau, 2016).

Orchid Island is a 45 square kilometer high island off the southeastern coast of Taiwan Island and separated from the Batanes of the Philippines by the Bashi Channel of the Luzon Strait and it is governed as Lanyu Township of Taitung County, Taiwan (Wikipedia, 2016d). The island is home to the Tao, an ethnic minority group who migrated to the island from the Batan Archipelago 800 years ago. The island is known to them as Ponso no Tao, "Island of the people", or Irala, and out of a total current population of 4,000, approximately 2,400 belong to the aboriginal Tao community and the remaining 1,600 are mainly Han Chinese. In the neighboring Philippines, the island is referred to as Botel Tobago (Wikipedia, 2016d). Orchid Island attracted 106,643 visitors in 2015 (Tourism Bureau, 2016).

Issues Confronting the Progress of Nature Tourism

Differences in Development Goals between Government Agencies

Since National Scenic Areas fall within the control of the Tourism Bureau of the Ministry of Transportation and Communications of Taiwan, while national parks fall within the jurisdiction of the Ministry of Interior of Taiwan, the policies/philosophies that govern the development of the two types of areas differ (Wikipedia, 2016e). For a national park the emphasis is on the preservation of natural and cultural resources, and development for human utilization definitely takes a backseat and for a national scenic area, the priorities are more balanced between preservation and tourism development (Wikipedia, 2016e). This has led to conflicts between preservationists and those more favorable towards the development of the area.

Seasonality

It has been evidenced that a short tourist season causes an unstable economic situation and may discourage further tourism development. Penghu, for instance, is a favorite summer tourist destination, attracting thousands of weekenders. However, this scenic area is mostly visited during the summer: when the autumn gales begin to blow in October, and the archipelago becomes deserted until April, when warmer weather seems to thaw the local tourism industry (Wikipedia, 2016e). The islands' climate has also a negative impact on its economy, as it is adverse for agriculture, and its isolated location rules out large-scale manufacturing development. Generations of Penghu residents have made their living from the sea, but over-fishing has severely depleted stocks and damaged the local fishing industry (Wikipedia, 2016e). Although tourism has become the favored way out of economic hardship for a county with a thinning population that receives more than 50 percent of its annual budget as subsidy from the central government, timely strategies to boost visitation are needed, given several projects aimed at attracting tourists in winter have been implemented with limited success (Wikipedia, 2016e).

Tourism Impacts on Small Islands

Concerning the problem and issues facing current development of small islands, Chen (2007a), investigating environmental footprints and tourism impacts of Penghu, revealed that tourism is the key economic driver of its islands. However, tourism activities would destroy the natural environment and affect the life and the culture of local residents if a comprehensive management plan is absent. In addition, the pressure on the environment resulting from tourists may alter the residents' perceptions toward tourism development. Moreover, for the case of Kinmen Island, Chen (2007b) found that Kinmen, like other small islands, suffers from a fragile environment that encounters environmental degradation and the paucity of utilities for living. For example, after Kinmen started tourism development, serious problems have surfaced, such as inappropriate waste disposal, water resource scarcity, and shortage of electricity. Lin (2007), in an investigation of the environmental loads and tourism impacts on Green Island, calculated the environmental footprint resulting from tourists and summarized the residents' perceptions of tourism impact into four categories: economy, social culture, environment, and health. The study shows that motorcycle and tour busses are the main contributor to greenhouse gas emission. The population level has exceeded the acceptable standard for human inhabitation of Green Island. For example, pollution levels during high visitation season was reported 9.4 times higher compared to low visitation season. In summary, the huge environmental overloads derived from tourism may affect the health of locals and lead to a negative attitude of residents toward tourism development (Lin, 2007).

Controversies over Establishing Casinos in Small Islands

The authority longs to legalize gambling as a way to attract tourists to Penghu, a move which some tourism experts view as an inappropriate way to promote tourism. This has invited a growing amount of concerns from the locals (Wikipedia, 2016e). In contrast, the casino supporters justify that the gaming business would attract additional investment to the islands and create jobs. They also argue that casinos would bring more than 20 billion New Taiwan Dollars in tax revenues to the local government. Other benefits would apparently be free medical treatment and transportation, 10,000 billion New Taiwan Dollars a month for elderly residents and free education for children, although details of these benefits were not explained. However, critics argue that gambling would jeopardize the islands' law and order along with nature environment so as to increase the cost of living (Wikipedia, 2016e).

Similarly, in a study by Lin (2013) concerning the casino industry in Lieyu Village which is off-island from Kinmen, an area of low income which totally relies on county and central government subsidies, the locals look to the casino industry as a solution to revive the economy. The village office sees it as its most urgent work to create its own financial resources. Thanks to the amendment of the Offshore Islands Development Act on January 12, 2009 off-island county governments are permitted to develop casinos. As such, the casino industry is no longer illegal in those small islands. The majority of Kinmen's residents think that the development of casinos could be a defining factor for the growth of the economy in Kinmen. The Lieyu's casino industry is currently in a primitive stage of development and above all, it is imperative to monitor the expansion of the casino in small islands to understand if it will be in conflict with the progress of nature tourism (Lin, 2013).

Developmental Strategies for Nature Tourism

Community-based Approach

Community-based tourism (CBT) is a concept which strives to balance local economic development and conservation via the active involvement of the host community economically and socially. Initiatives of CBT may be best exemplified in rural areas where local residents are generally economically marginalized and it has been a challenge to seek a finite boundary between economic development and conservation. As progressive development gives the local community positive economic benefit, social and environmental glitches may emerge such as blurring community identity, over-commercialization (Nicolics *et al.*, 2014), and damage to the natural environment (Ghaderi & Henderson, 2012).The key to success is to attract the right tourists embracing the ideology of CBT. In this regard, it is likely that at the embryotic stage for the development of CBT the size of visitor market may be small since the concept of CBT is not a prevailing development thought in Taiwan. To facilitate the growth of nature tourism in the preserved areas, local, regional, and central governments ought to pour into financial and human resources and provide incentives for the local tourism business operators in the shape of tax deductions.

The three kinds of barriers which exist in community participation are operational barriers, structural barriers, and cultural barriers; and these are also applicable in Taiwan. Operational levels include centralization of public administration of tourism, lack of co-ordination, and lack of information. Structural limitations include attitudes of professionals, lack of expertise, elite domination, lack of appropriate legal system, lack of trained human resources, relatively high cost of community participation, and lack of financial resources. Cultural limitations include limited capacity of poor people and apathy and a low level of awareness in the local community (Tosun, 2000). Taiwan is similar to the other developing countries such as Lao and only a small number of the local residents in the village were satisfied with their current and on-going participation expressing their strong willingness to continue participating in the process of tourism planning and development, whereas a large group of the residents were not willing to do it at all in the future(Kim *et al.*, 2014). Community participation has proven to be a successful model for tourism development in developed countries, but there exists some barriers in the case of developing countries (Tosun, 2000). The Taiwanese government can learn from the developed countries how to overcome barriers for developing successful sustainable nature-based tourism as CBT in Taiwan

Environmental Education

Environmentally friendly operations in the context of tourism have gradually received attention from the traveling public as well the suppliers of tourism (Han, 2015). However, recently, several studies (e.g. Chan, 2008) have shown that from the tourism operator's perspective, one barrier to practicing green operations is a lack of environmental expertise (Best & Thapa, 2013; Gleim *et al.*, 2013). The literature (e.g. Chang *et al.*, 2014) further urged that the timely delivery of environmental education should be considered as the key agenda to cope with the deficiency. Indeed, a well-crafted environmental education program would not only allow managers and staff to gain necessary skills in practicing green; it would also affect the innovativeness of service design that may indirectly shift the mind-set of the general population with regard to underlying benefits of experiencing environmentally friendly services.

Taiwan's central legislative body passed the final reading of the Environmental Education Act in May 18, 2010 making such education mandatory nationwide from 2011 (Taiwan Today, 2010; The China Post, 2010). This will ensure that people are environmentally conscious at school, in society, and in life, and this will make sustainable nature-based tourism in Taiwan more feasible and successful. According to the new law, all of the following are required to attend four hours or more of environmental education programs: employees of government institutions and public business organizations, the staff and students of junior high schools and below, and employees of legal professions that receive 50 percent or more of their funding from the government. The program will be paid for by environmental education funds to be established by central and local governments. The earning, safekeeping, and usage of the funds will be left for local governing agencies to decide, while central agencies will have to carry out certification programs for environmental education organizations and environmental educators (Taiwan Today, 2010; The China Post, 2010).

Social Responsibility

Corporate social responsibility (CSR) has been a frequently discussed subject in recent years. The goal of CSR is to forgo certain aspects of financial gain in search of socially appropriate behaviors. A few advantages may encourage tourism firms to be devoted to the practice of CSR, such as reputation building and customer loyalty (Benavides-Velasco *et al.*, 2014). In addition, it is to simultaneously generate both economic and social benefits for a firm (Mair *et al.*, 2006). Yeh *et al.* (2016) used the Analytical Hierarchy Process to study the factors of the hoteliers in Taiwan in adopting greener hotel management and found that the hoteliers' ability to create a greener image is the most important contributor to the managers' decisions to adopt greener management. In other words, marketing remains the highest priority. The other factors ranked by their importance include the following: the hotel's ability to go green (second), hotel's organizational and administrative ability (third), and customers' devotion to green behavior (fourth). Since the international tourism hotel industry relies heavily on natural resources, Liu (2013) took the international tourist hotels in Taiwan as an example to examine the relationships among leaders' transformational leadership, the company's green management, strategic social corporate responsibility, employees' green capabilities, and enterprise competitiveness. Liu (2013) found that transformational leadership can positively affect green management in hotels through the development of strategic social corporate responsibility and employees' green capabilities, and then enhance the hotels' competitiveness. Liu (2013) suggested that if enterprises want to implement environmental management, it depends on the supervisor's leadership style in promoting the implementation of green management policies, as well as providing education and staff training to cultivate green capabilities and lead the enterprises to enforce strategic social responsibility. Hence, enterprises can take advantage of their own expertise and resources to target goals and invest in charity to contribute to the society. Therefore, this article would like to explore if sustainable development enterprises are able to be competitive in the market.

Monitoring as a Way to Achieve Sustainable Development

Sustainable tourism is viewed as a development concept aiming to benefit the natural environment, social-cultural identity, and economy of a host community (Waligo *et al.*, 2013). These three aspects can also affect each other (Rio & Nunes, 2012). Certainly tourism could help lift the poverty level by generating a steady stream of revenues for the local community, but might cause environmental degradation as mentioned in the case of Kinmen National Park. Thus, it important to recognize issues that may impact the development of sustainability in preserved nature areas.

The United Nations World Tourism Organization (UNWTO) was one of the first international level organizations to develop and use indicators as an instrument to monitor and measure sustainable tourism; since 1993 UNWTO has worked on numerous monitoring projects in different parts of the world (Miller & Twining-Ward, 2006). For keeping nature-based tourism sustainable, the Taiwanese government should develop and improve the monitoring systems. Monitoring involves regularly assessing the state of an issue or phenomenon relative to particular goals, expectations, and objectives. It requires a degree of technical expertise and long-term commitment to monitor and report on indicators on a regular basis. The indicators can provide the Taiwanese government with information that can enable improved decision-making, help Taiwan's government develop and prioritize action plans, and improve the general level of awareness and understanding of sustainable tourism issues.

References

Benavides-Velasco, C. A., Quintana-García, C., & Marchante-Lara, M. (2014). Total quality management, corporate social responsibility and performance in the hotel industry. *International Journal of Hospitality Management*, 41, 77–87. doi:10.1016/j. ijhm.2014.05.003

Best, M. N., & Thapa, B. (2013). Motives, facilitators and constraints of environmental management in the Caribbean accommodations sector. *Journal of Cleaner Production*, 52(0), 165–175. doi:10.1016/j.jclepro.2013.03.005

Chan, E. S. W. (2008). Barriers to EMS in the hotel industry. *International Journal of Hospitality Management*, 27(2), 187–196. doi:10.1016/j.ijhm.2007.07.011

Chang, L.-H., Tsai, C.-H., & Yeh, S.-S. (2014). Evaluation of green hotel guests' behavioral intention. In J. S. Chen (Ed.), *Advances in Hospitality and Leisure* (Vol. 10, pp. 75–89). Bingley, U.K.: Emerald Group Publishing Limited.

Chen, P.-H. C. (2007a). *An Investigation on Environmental Loads and Tourism Impacts of Island Tourism: The Case Study of Penghu.* (Unpublished Master Thesis), National Taipei University of Nursing and Health Sciences., Taipei, ROC.

Chen, Y.-W. (2007b). *An Application of Health Impact Assessment to Island Tourism.* (Unpublished Masters Thesis), National Taipei University of Nursing and Health Science, Taipei, ROC.

Ghaderi, Z., & Henderson, J. C. (2012). Sustainable rural tourism in Iran: A perspective from Hawraman Village. *Tourism Management Perspectives*, 2–3, 47–54. doi:10.1016/j.tmp.2012.03.001

Gissibl, B., Hohler, S., & Kupper, P. (2012). *Civilizing Nature: National Parks in Global Historical Perspective* (Vol. 1). New York: Berghahn Books.

Gleim, M. R., Smith, J. S., Andrews, D., & Cronin Jr, J. J. (2013). Against the green: A multi-method examination of the barriers to green consumption. *Journal of Retailing*, 89(1), 44–61. doi:10.1016/j.jretai.2012.10.001

Han, H. (2015). Travelers' pro-environmental behavior in a green lodging context: Converging value-belief-norm theory and the theory of planned behavior. *Tourism Management*, 47(0), 164–177. doi:10.1016/j.tourman.2014.09.014

Kelly, R., & Brown, J. S. (2010). *Taiwan* (Vol. 7). Melbourne, Australia: Lonely Planet.

Kim, S., Park, E., & Phandanouvong, T. (2014). *Barriers to local residents' participation in community-based tourism: lessons from Houay Kaeng Village in Laos.* Paper presented at the SHS Web of Conferences.

Lin, C.-Y. (2007). *An Investigation on Environmental Loads and Tourism Impact of Green Island.* (Unpublished Masters Thesis), National Taipei University of Nursing and Health Sciences, Taipei, ROC.

Lin, C.-Y. (2013). *The Study on Casino Industry with Tourism in Lieyu Village of Kinmen County.* (Unpublished Masters Thesis), Ming Chuang University, Taipei, ROC.

Liu, G.-S. (2013). *Transformational Leadership on Competitiveness of Green Hotels: The Mediation effects of Employees' Green Competence, Green Management, Strategic Corporate Social Responsibility–A study on International Tourism Hotels in Taiwan.* (Masters Thesis), Chihlee University of Technology, New Taipei City.

Mair, J., Robinson, J., & Hockerts, K. (2006). *Social Entrepreneurship.* New York: Palgrave Macmillan

Miller, G., & Twining-Ward, L. (2006). Monitoring as an approach to sustainable tourism. In D. Buhalis & C. Costa (Eds.), *Tourism-Management-Dynamics: Trends, Management, and Tools* (pp. 51–57). Oxford, UK: Elsevier Butterworth-Heinemann

Nicolics, S., Richard, L., Jung, H., & Perfler, R. (2014). Environmental planning for cultural heritage management: An integrated planning approach for heritage site communities. *Regions Magazine*, 293(1), 11–14. doi:10.1080/13673882.2014.10806801

Rio, D., & Nunes, L. M. (2012). Monitoring and evaluation tool for tourism destinations. *Tourism Management Perspectives*, 4, 64–66.

Taiwan Today. (2010, May 19). *Environmental Education Act Passed in Legislature, Taiwan Today.* Retrieved from www.taiwantoday.tw/ct.asp?xItem=103733&CtNode=436

Tang, B.-L. (2014). *The Establishment and Orientation of Taiwan's National Parks in Japanese Colonial Period.* (Unpublished Masters Thesis), National Chengchi University, Taipei, ROC.

The China Post. (2010, May 19). *Environmental Education Mandatory in Taiwan, The China Post.* Retrieved from www.chinapost.com.tw/taiwan/national/national-news/2010/05/19/257057/Environmental-education.htm

Tosun, C. (2000). Limits to community participation in the tourism development process in developing countries. *Tourism Management*, 21(6), 613–633. doi:10.1016/S0261-5177(00)00009-1

Tourism Bureau, M. O. T. C. (2008). *Annual Report on Tourism 2007*. Taiwan: Tourism Bureau, M.O.T.C.

Tourism Bureau, M. O. T. C. (2016). *Visitors to the Principal Scenic Spots in Taiwan, January-December 2015*. Taiwan: Tourism Bureau, M.O.T.C.

Waligo, V. M., Clarke, J., & Hawkins, R. (2013). Implementing sustainable tourism: A multi-stakeholder involvement management framework. *Tourism Management*, 36, 342–353. doi:10.1016/j.tourman.2012.10.008

Wikipedia. (2016a). Geography of Taiwan. Retrieved 6th of May, 2016, from https://en.wikipedia.org/wiki/Geography_of_Taiwan

Wikipedia. (2016b). Green Island, Taiwan. Retrieved 6th of May, 2016, from https://en.wikipedia.org/wiki/Green_Island,_Taiwan

Wikipedia. (2016c). Kinmen. Retrieved 6th of May, 2016, from https://en.wikipedia.org/wiki/Kinmen

Wikipedia. (2016d). Orchid Island. Retrieved 6th of May, 2016, from https://en.wikipedia.org/wiki/Orchid_Island

Wikipedia. (2016e). Penghu National Scenic Area.. Retrieved 6th of May, from https://en.wikipedia.org/wiki/Penghu_National_Scenic_Area

Wikipedia. (2016f). Taiwan. Retrieved 6th of May, 2016, from https://en.wikipedia.org/wiki/Taiwan

Wikipedia. (2016g). Taiwan under Japanese Rule. Retrieved 6th of May, 2016, from https://en.wikipedia.org/wiki/Taiwan_under_Japanese_rule

Yeh, S.-S., Huang, M.-L., Fotiadis, A. K., & Huan, T.-C. (2015). Factors in adopting greener hotel management: An analytic hierarchy process approach. International Conference on Hospitality, Tourism and Leisure, 17th–18th May 2015, Shih-Chien University, Taipei, Taiwan.

17 Forest as a Venue for Recreational Therapy in Japan

Noriko Sato, Yu-Liang Tseng, Shih-Shuo Yeh and Tzung-Cheng Huan

Introduction

Development of Nature Tourism in Japan

Japan is a country of islands. It is made up of about 7,000 islands stretching along the Pacific coast of Asia. The islands lie over a large area bounded by latitudes 24° to 46°N and longitudes 122° to 146°E. Japan's islands are in a volcanic zone called the Pacific Ring of Fire. They are primarily the result of large oceanic movements occurring over hundreds of millions of years. In fact, at one time Japan was attached to the Eurasian continent until the subducting plates pulled Japan eastward which resulted in the sea of Japan (Barnes, 2003).

Though Japan has a high population density, a large portion of the land presents challenges that covers forest and mountain. Much of the mountainous terrain is not suitable for agricultural, industrial, or residential use. The habitable zones of Japan are mainly located in coastal areas and these zones have the highest population density in the world (Barnes, 2003; McCargo, 2013).

Details on early tourism activities in Japan are not abundantly available. However, there are records of excursions made by famous individuals. From about the year 1600 to 1867, domestic travel was by horse. So, there were porter stations and horse stables associated with places for lodging and food along well-traveled routes. For much of its history around the year 1600, Japan was a closed country to foreigners and therefore not much foreign tourism occurred during that time.

The Meiji Restoration around the year 1867 marked a big change which bolstered tourism development. It began with the building of a national railroad network which made tourism more affordable. The tourism boom includes both domestic and foreign tourists, as due to the Restoration, foreigners could enter Japan legally. In fact, by 1887, government officials had recognized the need for getting organized in order to attract foreign tourists. 1907 paved the way for the Hotel Development Law which allowed the Railways Ministry to begin constructing publicly owned hotels throughout Japan (Leheny, 2003).

Today domestic tourism is a vital part of the Japanese economy and also contributes to its culture. Japan features Disneyland Tokyo and many cultural and natural attractions and the extensive rail network has expanded much further from a modest beginning. The railroads together with domestic flights are the basis for efficient and speedy transport.

Japan has an Agency for Cultural Affairs that designates properties with legal protection which included monuments located in historical locations including ancient tombs, palaces, forts, and castles. As of April 1, 2016 there are 1,021 Natural Monuments and 1,760 Historic Sites, some of other destinations include places of scenic beauty (n = 398) and special national monuments (n = 75).

Japanese national parks are managed by the Ministry of the Environment and as of 27 March, 2015 there were 32 National Parks and 56 Quasi-National Parks. National Parks cover about 20,996 kilometers squared (5.6 percent of Japan's land area). Quasi-National Parks cover about 13,592 kilometers squared (3.6 percent of Japan's land) and Prefectural Parks (n = 314) cover about 19,726 kilometers squared (5.2 percent of land in Japan). The areas in National and Quasi-National Parks are divided into zones which are ordinary, special, and marine. Special zones include special protection and classes I, II, and III zones which are associated with restricted access for conservation purposes. Quasi-National Parks are generally seen as less prestigious (Ministry of the Environment, 2016).

Japan has been establishing parks for a long time. It established its first public parks in 1873 (Asakusa Park, Asukayama Park, Fukagawa Park, Shiba Park, and Ueno Park). In 1929 the National Parks Association was formed and the first National Parks Law was passed in 1931. This led to the establishment of the first National Parks in March 1934 and eight more parks were established soon after. Following the Second World War, eight National Parks were created by 1955.

The current administrative framework which is followed in Japan dates back to the Natural Parks Law that came into force in 1957 and replaced the earlier National Parks Law with minor amendments.

Forest Therapy as an Activity in Nature Tourism

Following a strategy of diversification of tourism offerings, Japan has recently focused on a new form of tourism which is forest therapy. The forest bath is a kind of popular leisure activity for the Japanese and the therapeutic effect from the forest bath is widely accepted by society. Hectic lifestyle in the present times often imposes enormous amounts of pressure on people and consequently individuals opt for different channels of recuperation. An aging society is also driving the recent demand for nature tourism which is regarded as a passive form of therapy. Elder people tend to prefer serene types of activities such as regressing back to nature and many individuals choose forests as recreational and therapeutic venues. In 2005, the Japanese government conducted a series of studies and hosted the World Exposition in Aichi, Japan with the theme "the life with forest, life for forest". The result indicated that 88 percent of Japanese citizens revealed strong attachment to the forest and in a 2003 study (Morita *et al.*, 2007), more than two-thirds of Japanese respondents expressed an interest in taking shinrin-yoku (forest bathing) to promote their health. The forest and its therapeutic property is therefore an invaluable resource that can be used to promote tourism and boost local economic activities.

Unlike Germany which has already legalized forest therapy as a medical practice, there is not yet any legal regulation regarding forest therapy in Japan. But in Japan, various investigation have been conducted, such as testing heart rate and saliva to examine the validity of forest therapy (Park *et al.*, 2010). Forest therapy is an activity that is able to promote personal healing and wellness through immersion in forest and other types of natural environment. Through scientific experiments, the effectiveness of forest therapy has been proven (Sung *et al.*, 2012) as well as its ability as preventive medicine (Park *et al.*, 2010). The Forestry Agency, Ministry of Health, various universities, and corporations have combined forces to study and promote the effectiveness of forest therapy. The National Land Afforestation Promotion Organization and a few non-profit organizations (NPO) host open-recruitment for corporations to compete for the contract to construct facilities and trails for forest therapy. A local governmental agency or organization which applies for the certification as a forest therapy base needs to prove the effectiveness of healing power through physical experiment. They also need to pass rigorous inspection for the lodging facilities and present plans for future development to gain governmental approval. After a destination achieves the status of a forest therapy base, they will have to propose trail paths that allow visitors to relieve stress and seek a healthier life. These trail paths also need to be reviewed and approved. For example, a trail path is required to exceed a certain width and be at a moderate slope for regular people to enjoy their stroll without enduring too much physical stress. It is also recommended that the trails are divided into 20 minutes of walking time per section so that people can electively end their walk.

Certification of Forest Therapy

In Japan, backed by scientific evidence, forests have been found to have relaxing effects. This grants good credentials to the forest therapy base, which is usually managed by local government (Karjalainen *et al.*, 2010). Forest therapy bases have two distinct characteristics. First, they must be smooth enough to promote enjoyable walking, and second, scientific tests must be conducted to measure the effectiveness of the forest therapy. In Japan, there are many forest lands that are privately owned and local government helps land owners to retain their credentials and manage the forest. For some remote areas, forest lands are government owned and therefore local automatous groups invite local residents to participate in the process of credential application and help local development through promoting tourism. The involvement of local residents is therefore very important for the success of these bases.

In order to fully utilize the space and resources of the forest, Forestry Agency hosted a preparatory meeting in January 2004 to establish a study group on forest therapy. This study group involved industry, academia, and cross-departmental cooperation of government to examine the healing and medical properties of forest therapy. The study group also devoted attention to the promotion of forest therapy in Japan and professional certification for accreditation of forests with notable and scientifically proven healing effects. In 2005, the members of the study group openly recruited local organizations or governments to establish forest therapy bases and forest therapy routes. The group plans to facilitate the accreditation of 100 forest therapy bases all over Japan. As of February 2016, 60 forests in Japan have received their credential as forest therapy bases and have actively participated in offering forest therapy activities. There is no statistical result that documents the economic effect of these 60 forest therapy bases, but local government has noticed an increase in hospitality demand by visitors to forest therapy bases.

Forest bathing is a term coined around the 1970s and 1980s. In 1982, the Agency of Japan introduced forest bathing trips as a way to retain good lifestyle. It is now a recognized way to pursue relaxation and facilitate stress-free treatment. The effectiveness of forest bathing is due to various volatile substances generally referred to as phytoncides derived from plants (Li *et al.*, 2006). They are antimicrobial volatile organic compounds, such as a-pinene and limonene, that trees give off to prevent themselves from rotting or being eaten by insects (Duka & Ardelean, 2010). Their healing properties have been recognized and used in many countries in holistic medicine and aromatherapy. During the 1990s, Japan sent researchers to study in Germany and adopt their way of scientifically examining the effects of forest therapy. In the Japanese colloquial definition, forest bathing is simply people enjoying strolls in the forest without any scientific evidence to back up its effectiveness. Once the title "therapy" is adopted, measurable scientific results are required to prove its validity. During the next decade, Japanese civilian organizations actively participated in the promotion of forest therapy and the study of its effect. There is no government involvement directly, but many retired officials of the Forestry Agency contribute to the effort.

As for the economic benefit from forest therapy, it depends on how the local government taps these benefits through their policies in regards to the forest therapy base. Some local governments strongly emphasize the economic benefit of the forest therapy base on the local community while others do not. Certain local governments do not receive substantial funds from the central government and are forced to rely on local taxes to maintain their forest and facilities which puts a damper on their commitment to forest therapy. There is also a pressing issue relating to the members of local legislative assemblies that may not possess enough knowledge about forest therapy and feel skeptical about its merits. It is therefore difficult to draw any conclusion about the economic benefit of forest therapy. However, the growing number of tourists that each base receives since their establishment in 2008 is an indication of economic progress.

Forest Therapy and Tourism in Japan

Forest therapy could be one of the methods that can help the Japanese government to revitalize its economy on the remote and/or mountainous areas (MacNaughton, 2003). Forest therapy can contribute to one's mental, physical (Pretty, 2004), emotional (Townsend, 2006), and spiritual wellbeing (Heintzman, 2002). Japan is covered by 64 percent of forest land and contains diversified forestry eco-systems. The forestry industry in the past was a major contributor toward Japan's economy and key revenue generator for local communities. However, the decline of the forest industry led to the dwindling of the industry and the trend of depopulation of surrounding community. Developing a tourism industry through the promotion of forest therapy is a possible solution for revitalizing these communities relying on forest resources (MacNaughton, 2003). Since 2010, the Japanese government has placed emphasis on the quality of life and happiness of its citizens (Tiefenbach & Kohlbacher, 2015). The Japanese government regularly collects nationwide data to assess the wellbeing of its citizens. Forest therapy has been scientifically proven to achieve wellbeing (Mitchell *et al.*, 2015) that has been strongly advocated by the Japanese government.

Forest therapy, which could be reviewed as a tourism activity, like eco-tourism, is generally not considered as a product for the masses (Hamdan & Low, 2014). Overcrowding may reduce the quality of forest therapy and damage the forest environment (Gallagher & Herrmann, 2014). Japanese forest therapy therefore tries to slow down tourist experiences by prolonging the walk; for example, a 2-kilometer-long walk is likely to take two hours. Forest therapy guides will allow visitors to take a break to indulge in yoga, stretch exercises, and other form of aerobic exercises. This also allows the visitors to experience the forest with their primal senses and immerse themselves in the experiences. Saliva samples of some participants were taken before and after the walk to scientifically measure the therapeutic effect and these quantifiable results were used to convince people that forest therapy is a viable venue to improve one's health. Forest therapy guides are different from conventional tourist guides as they not only well versed in local anecdote that can be used to charm visitors, but are also trained in basic therapeutic skills and health exercise regimen. This way, the guides will be able to clearly explain the effectiveness of the regimens and allow visitors to choose what they need. Life in Japan is considered as hectic which means the holidays are typically short as most citizens can afford half-day, one-day trip or sometimes a two-day trip. The regimen can vary based on the number of days a visitor has; for example, Japan possesses a lot of hot springs which can usually be found around forest areas. Such destinations are suitable to offer two-day trip for its visitors to incorporate hot spring services which also means that the visitors will have to utilize local lodging services that leads to additional expenditures and contribution to the local economy.

There are two possible ways for a forest therapy base to set its price structure. One is through a negotiation between the local government and residents to determine an optimal pricing strategy for services and the other is for locals to join as a member of a forest therapy group. The association plans itineraries and sets an average price range for all practitioners to follow. Many businesses attract customers on their own without involving intermediaries such as a travel agency. Most places that offer forest therapy are less well developed and therefore the price is relatively affordable for the average individual. Their primary goal is to attract visitors and promote the place as a tourism destination so that the visitors will purchase other services, such as massage or therapeutic treatment. These will then incur additional expenditure on the visitors' part and bring revenue to the local community.

Problem and Issues Facing Current Development

The recreational activities tend to differ among forest therapy bases, depending on the characteristics of the base. The activities range from different types of exercise, refreshment therapy (aromatherapy or forest yoga), to enjoying local delicacies (usually using local materials and featuring healthy cuisine). These bases also furnish various types of seminars to promote ways to lead healthy living while revealing scientific evidence relevant to the benefits of forest therapy. Indeed, combining forest therapy and tourism has been merged as an innovative venture that is quickly gaining acceptance (Konu, 2015) by vigilant travelers. There are more than 60 bases scattered around Japan. The following section discusses unique situations transpiring in three different forest bases in Kyushu Island where it is mountainous with active volcanos and surrounded by abundant forests and hot springs.

Cases in Forest Therapy Development

1: Sasaguri Town in Fukuoka Prefecture: Combine Pilgrimage Tourism and Forest Therapy

Sasaguri is famous for its Shikoku 88 Kasho (also known as Shikoku Henro or Shikoku Junrei), which is a multi-site pilgrimage route consisting of 88 temples associated with the Buddhist monk K kai. It is one of the most distinct cultural landscapes of Japan that attracts tourists and pilgrims from around the world. Visitors undertake a journey through 88 temples for ascetic, pious, and tourism purposes (Reader, 2015). The temples and trails are mostly located in and surrounded by the nature environment. Nature often provides a sense of spiritual fulfillment (Jepson & Sharpley, 2015), and so pilgrims are more likely to be susceptible to the idea of forest therapy. This place already attracts a good number of visitors to appreciate nature and spiritual experiences. The combination of pilgrimage, tourism, and forest therapy can therefore contribute to the development of the hospitality industry. When one speaks of the development, it doesn't necessarily refer to the new construction of buildings or development of new lands; it simply refers to the development of regimens and itineraries that allows tourists to appreciate what is already here. This way, one can preserve the environment, maintain the quality of tourism experiences regarding forest therapy, and still manage to contribute to the economy.

2: Ukiha City in Fukuoka Prefecture: Synergy with the Local Tourism Industry

Ukiha City was established in 2005 by merging two towns, which is now estimated to contain 33,000 citizens. The Ukiha City forest therapy and aroma experience is available for anyone to join for 3,500 yen—an inexpensive cost. The fee includes an Ukiha Hokkori boxed meal or bento, guide, and materials for an aromatic workshop. The itinerary is available three or four times a month, typically on Fridays and weekends. The trail is about 1.8 kilometers by the Tsuzura rice field. The meal box is made of biodegradable materials and visitors are encouraged to take their litter back as no trash bin is provided at the trail. The hiking trail in the forest has a maximum capacity of 80 people and the lodging around the trail area is only able to accommodate 30 people. This arrangement allows the local forest therapy practitioner to control the quality of the therapy by not exceeding the carrying capacity. Half of Ukiha City consists of roughly half mountainous and half flatland area. As the forest therapy often takes place in mountainous areas, the local government encourages visitors to stay in the urban areas after their visit to the mountain by developing a variety of tourist services, such as hot spring lodging and the Old Street for nostalgia buffs to enjoy.

3: Hinokage Town in Miyazaki Prefecture: Using Non-profit Organizations to Allow Prosperity of Private Firms

Hinokage is a small town with approximately 5,000 residents and located next to Takachiho which is a historically significant town. Both offer heritage experiences to the visitors, such as Kagura dances and traditional handicrafts. The forest therapy group started gaining its reputation by hosting events to promote the effect of the therapy via a collaboration with the host community. The group offers the locals access to therapy services, so that the locals can be familiar with them. Two years after the forest therapy base was established, locals were well versed in forest therapy and were able to advocate the various effects of therapy in front of the visitors. The locals also benefited economically by providing hospitality and guide services to the visitors. In 2011, the local practitioners and forest therapy group members formed a non-profit organization (NPO) to privatize the training of forest therapy. Thus, more private firms could receive economic benefit from forest therapy.

Key Success Factors of Promoting Forest Therapy

Rural tourism is often dominated by small-scale businesses, which leads to competition rather than co-operation amongst them (Haven-Tang & Jones, 2012). They tend to lack the expertise for staging a central theme in order to create a sense of place identity and therefore, local leadership is one of the most important components contributing to the success of rural tourism development (Haven-Tang & Jones, 2012; Waligo *et al.*, 2013). Tourism based on forest therapy is a sustainable operation that could become the industry leader, able to unite local efforts which are essential to co-create value and offer unique experiences for its visitors. The local government is a possible stakeholder which can assume this leadership role. As an objective third party, local government can bring about partnership and collaboration among local practitioners. NPO is also another good idea as discussed in the previous section. The practitioners are still in competition with each other, but as they are all part of the same economic eco-system, they are also co-dependent on one another to attract visitors. Healthy coopetition (combination of co-operation and competition) is often necessary to achieve successful economic development (Lombard & Morris, 2012).

The involvement of stakeholders is vital to the success of rural tourism development. It enlists local residents (Harrill, 2004; Lee, 2013; Wilson *et al.*, 2001), business, government, and special interest groups (Waligo *et al.*, 2013). As researchers (e.g., Albassami *et al.*, 2015) asserted that internal marketing is essential to the promotion of external images, local residents should be involved in building a brand image of forest therapy. Meanwhile, governments need to have a strategy that allows the local residents and stakeholders to successfully take over the operation and thrive on their own (Salazar, 2012).

The training of tour guides is an important task in developing community-based tourism. Professional tour guides are able to transform a simple trip into memorable experiences for the tourists (Carmody, 2013). Apart from traditional tour guide skills and cheerful demeanor, forest tour guides also need to be well versed in alternative therapy methods and fully embrace them.

Constraints of Promoting Forest Therapy

The Fukuoka and Miyazaki Prefectures shows very different attitudes toward establishing forest therapy venues. Also, Fukuoka Prefecture receives no funds in regards to the establishment of forest therapy system and they have to rely on local automatous groups to promote the idea of forest therapy. As a result, they have a very tight budget compared to the Miyazaki Prefecture counterpart.

Sasaguri Town in Fukuoka Prefecture is a more urbanized area that possesses forests in its vicinity and traveling by tram from Fukuoka downtown to Sasaguri only takes 20 minutes, which means it is able to attract forest lovers from the metropolis. On the other hand, this also implies that the visitors are less likely to stay overnight. Ukiha City is located in a rural area, which requires one hour of travel from Fukuoka downtown by tram. Despite its remoteness, Ukiha City possesses some of Japan's best terrace scenery, the 400-year-old Old Street, a hot spring, and offers a variety of agricultural experiences. Hinokage Town is in a far-flung region and the only means of transportation that can get there is bus which takes four hours from Fukuoka downtown, and all recreational resources are scattered quite far apart from each other, so it is difficult to attract a large number of visitors. The town has recently focused their efforts on promoting train hotels (decommissioned trains made into accommodatiojn) and reinforcing the forest therapy that could hopefully entice those enjoying peace and serenity.

Prospect of Forest Therapy

Social Development in the 21st Century

The 20th century was marked by a series of wars and conflicts, most notably by two world wars in the first half. The second half was tarnished by the fight between capitalists and communists. This barrier falls after the dissembling of the Union of Soviet Socialist Republics that marks the end of the 20th century. The 21st century has entered into a new era where people increasingly yearn for peace and a world with less conflict. The world's economy also tends to be united through collaboration, such as the establishment of the single-European currency, the Euro. Internationalization seems an inevitable trend in the years to come.

The development of forest therapy, and its ideal for a better life for all mankind, also needs to consider trends in internationalization. For example, the International Society of Nature and Forest Medicine (INFOM), headquartered in Tokyo, is one such organization that is devoted to the progress and development of research involving nature and forest medicine. The Ministry of Agriculture, Forestry and Fisheries of Japan initiated a research project beginning in 2004 to study the effect of the forest environment on people's mental and physical health and based on the findings of the project, the Japanese Society of Forest Medicine was formed in 2007 and later, to reach the international community, INFOM was formed.

The Information Era

Social media is an effective tool for promoting niche tourism destinations (Alonso & Bressan, 2014). It is a new form of word-of-mouth advertisement where user interaction and user-generated content disseminates information more broadly and faster (Phang *et al.*, 2013). There are now various websites promoting forest therapy bases and forest medicines and social media can be quite effective in foresting one's knowledge, attitude, and perception about a nature-based leisure activity (e.g. Gupta *et al.*, 2015).

Change in Population Structure

The Japanese population reached its peak in 2007 and has been declining ever since. It is estimated that, by 2025 people above 65 years of age will account for 25 percent of the entire population. It means that the market for forest therapy will grow as older visitors tends to be more susceptible to the idea. On the other hand, this implies that the industry may need to operate with a limited labor force.

Future Paths of Forest Therapy

The changes of the 21st century usher in a new era of new tourism development as phrases such as sustainable tourism, community-based tourism, eco-tourism, and nature-based tourism became increasingly popular. Despite the name, the new tourism development is not free from the influence of the changes that the 21st century has to face.

Tourism can be subdivided into domestic and international travel. However, a growing sense of global village and new technology-inspired traveling methods blur the boundaries between countries. Domestic tourism also suffers serious competition even with overseas destinations. Many Asian populations, such as in Malaysia and Japan, are fascinated by Western culture and prefer overseas holiday (Boniface *et al.*, 2016). For example, the beach destinations in Japan have to compete with Hawaii which to most Asians is a more exotic place. The Japanese domestic ski resort also needs to compete with its counterpart in Austria. Therefore, domestic tourism destinations also need to build a competitive edge over alike international destinations. Nature tourism, specifically forest therapy, is one way to differentiate Japanese tourism products from their global competitors. It is important to use these unique, authentic characteristics to attract inbound tourists (Carlisle *et al.*, 2013).

Long life expectancy is seemingly a distinct trait of the Japanese owing to a healthy lifestyle in eating and recreation. It is estimated that Japan will have the highest proportion of elderly in the world by the year 2020 (Campbell, 2014). Thus the demand for forest therapy from seniors is expected to grow. On a different but related note, hiring retirees to serve as tour guides and receptionists for the therapy services could be considered as a new service alternative.

Environmental protection is one of the contemporary issues facing tourism development. The aim of eco-tourism and nature tourism is to maintain the natural environment while providing a certain level of economic growth. It also promotes the idea of immersion in nature to improve one's wellbeing as low-energy and low-pollution transportation modes have been often employed, such as train, cable car, and electric car. As for forest therapy, integrating such eco-friendly methods becomes a vital step in enhancing visitor experiences.

In conclusion, future tourism businesses ought to embrace global agendas to maintain competitiveness in an overcrowded marketplace (Hassan, 2000). Developing environmentally friendly tourism products is also a prevailing trend (Han, 2015; Yeh *et al.*, 2016). Such a factor contributes to tourism development, especially in sustainable tourism which needs to reach a balance between economic growth and environmental protection.

References

Albassami, F. A., Al-Meshal, S. A., & Bailey, A. A. (2015). An investigation of internal marketing and its effects on employees in the banking sector in Saudi Arabia. *Journal of Financial Services Marketing*, 20(3), 176–190. doi:10.1057/fsm.2015.11

Alonso, A. D., & Bressan, A. (2014). Social media usage among micro and small winery businesses in a 'niche' market: A case study. *International Journal of Innovation and Regional Development*, 5(3), 243–265. doi:10.1504/IJIRD.2013.059877

Barnes, G. L. (2003). Origins of the Japanese islands: The new "Big Picture". *Nichibunken Japan Review*, 15, 3–50.

Boniface, B., Cooper, R., & Cooper, C. (2016). *Worldwide destinations: The geography of travel and tourism* (7th ed.). New York: Routledge.

Campbell, J. C. (2014). *How policies change: The Japanese government and the aging society*. New Jersey: Princeton University Press.

Carlisle, S., Kunc, M., Jones, E., & Tiffin, S. (2013). Supporting innovation for tourism development through multi-stakeholder approaches: Experiences from Africa. *Tourism Management*, 35, 59–69. doi:10.1016/j.tourman.2012.05.010

Carmody, J. (2013). Intensive tour guide training in regional Australia: An analysis of the Savannah Guides organisation and professional development schools. *Journal of Sustainable Tourism*, 21(5), 679–694. doi:10.1080/09669582.2012.744412

Duka, R., & Ardelean, D. (2010). Phytoncides and phytoalexins–vegetal antibiotics. *Jurnal Medical Aradean (Arad Medical Journal)*, 13(3), 19–25.

Gallagher, D., & Herrmann, N. (2014). *Antiepileptic drugs for the treatment of agitation and aggression in dementia: Do they have a place in therapy? Drugs*, 74(15), 1747–1755. doi:10.1007/s40265-014-0293-6

Gupta, N., Raghavan, R., Sivakumar, K., Mathur, V., & Pinder, A. C. (2015). Assessing recreational fisheries in an emerging economy: Knowledge, perceptions and attitudes of catch-and-release anglers in India. *Fisheries Research*, 165, 79–84. doi:10.1016/j.fishres.2015.01.004

Hamdan, M., & Low, K. C. P. (2014). Ecotourism development in Brunei Darussalam. *Transnational Corporations Review*, 6(3), 248–272.

Han, H. (2015). Travelers' pro-environmental behavior in a green lodging context: Converging value-belief-norm theory and the theory of planned behavior. *Tourism Management*, 47, 164–177. doi:10.1016/j.tourman.2014.09.014

Harrill, R. (2004). Residents' attitudes toward tourism development: A literature review with implications for tourism planning. *Journal of Planning Literature*, 18(3), 251–266. doi:10.1177/0885412203260306

Hassan, S. S. (2000). Determinants of market competitiveness in an environmentally sustainable tourism industry. *Journal of Travel Research*, 38(3), 239–245. doi:10.1177/004728750003800305

Haven Tang, C., & Jones, E. (2012). Local leadership for rural tourism development: A case study of Adventa, Monmouthshire, UK. *Tourism Management Perspectives*, 4, 28–35. doi:10.1016/j.tmp.2012.04.006

Heintzman, P. (2002). A conceptual model of leisure and spiritual wellbeing. *Journal of Park & Recreation Administration*, 20(4), 147–169.

Jepson, D., & Sharpley, R. (2015). More than sense of place? Exploring the emotional dimension of rural tourism experiences. *Journal of Sustainable Tourism*, 23(8–9), 1157–1178. doi:10.1080/09669582.2014.953543

Karjalainen, E., Sarjala, T., & Raitio, H. (2010). Promoting human health through forests: Overview and major challenges. *Environmental Health and Preventive Medicine*, 15(1), 1–8. doi:10.1007/s12199-008-0069-2

Konu, H. (2015). Developing a forest-based wellbeing tourism product together with customers: An ethnographic approach. *Tourism Management*, 49, 1–16. doi:10.1016/j.tourman.2015.02.006

Lee, T. H. (2013). Influence analysis of community resident support for sustainable tourism development. *Tourism Management*, 34, 37–46. doi:10.1016/j.tourman.2012.03.007

Leheny, D. R. (2003). *The rules of play: National identity and the shaping of Japanese leisure*. Ithaca, New York: Cornell University Press.

Li, Q., Nakadai, A., Matsushima, H., Miyazaki, Y., Krensky, A. M., Kawada, T., & Morimoto, K. (2006). Phytoncides (wood essential oils) induce human natural killer cell activity. *Immunopharmacology and Immunotoxicology*, 28(2), 319–333. doi:10.1080/08923970600809439

Lombard, J. R., & Morris, J. C. (2012). Using privatization theory to analyze economic development projects: Promise and performance. *Public Performance & Management Review*, 35(4), 643–659. doi:10.2753/PMR1530-9576350404

McCargo, D. (2013). *Contemporary Japan* (3rd ed.). London: Palgrave Macmillan.

MacNaughton, A. (2003). Placing tourism among the options for small forest owners in Northern Japan. *Small-scale Forest Economics, Management and Policy*, 2(1), 81–91. doi:10.1007/s11842-003-007-5

Ministry of the Environment. (2016). National Parks & Important Biodiversity Areas of Japan. Retrieved 30th of May, 2016, from www.env.go.jp/park/topics/review/attach/pamph1/en_01.pdf

Mitchell, R. J., Richardson, E. A., Shortt, N. K., & Pearce, J. R. (2015). Neighborhood environments and socioeconomic inequalities in mental wellbeing. *American Journal of Preventive Medicine*, 49(1), 80–84. doi:10.1016/j.amepre.2015.01.017

Morita, E., Fukuda, S., Nagano, J., Hamajima, N., Yamamoto, H., Iwai, Y., ... Shirakawa, T. (2007). Psychological effects of forest environments on healthy adults: Shinrin-yoku (forest-air bathing, walking) as a possible method of stress reduction. *Public Health*, 121(1), 54–63. doi:10.1016/j.puhe.2006.05.024

Park, B. J., Tsunetsugu, Y., Kasetani, T., Kagawa, T., & Miyazaki, Y. (2010). The physiological effects of Shinrin-yoku (taking in the forest atmosphere or forest bathing): Evidence from field experiments in 24 forests across Japan. *Environmental Health and Preventive Medicine*, 15(1), 18–26. doi:10.1007/s12199-009-0086-9

Phang, C. W., Zhang, C., & Sutanto, J. (2013). The influence of user interaction and participation in social media on the consumption intention of niche products. *Information & Management*, 50(8), 661–672. doi:10.1016/j.im.2013.07.001

Pretty, J. (2004). How nature contributes to mental and physical health. *Spirituality and Health International*, 5(2), 68–78. doi:10.1002/shi.220

Reader, I. (2015). *Pilgrimage: A very short introduction*. Oxford, UK: Oxford University Press.

Salazar, N. B. (2012). Community-based cultural tourism: Issues, threats and opportunities. *Journal of Sustainable Tourism*, 20(1), 9–22. doi:10.1080/09669582.2011.596279

Sung, J., Woo, J.-M., Kim, W., Lim, S.-K., & Chung, E.-J. (2012). The effect of cognitive behavior therapy-based "forest therapy" program on blood pressure, salivary cortisol level, and quality of life in elderly hypertensive patients. *Clinical and Experimental Hypertension*, 34(1), 1–7. doi:10.3109/10641963.2011.618195

Tiefenbach, T., & Kohlbacher, F. (2015). Happiness in Japan in times of upheaval: Empirical evidence from the national survey on lifestyle preferences. *Journal of Happiness Studies*, 16(2), 333–366. doi:10.1007/s10902-014-9512-9

Townsend, M. (2006). Feel blue? Touch green! Participation in forest/woodland management as a treatment for depression. *Urban Forestry & Urban Greening*, 5(3), 111–120. doi:10.1016/j.ufug.2006.02.001

Waligo, V. M., Clarke, J., & Hawkins, R. (2013). Implementing sustainable tourism: A multi-stakeholder involvement management framework. *Tourism Management*, 36, 342–353. doi:10.1016/j.tourman.2012.10.008

Wilson, S., Fesenmaier, D. R., Fesenmaier, J., & Van Es, J. C. (2001). Factors for success in rural tourism development. *Journal of Travel research*, 40(2), 132–138. doi:10.1177/004728750104000203

Yeh, S.-S., Ma, T., & Huan, T.-C. (2016). Building social entrepreneurship for the hotel industry by promoting environmental education. *International Journal of Contemporary Hospitality Management*, 28(6). doi:10.1108/IJCHM-03-2014-0122

18 Final Remarks

Challenges and Research Directions

Nina K. Prebensen, and Joseph S. Chen

The preceding chapters describe the issues and phenomena due to the interaction among nature environment, host community and the tourist indulging in and consuming the resources that nature offers. From the tourist's point of view, nature is a setting, a venue or a location providing health, wellness, hedonic, and eudaimonic experiences demanding a variety of mental and physical exertions. Tourism activities may produce pressures on resources on which they rely. In order to manage nature tourism in a sustainable way appropriate monitory mechanisms ought to be developed systematically. This book offers examples of nature tourism from different countries including Australia, China, France, Finland, Germany, Japan, Hungary, India, Israel, Kenya, Namibia, Norway, Poland, Romania, South Africa, Taiwan, and South Korea.

The countries studied here show different types and levels of challenges regarding preservation of nature in a sustainable way. The works can be categorized based on two perspectives. First a governmental and managerial perspective, dealing with environmental issues. In this they reveal challenges such as environmental education and learning, sustainability, conservation, restrictiveness, benefits to locals, and ethics, among others which need to be acknowledged and discussed and handled locally as well as internationally. The second perspective deals with individual tourist and how businesses can develop their offers in a sustainable way by meeting the needs of various types of nature-based tourists. From this perspective nature may be a wonderful place to offer valued experiences to customers through ethical, responsible, and sustainable tourist firms.

In Chapter 2 Jennifer Laing and Warwick Frost articulate the travel narratives of explorers within the framework of well-being in nature. The authors discuss how nature may function as a place to recover and to improve health, quality of life, individual well-being, and even happiness. In particular, the chapter employs the existential authenticity concept suggested by Wang (1999) to discuss how travellers use nature-based experiences, involving potential or real risks to challenge themselves, transcend self-imposed boundaries, and achieve goals or to be receptive to new identities. The chapter shows the value of applying positive psychology theories in a tourism setting in order to gain a deeper understanding of the hedonic and eudaimonic well-being and benefits of nature-based travel.

The authors discuss challenges when it comes to the concept of well-being and how it should be interpreted and comprehended over time.

In Chapter 3 Giovanna Bertella examines how and to what extent human well-being is related to—and could be explained in terms of—empathy toward the animals. Bertella employs both hedonic and eudaimonic aspects of well-being in her study as nature and animal-based experiences may reflect both aspects, in particular regarding empathy and empathic well-being. Bertella suggests that the value attached to wildlife encounters by some people is both hedonic and eudaimonic and that the four dimensions of empathy; attentiveness, knowledge, connectedness, and responsibility, are relevant to these cases. The study suggests that the way nature-related activities (e.g. whale watching) are organized impact the level of empathy or that tourists with less knowledge choose certain types of organized tours. The sense of responsibility at the individual level has emerged as a particularly critical element and its absence is particularly observed in the cases of whale watchers who join organized tours and are not especially knowledgeable or interested in whales. Although showing some elements relative to perspective taking, these tourists might have the tendency to attribute the responsibility exclusively to the tourism providers. The chapter ends with reflections regarding the underlying perception of animals as resources, which should be further acknowledged and studied.

In Chapter 4 Timothy J. Lee and Jinok Susanna Kim discuss how nature-related activities provide people with a range of health-related benefits including stress-relief, attention-improvement, social relationships, physical health, and emotional well-being. The authors use attention restoration theory as an underpinning to examine the effect of those activities, a part of health tourism, on the subjective happiness of tourists. The chapter shows that the subjective happiness of tourists can be improved through nature-based activities and furthermore, the tourists perceived that environmental restrictiveness of nature-based activities significantly influences satisfaction. In line with previous research, the authors note how perceived environmental restrictiveness could be a defining agent to enhance tourist satisfaction through emotions by participating in nature-based activities.

In Chapter 5 Melanie Smith focuses on the younger generation and their contact with nature. Building on literature revealing the benefits humans can gain from nature environments, Smith discusses in more depth the relationship among nature, well-being, quality of life, and tourism with a particular emphasis on young people. People aged 18–33 from Hungary, Romania, Poland, and Israel are interviewed. The chapter reveals that the majority of the respondents go to the countryside for leisure or tourism purposes in addition to visiting friends and relatives and around 40 percent claimed that relaxation is the major purpose. The study further reveals that the most interesting activities, in rank of importance, are hiking/walking, cycling, and visiting lakes/rivers (swimming), followed by eating local farm-fresh foods. Smith argues that these results are promising due to the importance of being close to and benefitting from nature.

In Chapter 6 Nina K. Prebensen, Young-Sook Lee, and Joseph S. Chen adopt the concepts and scales of nature connectedness and nature relatedness to study

210 Nina K. Prebensen and Joseph S. Chen

East Asian tourists. As the scientific community is increasingly focusing on human–nature relationship and their impact on environmentally sustainable behavior, the chapter explores and compares how tourists from China, South Korea, and Japan relate to and connect with nature. The theoretical underpinning of the comparison rests on how changing cultural values also referred to as Neo-Confucianism, are playing a role in influencing nature tourists from East Asia. Scholars such as Mayer and Franz (2004) claim that connection to nature is a defining predictor of ecological behavior and subjective well-being and that scales such as people's connectedness to nature promise to be a useful empirical tool for research on the relationship between humans and the natural world. This chapter suggests the scale should be further developed and tested in various markets.

In Chapter 7 Oystein Jensen, Frank Lindberg, Damiannah Kieti, Bjorn Willy Aamo, and James Nampushi narrate how local traditions and values are represented by two different wildlife resort companies, i.e. Basecamp Masai Mara (BCM) in Kenya and Basecamp Spitsbergen (BCS) in the Arctic. As the idea that ecotourism can be locally beneficial has been promoted within tourism research, it has also been argued that the involvement of local communities in ecotourism operations additionally can also contribute to improving the quality of the tourist experience, such as through the provision of knowledge and services. For tourists the appreciation of such local skills and attitudes to nature can also be perceived as an extension of their nature-related experience. This can take place, for example, through interaction with trained local guides who combine professional skills with their local traditional knowledge and philosophy which enables the tourists access to dimensions of a natural and spiritual world that they otherwise would not have been aware of. The case studies illustrate how traditions of dealing with wilderness and extreme environment can increase the tourists' physical and spiritual access to such areas, even in the case of traditions from past settlements.

In Chapter 8 Bruce Prideaux and Michelle Thompson deal with the impact of climate change on tourism in world heritage sites. By employing the Wet Tropics region of Australia as a case study, the chapter investigates the status of research into climate change-related issues, outlines the role of tourism in the Wet Tropics region, and examines how climate change is expected to affect the World Heritage Areas (WHAs) located in the Wet Tropics. The authors supply a number of strategies that may be used to prepare the tourism business for the possible impacts of climate change.

In Chapter 9 Lynn M. Jamieson urges that venturing into a natural environment is a challenging experience and tourism professionals ought to consider planning every aspect of the tourist experience. This chapter delineates the process of generating positive tourist experiences that involve anticipation-envisioning, engagement-interacting and reflection-returning. In order to effectively deliver a positive nature experience, it is vital to train the service staffs and educate the tourists concerning the concept of sustainability. Meanwhile the educative messages towards green awareness and practices should be placed on diverse information channels. Regulatory and safety information concerning activities taken should also be manifested in all information conduits to avoid unpleasant recreational experiences due to violation of rules or unexpected sports injury. After the trip, it is advantageous for service firms to reconnect the tourists with the nature environment visited beforehand that may enable the tourist to reflect the exciting experience and promote memorable experiences in the long run.

In Chapter 10 Isabelle Frochot introduces a case study of the Vanoise National Park in the Alps and the chapter describes the history of national parks in France. Frochot reviews the history of national parks in France and centers on the specific case of the Vanoise National Park in the French Northern Alps and discusses stakeholder involvement in park governance. The proximity of profit-making ski resorts certainly has a role to play, but rightly or not, local inhabitants in the peripheral area also feel that the rules of the park are too constraining and imposed from above. Frochot converses with power structures, decision making, and destination management regarding who is best suited to preserve and protect nature: local authorities or the national governments.

In Chapter 11 Raija Komppula, Henna Konu, and Noora Vikman investigate two different types of tourist experiences in nature from a well-being perspective. In particular, they focus on the impact of sensing the nature, i.e. sound (silence) and the sight (scenery) in forest-based well-being. The authors discuss how nature, especially forests have been proved to have beneficial effects on the physical and mental health and well-being of human beings. Interviews with test groups show that they do appreciate the active role of the guides in enabling the nature experience by facilitating opportunities to see, hear, taste, smell, and feel, and explaining the sources of the different experiences for the tourists. The informants furthermore show a variety of positive experiences in the forest environment and the forest has a soothing and calming effect, helping people to gain a silent mood, revealing the imperative of nature as an important setting for enhanced personal well-being.

In Chapter 12 René van der Duim, Jakomijn van Wijk, and Machiel Lamers descibe the phenomenon of nature tourism in Africa. The chapter provides an overview of this transition in the governance of nature tourism by describing the main logics of the conservation discourse over time. Furthermore, it discusses four institutional arrangements for nature tourism in Africa—conservancies in Namibia, private game reserves in South Africa, tourism conservation enterprises in Kenya, and transfrontier conservation areas. The chapter illustrates how communal and private landowners have come to play a pivotal role in conservation on the one hand and how conservation increasingly is undergirded by neoliberal principles on the other. The authors discuss how commodification and financialization of conservation are the root of many governance problems associated with these arrangements, and it is unlikely that the market logic will become subordinate in the conservation discourse in the near future.

In Chapter 13 Marius Mayer and Manuel Woltering evaluate protected areas in Germany. This chapter demonstrates that only a relatively small share of visitors in Germany are motivated to visit protected areas. Interestingly, the study reveals that the economic impact analyses of German protected area tourism proves that tourism plays a pivotal role in mostly the peripheral rural protected area regions in Germany which are often part of the regional development strategies involving stimulation of local tourism. The chapter also shows synergy between case studies that use the same methodology, in that they can function as a database for national socio-economic protected areas and these databases could not only be used as monitoring systems but also for international comparisons.

In Chapter 14 Krithi K. Karanth, Shivangi Jain, and Dincy Mariyam underline emerging trends in wildlife and tiger tourism in India. The chapter focuses on examining wildlife, including 36 tiger reserves, tourism in terrestrial and penin-sular marine National Parks, and Wildlife Sanctuaries, and the study further com-pares tiger and non-tiger reserves. Tiger-focused tourism is a major force within wildlife tourism in and outside India, comprising 32 percent of all visitors and generating higher gate fees and revenues. This assessment of tourism in a selec-tion of Indian wildlife reserves finds that tourism growth is not universal and that there are many wildlife reserves that are visited by few people and/or that have experienced negative growth rates. This makes it challenging to sustain conserva-tion efforts in these places in the absence of sufficient funds, as well as of broader public support and interest in these reserves. In agreement with the current lit-erature, the authors state that conservation efforts directed at threatened mammal species has become reliant on revenue from tourism to a previously unsuspected degree. Therefore, raising funds to monitor and conserve such forms of tourism are highlighted as a vital future issue.

In Chapter 15 Rui Song highlights the challenges of nature tourism in China while illuminating upcoming challenges regarding sustainability with the Chinese tourism business. Song furnishes suggestions concerning how to manage the tourism industry in a sustainable way. As China has witnessed a booming devel-opment of nature tourism in the last three decades, sustainable management is of extreme importance. Sustainable development which incorporates ecological, social, and economic aspects has been confirmed as the goal and framework of tourism development in China. The author adds that a Chinese cultural context should be considered for the development of sustainability. The different imple-mentation of western concepts of sustainability via a Chinese approach is the general anthropocentrism and anthropomorphism inherent in the Chinese value system that is derived from Confucian philosophy and Daoism. The author also points to the need for "enlightened mass tourism" that should be regarded as the philosophy of tourism development in general and natural tourism specifically. The article also frames issues such as efforts toward natural resource sites should be reformed, reforms should be implemented to increase the collective partici-pation of natural resource-dependent communities in the development/manage-ment of nature tourism, and that scientific research should be carried out at the national level.

In Chapter 16 Yu-Liang Tseng, Noriko Sato, Shih-Shuo Yeh, and Tzung-Cheng Huan portray the future of nature tourism in Taiwan and recommend sustain-ability as a theoretical underpinning. Accordingly, they offer three different developmental strategies, i.e. community-based tourism which strives to balance local economic development and conservation via the active involvement of host community economically and socially; supporting environmental education; and practicing corporate social responsibility which involves forgoing certain aspects of financial gain in search of socially appropriate behaviors.

In Chapter 17 Noriko Sato, Yu-Liang Tseng, Shih-Shuo Yeh, and Tzung-Cheng Huan explore the forest as a venue for recreational therapy in Japan. Japan has recently focused on forest therapy as part of their tourism strategy and forest baths are considered as a popular leisure activity. In Japanese society the therapeutic effects of forest bathing are widely accepted and the demand for such activities is driven by the enormous amount of pressures that people routinely encounter. An aging society is also driving the recent demand for nature tourism which is regarded as a passive form of therapy. The chapter discusses three cases delineating underlying constraints and challenges in developing and promoting forest therapy. One of the issues debated in the chapter is the integration of eco-friendly methods as a vital step to enhancing the visitor experience in forest therapy and to seek for a balance between economic growth and environmental protection.

This book shows the importance of collaboration and knowledge sharing when it comes to nature tourism. Countries need to learn from other countries, destinations need to learn from other destinations, and firms need to learn from other firms about how best can they use nature in a responsible and sustainable way. Learning and knowledge sharing in a systemic framework should be further advocated and all these stakeholders should also ensure that nature tourists can learn as they benefit from nature. How can tourists learn to protect nature and be responsible in their behavior? Ethical issues in particular when it comes to animals should be further discussed and cultural differences and cultural understanding are major topics that need to be addressed in the future.

Moreover, this study seems to point to a research direction concerning what the underlying meanings of valuable tourist experiences in relation to nature tourism are. Meanwhile, while studying a rewarding tourist experience, it is also important to consider the moderators of tourist experiences as presented in the book that include but are not limited to activity pattern (e.g. wildlife viewing), cultural background (e.g. Neo-Confucian), generation cohort (e.g. Generation Y), recreational settings (e.g. forest), space intensity (e.g. perceived crowdedness in forest), and the traits of service personnel (e.g. a trained tour guide from the host community). Further, to cope with lifestyle change and an aging society occurring in the developed world, future research may also tackle types of nature-related activities that could better promote well-being (as a holistic benefit of traveling) among different segments of constituencies.

It is also critical to look at the contemporary issues regarding rules and regulations affecting the development of nature tourism. As shown in the case study on nature tourism in Germany, like the phenomenon of rich economies, protected nature areas have been utilized as attractions to boost the tourism economy. Indeed, the perception of environmental restrictiveness may lead to a satisfactory visiting experiences in nature as revealed in the study from South Korea. However, those regulations imposing restrictions on exploiting nature resources would largely affect the livelihood of local communities within the protected arears even in a developed nation like France. Undoubtedly, in an under-developing or developing nation, locals are likely to revert to exploiting nature resources in the hope of maintaining their living regardless of the regulations. For example, the number of tigers in India may be gradually diminished in the event of poaching by the locals. In sum, the regulatory challenges appear to differ among countries with a different magnitude of economy. As the lessons learnt from the past, government positive intervention including tax incentives and subsides may alleviate the issue. The above observations may serve as an information conduit for future research on regulation and policy making.

The effect of climate change may threaten tourism development as advocated in the case study of the wet tropic region of Australia. The climate change has been a globe issue of significance in the mind of the masses and certainly this challenge could not only undermine the growth of the tourism business but also helps the civilization to thrive. For example, as the abnormal pace of glacier retreat continues it causes rising sea levels and could inevitably destroy ocean-front and small-island resorts. The climate issue is indeed urgent and requires timely attention from tourism researchers. Scholars may address this topic from two perspectives: supply and demand. The supply side, for instance, may relate to development and managerial strategies that apply to nature tourism, while tourists' behavioral intentions and coping mechanisms regarding the climate change problem could constitute a valuable investigative topic.

Nevertheless, in response to the concept of conservation, eco-tourism, as well as other environmentally friendly forms of nature tourism, seemingly render viable alternatives in safeguarding the integrity of nature, incorporating the survival of inhabitants, species, and vegetation within nature attractions. In principle, environmental conservation is respected as a way of wisely utilizing nature resources as promoted in the case study of sustainable nature tourism in China. However, in the face of pressing issues like climate change and scarcity of food and water in under-developing countries which often aspire to nature tourism as an economic alternative, uncontrolled development could also acerbate unhealthy living conditions in host communities affected in the long run. To what extent does the development in nature tourism progress? What could be the optimal form of nature tourism that minimizes the environmental impacts and benefits the growth of economy? Are less intrusive forms (e.g. whale watching and forest bathing) of nature tourism better alternatives for both the economy and environment? These fundamental issues may remain largely unsolved as development progresses regardless. With the prevalence of information technology, it may be advantageous to systematically enlist research ideas in the context of nature tourism from different parts of world to create synergy for service delivery and policy making.

Index

Africa (eastern and southern), governing
nature tourism in 146–55; agreements
on objectives 152; conservancies
148–51; contemporary institutional
arrangements in Africa 148; donor
funding 147; external challenges
153–5; "fortress conservation" 147;
internal challenges 151–3; logics in the
conservation discourse 148; NGOs 150,
155; policy levels 154; private game
reserves 146, 151; shifting conservation
logics 146–7; tourism conservation
enterprises 146, 148, 150; Transfrontier
Conservation Areas 146, 151; wildlife
protection 147
Alps, Vanoise National Park *see* national
park in turmoil
Americans with Disabilities Act (ADA) 96
Analytical Hierarchy Process 192
animals, empathy toward 23–4, 210
antimicrobial volatile organic
compounds 199
Attention Restoration Theory (ART) 34
Australia, Wet Tropics region of *see* World
heritage sites, impact of climate change
on tourism in

Basecamp Explorer (BCE) in Maasai
Mara, Kenya and Svalbard, Norway
see local traditions and way of living,
influence of on tourism
Basecamp Maasai Brand (BMB) 71
Basecamp Masai Mara (BCM) 72, 210
Basecamp Spitsbergen (BCS) 76, 210
biosphere reserves (Germany) 137
Bird Protection League (LPO)
(France) 109
'blue spaces' 49
Botel Tobago 188

Build-Operate-Transfer (BOT)
contracts 175
Bwindi National Park (Uganda) 5

casino industry 190
challenges and research directions
208–14; Basecamp Masai Mara
210; Basecamp Spitsbergen 210;
challenges, perspectives of 208; China
212; community-based tourism 212;
empathy toward animals 209; integrity
of nature 214; Neo-Confucianism
210; private game reserves 211;
Taiwan 212–13; tourism conservation
enterprises 211; travel narratives of
explorers 208; World Heritage Areas
210
Chinese approach to sustainability 172–82;
Build-Operate-Transfer contracts
175; challenges of sustainability
of nature tourism 177–80; China
National Tourism Administration
173; community involvement 176;
ecologically sustainable development
176; Five-Year Plan 175; Golden
Week Policy Two 177; mass tourism
nature-based development model
177; National People's Congress 176;
nature-based tourism 172; nature
tourism resource administration
system 173–5; official agenda 175;
resource administration system 179;
State Environmental Protection
Administration 176; suggestions
180–2; tourism and natural resource
administration in China 172–3
Chinese tourists *see* neo-Confucianism
among Chinese, South Korean and
Japanese tourists

climate change *see* World heritage
    sites, impact of climate change on
    tourism in
"closed shutters" 116
"communicative staging" 77
community-based tourism (CBT)
    190–1, 212
connectedness and relatedness to nature
    see neo-Confucianism among Chinese,
    South Korean and Japanese tourists
coral bleaching 89
corporate social responsibility (CSR) 192
creative transformation 59

Davidson, Robyn 17–19
decision tree 142

'earth-centered therapy' 48
ecologically sustainable development
    (ESD) 176
Eco Retreats 48
Eco-warrior award 71
empathy toward animals 23–4, 210
Energy Star Home Energy Rating
    System 100
EU COST Project on Tourism, Wellbeing
    and Ecosystem Services 50
eudaimonia 12–19, 29–30

forest-based wellbeing tourism
    (Finland) 120–7; case silence 122–4;
    "emptiness" 123; forest therapy 121;
    ice fishing 123–4; Japanese case 124–7;
    "listening walk" 122; wellbeing effects
    of nature and forests 121–2
'forest schools' 52
forest therapy *see* Japan, forest as a venue
    for recreational therapy in
Formosa *see* Taiwan, tourism in preserved
    nature areas in
"fortress conservation" 147
French Northern Alps *see* national park
    in turmoil

Generation Y 46–54; 'blue spaces' 49;
    'earth-centered therapy' 48; Eco
    Retreats 48; 'forest schools' 52; 'green
    therapy' 47; 'Nature-Deficit Disorder'
    49; recommendations 53–4; relationship
    between nature, wellbeing and tourism
    46–50; 'slow cities' 49; Survey Monkey
    50; young people and their connection
    to nature 50–3

Germany's protected areas, nature tourism
    in 131–43; biosphere reserves 137;
    day-trips 133; decision tree to determine
    visitors with high national park
    affinity 142; economic impact 138–42;
    Germany as tourism destination
    131; national parks 135–7; nature-
    based tourism 132–7; nature parks
    137; official tourism statistics 138;
    protected areas 133–7; representative
    surveys 137–8; tourism in Germany's
    large-scale protected areas 137–42;
    tourism indicators 140–1; UNESCO
    biosphere reserves 137; visitors with a
    high PA affinity 139
Golden Week Policy Two 177
governing nature tourism *see* Africa
    (eastern and southern), governing nature
    tourism in
Great Barrier Reef Marine Park
    (GBRMP) 83
green programs 100–1
'green therapy' 47

hedonia 12–19, 29–30

India, emerging trends in wildlife and tiger
    tourism in 159–68; demand for wildlife
    tourism 160; economic benefits 159;
    gate fees 165–8; methods 161; results
    and discussion 161–5; visitors 162–5;
    Wildlife Sanctuary, areas covered
    by 161
"integral reserve" 111
International Whaling Commission 26

Japan, forest as a venue for recreational
    therapy in 196–205; Agency for
    Cultural Affairs 197; antimicrobial
    volatile organic compounds 199; cases
    201–2; certification of forest therapy
    198–9; constraints of promoting forest
    therapy 203; development of nature
    tourism in Japan 196–7; forest therapy
    as an activity in nature tourism 197–8;
    forest therapy and tourism in Japan
    199–200; future paths of forest therapy
    204–5; Hinokage Town in Miyazaki
    Prefecture 202; information era 204;
    key success factors of promoting forest
    therapy 202–3; Meiji Restoration 197;
    Natural Parks Law 197; overcrowding
    200; Pacific Ring of Fire 196;

phytoncides 199; population structure, change in 204; price structure 200; problem and issues facing current development 201; prospect of forest therapy 203–5; Quasi-National Parks 197; Sasaguri Town in Fukuoka Prefecture 201; Shikoku 88 Kasho 201; social development in the 21st century 203–4; tour guides, training of 203; Ukiha City in Fukuoka Prefecture 201–2

Japanese tourists *see* neo-Confucianism among Chinese, South Korean and Japanese tourists

"Japan National Park Law" 184

Kenya *see* local traditions and way of living, influence of on tourism

Koiyaki Guiding School (KGS) 71

Korea's nature-based recreation settings, impact of 34–42; Attention Restoration Theory 34; data analysis 38; emotion 35–6; measurement 37; measurement model 39; methods 37–8; perceived environmental restorativeness 34–5; respondents' demographic characteristics 38–9; results 38–41; sampling and data collection 37–8; satisfaction 36; structural model 39; subjective happiness 37

Kyoto Protocol on Climate Change 82

landscape preservation 112

LEED certification 100

Lieyu's casino industry 190

local traditions and way of living, influence of on tourism 68–79; Basecamp Masai Mara, description of 70–1; Basecamp Spitsbergen 76–7; BCM Maasai staff's intended influence on the tourist experiences 72–5; "communicative staging" 77; Eco-warrior award 71; Koiyaki Guiding School 71; Maasai people 71–2; perspectives 68

Maxwell, Gavin 15–17

Meiji Restoration (Japan) 197

Muir, John 13–15

My First Summer in the Sierra 13–15

Naboisho Wildlife Conservancy 71

NAHB Green 100

National Oceanic and Atmospheric Administration (NOAA) 85

National Park Service 103

national park in turmoil 109–18; Bird Protection League 109; "closed shutters" 116; concept of national parks in the French context 110–11; farmers, objection from 116; "integral reserve" 111; landscape closure 112; landscape preservation 112; National Society for Nature Preservation 109; new statuses established in 2006 112–13; objectives of national parks 111–13; original objectives 111–12; peripheral zone 111; Vanoise National Park, crisis since 2015 115–17; Vanoise National Park, history of 113–14; Vanoise National Park, regulations and administrative bodies 114–15; zones 111

National People's Congress (NPC) (China) 176

National Society for Nature Preservation (France) 109

nature-based tourism (NBT) 132, 172

'Nature-Deficit Disorder' (NDD) 49

nature relatedness (NR) 60; *see also* neo-Confucianism among Chinese, South Korean and Japanese tourists

Neo-Confucianism 210

neo-Confucianism among Chinese, South Korean and Japanese tourists 57–66; Chinese neo-Confucianism and nature 58–9; connectedness to nature 60; creative transformation 59; findings and discussions 63–5; Japanese neo-Confucianism 60; measuring oneness between nature and human 60–1; method 61–3; motives driving inquiry 57; nature relatedness 60; neo-Confucianism and nature 58; new environmental paradigm 61; procedure 62; South Korean neo-Confucianism 59; study population 61–2; Tourist Connectedness to Nature scale 62; Tourist Nature Relatedness scale 62–3

new environmental paradigm (NEP) 61

Norway *see* local traditions and way of living, influence of on tourism

Orchid Island 188

'organic holism' 57

Pacific Ring of Fire 196
PERMA (positive emotions, engagement, relationships, meaning and achievement) 12
phytoncides 199
private game reserves (PGR) 146, 151, 211

Quasi-National Parks (Japan) 197

recreation settings *see* Korea's nature-based recreation settings, impact of
relatedness to nature *see* neo-Confucianism among Chinese, South Korean and Japanese tourists
research directions *see* challenges and research directions
research progress 1–7; environmental rows and conservation 2–3; impacts on community and nature 5; management and development 5–7; place attachment 4; progress and woes of nature tourism development 1–2; pro-poor intervention 5; tourist experiences 3–4; visitor experience, influences of 4
Retreat Company 49
Ring of Bright Water 15–17
Rs of green 99

Shikoku 88 Kasho 201
Sierra Club 107
'slow cities' 49
South Korean tourists *see* neo-Confucianism among Chinese, South Korean and Japanese tourists
subjective well-being 12–19
Survey Monkey 50
sustainability messaging 98, 104

Taiwan, tourism in preserved nature areas in 184–93; Analytical Hierarchy Process 192; Botel Tobago 188; Chinese Civil War 184; community-based tourism 190–1; controversies over establishing casinos in small islands 190; development of nature tourism in Taiwan 184–8; differences in development goals 189; environmental education 191–2; First Sino-Japanese War 184; Fort Zeelandia 184; issues confronting the progress of nature tourism 189–90; "Japan National Park Law" 184; monitoring 193; Orchid Island 188;

seasonality 189; small islands, tourism impacts on 189–90; social responsibility 192–3; Taroko National Park 186; Tourism Bureau of Taiwan 185; unique nature tourism in Taiwan 186–8; Yellowstone Park of Penghu 199
Taroko National Park 186
tiger tourism *see* India, emerging trends in wildlife and tiger tourism in
tourism conservation enterprises (TCE) 146, 148, 150, 211
Tourist Connectedness to Nature (TCN) scale 62
Tourist Nature Relatedness (TNR) scale 62–3
Tracks 17–19
transformation, explorer travel narratives of *see* well-being, nature and
Transfrontier Conservation Areas (TFCAs) 146, 151
"Tuhao" 122

Uganda 5
UNESCO biosphere reserves 137
United Nations Climate Change Conference 82, 90

visitor experience, influences of 4
visitor experiences, quality perspectives in management of 95–108; ability 96; anticipation (envisioning) 95–6; challenge 98; comfort 97; cultural competence 96–7; delivery 104–7; education for sustainability 99–104; engagement (interacting) 97; fear of the unknown 96; green programs 100–1; importance of accuracy in presenting the natural world 103–4; importance of and components for a positive visitor experience 95–9; LEED certification 100; marketing 103; medical constraints 96; mental preparation 97; message 95–9; operating in a natural environment 107; outcome 107–8; reflection (returning) 98; regulatory process 105–7; resources 103; return rate 98–9; Rs of green 99; safety and security 104–5; sustainability messaging 98, 104; visitor expectations 106–7; visitor satisfaction 99
visitors with a high PA affinity (VHPAA) 139

way of living *see* local traditions and way of living, influence of on tourism

well-being, nature and 11–20; eudaimonia, hedonia and subjective well-being 12–19; PERMA 12; texts 13–19; *see also* wildlife experiences, well-being in

Wet Tropics Rainforests (WTR) (Australia) 83

wildlife experiences, well-being in 23–31; empathy and empathic well-being 23–4; eudaimonic aspect of well-being 29–30; findings from the explorative phase 26–7; hedonic aspect of well-being 29–30; in-depth interviews, respondents of 28; main findings 27–8; method 25–6; no well-being experienced 28–9; whale watchers' and whales' well-being 24–5

wildlife protection (Africa) 147

Wildlife tourism *see* India, emerging trends in wildlife and tiger tourism in

World Heritage Areas (WHAs) 83, 210

World heritage sites, impact of climate change on tourism in 82–91; coral bleaching 89; discussion 90–1; flow diagram 84; Great Barrier Reef Marine Park 83, 88–90; out-migrating organisms 82; previous research 83–5; species facing extinction 82; 'tipping points' 90; tourism in Wet Tropics region 85–8; Tropical Cyclone Larry 87; Wet Tropics Rainforests 86–8

Yellowstone National Park 105, 106

Yosemite National Park 105, 106